Safe Practice
in Physical Education and Sport

association for
Physical Education

Eighth edition © The Association for Physical Education, 2012

Reprinted 2014

First published 2012

ISBN: 978-1-905540-94-5

Author:

Peter Whitlam

afPE appreciates the contributions through review made by:

Yvonne Ball – British Wrestling Association

Lerverne Barber – University of Worcester

Glen Beaumont – co-author of the 2008 edition

Nick Booth – Continental Sports

Denise Fountain – Calthorpe Special School

Lindsy Gray – Rossington All Saints Academy

Vanessa Incledon – University of Worcester

Angela James – afPE Safety Officer

Eileen Marchant – afPE NCfPL Lead Consultant

Jan Parker – Aspire School Improvement Partnership

Norman Randall – England Fencing

Martin Reddin – British Gymnastics

Chris Smith – City of London School

Peter Sutcliffe – UK Athletics

Janet Thorpe – Linthwaite Clough JI & EY Unit

Adrian Tranter – British Taekwondo Control Board

Karen van Berlo – University of Worcester

Aiden Wilkinson – Student, Leeds University

Sue Wilkinson – afPE Strategic Manager

Colin Wood – University of Worcester

Jes Woodhouse – ITTE Consultant

afPE project lead officer: Sue Wilkinson

Coachwise editor: Christopher Stanners

Coachwise designer: Saima Nazir

Photographs © Alan Edwards

Indexer: Glyn Sutcliffe

Published on behalf of afPE by

Room 117

Bredon

University of Worcester

Henwick Grove

Worcester

WR2 6AJ

Tel: 01905-855 584

Fax: 01905-855 594

Coachwise Ltd

Chelsea Close

Off Amberley Road, Armley

Leeds LS12 4HP

Tel: 0113-231 1310 Fax: 0113-231 9606

Email: enquiries@coachwise.ltd.uk

Website: www.coachwise.ltd.uk

Foreword

I am delighted to write the foreword for this eighth edition of *Safe Practice in Physical Education and Sport* published by the Association for Physical Education (afPE). This resource is an essential reference for everyone who is involved in providing physical education and sport activities at all levels. It provides definitive guidance in all aspects of the subject, and the author, Peter Whitlam, who is afPE's Health and Safety Project Manager, sought confirmation and reinforcement through review from a wide range of experts to ensure accuracy and current best practice. Advice in the resource is in line with recent developments in practice and is underpinned by reference to recent case law.

This eighth edition is significantly different from those previously published and focuses very much on safe teaching and learning principles, which are underpinned by those of safe management. It also supports and complements best practice in standards, while remaining user-friendly and simple to navigate.

Within the five sections in the handbook, you will be able to access advice and support in every aspect of physical education and sport. They are structured in a clear and simple way, thus making it easy to find the answer to any query, whether you are a practitioner, head teacher, governor or coach. The sections on safe teaching, essential learning and safe management principles are important reading for all those who teach or coach the subject and for those who are subject leaders, members of leadership teams and governors. There is also a wealth of advice in the section that applies and reinforces the principles outlined in other sections to specific areas of activity. Appendices are included on a CD-ROM to be downloaded and used appropriately.

Past editions of this handbook have always provided crucial and relevant advice at all levels. With the ever-changing educational landscape, advice on health and safety remains critical, and afPE has the expertise within this field. I commend this new edition to you as it will help to ensure young people are kept safe, as well as reinforcing the message that the law protects careful teachers and coaches.

Eileen Marchant
Chair of the afPE Board

Contents

Case Law Listed in the Text   1

Glossary of Terms   6

Abbreviations   7

Introduction   11
Terminology Used in the Handbook   11
Navigating this Handbook   12

Section 1: Basic Principles   13
1.1 Overview   14
1.2 Relevant Case Law   18

Section 2: Safe Teaching Principles   19
2.1 Overview   20
2.2 Safe Teaching: A Summary   20
2.3 Safe Teaching: Some Additional Information for the Teacher   25

Section 3: Safe Management Principles   51
3.1 Overview   52
3.2 A Generic Policy Statement for PES   54
3.3 Guidance to Develop and Manage Safe-practice Procedures in PES   55
3.4 Staff Management   56
3.5 Student Management   78
3.6 Equipment Management   110
3.7 Facility Management   120
3.8 Transport Management   127
3.9 Group Management   135
3.10 Programme Management   140
3.11 Risk Management   154

Section 4: Essential Learning about Safe Practice   165
4.1 Safety Education   166
4.2 Overview   166
4.3 What Safe-practice Principles Should Students Learn?   167
4.4 How Can Students Learn and Effectively Apply the Principles of Safe Practice?   172

Section 5: Applying the Principles to Specific Areas of Activity   175
5.1 Adventure Activities   176
5.2 Aquatic Activities   202
5.3 Athletics Activities   213
5.4 Combat Activities   218
5.5 Dance Activities, Movement and Creative Development   228

5.6 Games Activities   230

5.7 Gymnastics and Trampolining Activities   242

5.8 Health-related Physical Activities   248

5.9 Physically Active Play in the School Environment   253

Index   **256**

Appendices (on CD-ROM only)

Appendix 1:   **The Triangle Model for Safe Practice/Managing Risk in Physical Education and Sport**

Appendix 2:   **Safe Teaching: A Summary**

Appendix 3:   **First Aid Qualifications and First Aid Kits: An Explanation of the Health and Safety Executive Approved Code of Practice (HSE ACOP) on First Aid 1997 (First Aid Kit Contents Revised 31 December 2011)**

Appendix 4:   **School Accident Report Form**

Appendix 5:   **Standard Accident Procedures**

Appendix 6:   **Department for Education Recommended Annual Consent Form for Participation in Optional School Trips and Other Off-site Activities**

Appendix 7:   **Sample Consent Form for the Use of Digital Imagery in School**

Appendix 8:   **Parental Consent Form for a Student to be Transported in Another Adult's Vehicle**

Appendix 9:   **Aspects Relevant to Safeguarding Within a Physical Education and Sport Context**

Appendix 10: Risk Assessment for On-site Physical Education, Including Level 1 School Games Intra-school Sport

Appendix 11: Risk Assessment Form for School Games Level 2 Inter-school Sport, Level 3 Centrally Organised Events and Other Off-site Fixtures

Appendix 12: Welsh Language Risk Assessment Form

Appendix 13: Welsh Language Version of Risk Assessment Form for Off-site Inter-school Away Fixtures

Appendix 14: A Generic Policy Statement for Physical Education and Sport

Appendix 15: Teachers' Standards: Effective from 1 September 2012

Appendix 16: Potential Roles and Responsibilities when Support Staff Lead School Groups Off Site

Appendix 17: Volunteer Driver's Declaration

Appendix 18: Exemplar Code of Conduct for Students

Appendix 19: Students with Special Educational Needs and Disability

Appendix 20: Quality Assurance and Quality Standards on the Inspection and Maintenance of Gymnastics, Fixed Play, Sports and Fitness Equipment

Appendix 21: Minibus Driver's Hours of Work Allowed – British Domestic Rules (Transport Act 1968)

Appendix 22: Car Seats, Boosters and Seat Belts – Department for Transport

Appendix 23: Managing a Sports Event – Some Planning Issues Identified

Appendix 24: Summary of British Gymnastics' Advice on the Use of Spotting

Appendix 25: List of Sport Organisations Relevant to Schools with Website Details

Case Law Listed in the Text

No.	Title	Issue	Section	Paragraph
Section 1: Basic Principles				
1	R versus Porter (2008)	Real not hypothetical risk situation	*Basic Principles: Relevant Case Law* and *Risk assessment*	1.2.1 3.11.19
2	R versus Chargot and Ruttle Contracting (2008)	Common sense approach to risk	*Basic Principles: Relevant Case Law* and *Risk assessment*	1.2.2 3.11.20
Section 2: Safe Teaching Principles				
3	Farmer versus Hampshire County Council (2006)	Footwear for activity	*Footwear – staff and students*	2.3.29
4	Villella versus North Bedfordshire Borough Council (1983)	Footwear for activity		2.3.30
5	Denbighshire County Council versus McDermott (2005)	Clear instructions	*Forethought*	2.3.36
6	R (ex parte Roberts) versus the Chair and Governors of Cwnfelinfach Primary School (2001)	Jewellery	*Personal effects, including jewellery and cultural or religious adornments*	2.3.55
7	Morrell versus Owen (1993)	Facility unsafe for participants	*Equipment*	2.3.98
8	Hippolyte versus Bexley London Borough (1994)	Following school policy	*Policies and procedures*	2.3.112
9	Moore versus Hampshire County Council (1981)	Reintegration into lessons after absence	*Registers and records*	2.3.117
10	Taylor versus Corby Borough Council (2000)	Unsafe facility	*Work area*	2.3.127
11	Mountford versus Newlands School (2007)	Playing out of age group	*Matching the students* and *Mixed-age sport*	2.3.150 3.9.17
12	Anderson versus Portejolie (2008)	Working beyond ability	*Progression*	2.3.169
13	Woodroffe-Hedley versus Cuthbertson (1997)	Not following established procedure	*Regular and approved practice*	2.3.175

14	Shaw versus Redbridge LBC (2005)	Regular and approved practice typical of profession	*Regular and approved practice and Duty of care*	2.3.176 3.4.33
15	Affutu-Nartay versus Clark (1994)	Teacher taking full role in game	*Staff participation and Physical contact and staff participation in student activities*	2.3.191 3.4.101
16	Harris versus Perry (2008)	Constant supervision not essential		2.3.195
17	McDougall versus Strathclyde Regional Council (1995)	Constant supervision not essential	*Supervision*	2.3.196
18	Palmer versus Cornwall County Council (2009)	Inadequate ratios		2.3.197
19	Orchard versus Lee (2009)	Students owe staff a duty of care		2.3.198

Section 3: Safe Management Principles

20	Williams versus Eady (1893)	Standard of care		3.4.27
21	Lyes versus Middlesex County Council (1962)	Standard of care as a teacher		3.4.28
22	Bolam versus Friern Hospital Management Committee (1957)	Standard of care as a teacher		3.4.29
23	Gower versus LB of Bromley (1999)	In loco parentis applies to all in schools	*Duty of care*	3.4.30
24	Stokes versus Guest, Keen and Nettleford (Bolts and Nuts) Limited (1968)	Higher duty of care		3.4.31
25	Woodbridge School versus Chittock (2002)	Range of reasonable options in teaching		3.4.32
26	Bolton versus Stone (1951) and Harrison versus Wirral MBC (2009)	Rare event means no liability		3.4.34
27	Jones versus Manchester Corporation (1958)	Management responsibility to deploy competent staff	*Qualifications and competence*	3.4.46
28	R versus Kite (1996)	Management responsibility to employ competent staff		3.4.47

29	Heffer versus Wiltshire County Council (1996)	Staff to check student confidence and provide appropriate progression	*Qualifications and competence*	3.4.48
30	Kenyon versus Lancashire County Council (2001)	Injury caused by incorrect tuition		3.4.49
31	Viasystems (Tyneside) Ltd versus Thermal Transfer (Northern) Ltd (2005)	Head teachers legally responsible for actions of visiting staff	*Support staff, volunteers and visiting coaches*	3.4.65
32	Burton versus Canto Playgroup (1989)	Leaving a minor to manage young students		3.4.66
33	Porter versus City of Bradford MBC (1985)	Head teacher responsible for deploying incompetent staff	*Supervision, control, behaviour management and group management*	3.4.78
34	Wooldridge versus Sumner (1962)	Officials have a duty of care for spectators when on pitch		3.4.79
35	Smolden versus Whitworth (1996)	Officials must apply rules of sport correctly		3.4.80
36	Norfolk County Council versus Kingswood Activity Centre (2007)	Staff not trained adequately	*Professional learning for staff*	3.4.86
37	van Oppen versus the Clerk to the Bedford Charity Trustees (1988)	Parental responsibility to insure students	*Insurance*	3.4.113
38	Jones versus Northampton Borough Council (1990)	Not informing participants of hazard		3.4.114
39	G (a child) versus Lancashire County Council (2000)	Duty to inform parents about critical information	*Consent forms and keeping parents informed*	3.5.7
40	R versus Church (2008)	Teacher downloading pornography	*Safeguarding*	3.5.138
41	R versus Drake (2011)	Teacher abusing position of trust		3.5.140
42	R versus Thompson (2008)	Teacher abusing position of trust		3.5.141
43	R versus Walsh (2007)	Teacher abusing position of trust		3.5.142
44	R versus Brooks (2007)	Teacher abusing position of trust		3.5.143

45	R versus Lister (2005)	Teacher abusing position of trust	Safeguarding	3.5.144
46	R versus Unsworth (2000)	Teacher abusing position of trust		3.5.145
47	Dickinson versus Cornwall County Council (1999)	Possibility becomes foreseeable after one instance		3.5.152
48	R versus Calton (1998)	Violent play by student	Violent play	3.5.153
49	Hattingh versus Roux (2011, South Africa)	Dangerous and illegal play		3.5.154
50	Gravil versus Carroll (1) and Redruth RFU Club (2) (2008)	Vicarious responsibility		3.5.155
51	R versus Stafford (2009)	Golf rage		3.5.156
52	Beaumont versus Surrey County Council (1968)	Inadequate disposal of faulty equipment	Purchase, maintenance, disposal and movement of equipment	3.6.43
53	Steed versus Cheltenham Borough Council (2000)	Faulty goalposts		3.6.44
54	Greenwood versus Dorset County Council (2008)	Injury folding trampoline		3.6.45
55	Hall versus Holker Estate Co Ltd (2008)	Goal netting not secured, causing injury	Purchase, maintenance, disposal and movement of equipment and Equipment	3.6.46 / 2.3.97
56	Jones versus Monmouthshire County Council (2011)	Tripping hazard	Work areas and playing surfaces	3.7.51
57	Young versus Plymouth City Council (2010)	Tripping hazard		3.7.52
58	Bassie versus Merseyside Fire and Civil Defence Authority (2005)	Dusty floor as slipping hazard		3.7.53
59	Douch versus Reading Borough Council (2000)	Undulating playing surface		3.7.54
60	Taylor versus Corby Borough Council (2000)	Holes in playing surface		3.7.55
61	Futcher versus Hertfordshire LA (1997)	Compacted sand causing long-jump injury		3.7.56
62	R versus Unwin (2011)	Importance of reputable transport companies	Transport Management	3.8.53
63	Jones versus Cheshire County Council (1997)	Exceeding set ratios	Ratios and group sizes	3.9.9

64	Begum versus the Head Teacher and Governors of Denbigh High School (2006)	School's right to set uniform policy		3.10.31
65	Watkins-Singh versus the Governing Body of Aberdare High School and Rhondda Cynon Taff Unitary Authority (2008)	Covering or removal of religious artefacts in PES	*Religious and cultural issues*	3.10.32
66	R versus HTM (2008)	Foreseeability as to the likelihood of injury occurring		3.11.21
67	Liverpool City Council versus The Adelphi Hotel (2010)	Inadequate risk assessment	*Risk assessment*	3.11.22
68	R versus Ellis (2003)	Not communicating risk		3.11.29
69	Poppleton versus Portsmouth Youth Activities Committee (2008)	Ignoring warnings of risk	*Reporting, recording and communicating risk*	3.11.30
70	Edwards versus NCB (1949)	Definition of 'reasonably practicable'		3.11.31

Glossary of Terms

Additional educational needs	Specific requirements relating to issues such as ability, cultural background, ethnicity and language, which may have safety implications and should be considered by those delivering physical education and sport.
Adults	Occasionally used as a collective term for school staff, volunteers and paid coaches.
Adults supporting learning	See *Support staff*.
Class teachers or qualified teachers (QTS)	Used specifically in circumstances where qualified teachers have a particular responsibility (includes lecturers in further and higher education).
Coaches	All those who are not members of school staff who are contracted (ie paid) to deliver an agreed physical education or school sport programme.
Cover staff/cover supervisors	Adults employed to supervise groups doing pre-prepared work. They may not have any expertise in physical education and, as such, should take groups for classroom-based lessons.
Employers	Includes local authorities, local authority children's services, departments of education and education service, education and library boards, school governing bodies, trustees, managers of other premises (including school grounds and outdoor centres) and self-employed people who employ others.
Foundation/Key Stage 1	In Northern Ireland, students aged 5–7 years.
Head teachers	All those responsible for managing educational establishments (includes principals).
Helpers	Used specifically in the context of special educational needs and disability.
Key Stage 1	Students aged 5–7 years (now covered by the Foundation Phase in Wales, which includes students aged 3–7).
Key Stage 2	Students aged 7–11 years.
Key Stage 3	Students aged 11–14 years.
Key Stage 4	Students aged 14–16 years.
Parents	Includes carers, guardians and other next-of-kin categories.
Physical education	Short for the term *physical education and sport* – abbreviated to *physical education* or *PES* for convenience.
School sport	All sessions that take place outside of lesson time (formerly known as *extra-curricular activities* or *out-of-school-hours learning*).
Students	All young people attending any form of educational establishment.
Subject leaders	All those responsible for managing physical education and sport in any phase or educational establishment.
Support staff	Adults without qualified teacher status (QTS) who contribute to education programmes whether in a paid or voluntary capacity. (The term *practitioners* is used in Wales.) Use of this term excludes trainee teachers.

Teachers (occasionally referred to as *staff*)	Any adult delivering physical education to students with the approval of the head teacher, including qualified teachers, volunteers and paid coaches, agency staff and those on a school staffing roll without qualified teacher status, such as learning mentors, classroom assistants and teaching assistants.
Trainee teachers	Those undergoing courses, whether school- or university-based, leading to qualified teacher status who participate in school placements for the key purpose of learning the skills of teaching. Trainee teachers do not fall within the category of 'support staff' and should not be considered substitute teachers.
Young leaders	Students under the age of 18 (who are closely managed by school staff) who are not paid for their work within physical education or school sport programmes.

Abbreviations

AALA	Adventure Activities Licensing Authority
ABAE	Amateur Boxing Association of England
ABRS	Association of British Riding Schools
ADHD	attention deficit hyperactivity disorder
AETR	European Agreement Concerning the Work of Crew of Vehicles Engaged in International Road Transport
afPE	Association for Physical Education
AIDS	acquired immune deficiency syndrome
ARP	accident reporting point
ASA	Amateur Swimming Association
ASD	autistic spectrum disorder
ASL	adult supporting learning
BAB	British Aikido Board
BAHA	British Adventure Holidays Association
BASI	British Association of Snowsport Instructors
BCA	British Caving Association
BCU	British Canoe Union
BG	British Gymnastics
BHFNC	British Heart Foundation National Centre for Physical Activity and Health
BHS	British Horse Society
BJA	British Judo Association
BKA	British Karate Association
BMA	British Medical Association
BMC	British Mountaineering Council
BMG	British Mountain Guides
BSAC	British Sub-Aqua Club
BS EN	British Standards European Norm
BSI	British Standards Institute
BSSA	British Street Surfing Association
BSUK	BaseballSoftball*UK*

BTCB	British Taekwondo Control Board
CANI	Canoe Association of Northern Ireland
CE	Conformité Européene
CIMSPA	Chartered Institute for the Management of Sport and Physical Activity
CLOtC	Council for Learning Outside the Classroom
CPR	cardiopulmonary resuscitation
CRB/DBS	Criminal Records Bureau/Disclosure and Barring Service (also Disclosure Scotland and AccessNI)
DfE	Department for Education (formerly Department for Children, Schools and Families or Department for Education and Skills [DfES])
EAL	English as an additional language
EAP	emergency action plan
ECB	England and Wales Cricket Board
EKF	English Karate Federation
EU	European Union
EVC	educational visit coordinator
FA	Football Association
FAQs	frequently asked questions
FAW	Football Association of Wales
FARS	Federation of Artistic Roller Skating
FCO	Foreign and Commonwealth Office
FILA	Fédération Internationale des Luttes Associées
GAA	Gaelic Athletic Association
GUI	Golfing Union of Ireland
HIV	human immunodeficiency virus
HLTA	higher level teaching assistant
HRPA	health-related physical activity
HSE	Health and Safety Executive
HSWA	Health and Safety at Work Act 1974
HT	head teacher
IABA	Irish Amateur Boxing Association
IOL	Institute for Outdoor Learning
ITE	initial teacher education
LA	local authority
LOtC	Learning Outside the Classroom
LSCB	local safeguarding children board
LTA	Lawn Tennis Association
MCA	Maritime and Coastguard Agency
MiDAS	Minibus Driver Awareness Scheme
MLT	Mountain Leader Training
NaRS (PL)	National Rescue Standard Pool Lifeguard
NaRS (SAT)	National Rescue Standard for the Pool Safety Award for Teachers

NCPL	National College for Professional Learning
NCSS	National Council for School Sport
NDCS	National Deaf Children's Society
NDTA	National Dance Teachers Association
NICAS	National Indoor Climbing Award Scheme
NISA	National Ice Skating Association
NIVB	Northern Ireland Volleyball
NOPs	normal operating procedures
NRASTC	National Rescue Award for Swimming Teachers and Coaches
NSAI	National Standards Authority of Ireland
NSSA	National School Sailing Association
OEAP	Outdoor Education Advisers' Panel
OT	occupational therapist
PADI	Professional Association of Diving Instructors
PAS	Publicly Available Specification
PAT	portable appliance test
PCV	passenger-carrying vehicle
PL	professional learning
PPA	planning, preparation and assessment
PPE	personal protective equipment
PSOPs	pool safety operating procedures
PSV	public service vehicle
PUWER	Provision and Use of Work Equipment Regulations 1998
QTS	qualified teacher status
R	Regina (more commonly stated as 'the Crown')
REPs	Register of Exercise Professionals
RFL	Rugby Football League
RFU	Rugby Football Union
RIDDOR	Reporting of Injuries, Diseases and Dangerous Occurrences Regulations 1995
RLSS UK	Royal Life Saving Society UK
RNIB	Royal National Institute of Blind People
RoSPA	Royal Society for the Prevention of Accidents
RPII	Register of Play Inspectors International
RYA	Royal Yachting Association
RYANI	Royal Yachting Association Northern Ireland
SALT	speech and language therapist
SAPs	standard accident procedures
SCA	Scottish Canoe Association
SEBD	social, emotional and behavioural difficulties
SEBDA	Social, Emotional and Behavioural Difficulties Association
SENCO	special educational needs coordinator
SEND	special educational needs and disability

SGU	Scottish Golf Union
SL	subject leader
SLSGB	Surf Life Saving GB
STA	Swimming Teachers' Association
SVA	Scottish Volleyball Association
UKA	UK Athletics
VOSA	Vehicle and Operator Services Agency
WABA	Welsh Amateur Boxing Association
WLA	Welsh Lacrosse Association
WRU	Welsh Rugby Union
WYA	Welsh Yachting Association
YET	Young Explorers' Trust
YMCAfit	YMCA Fitness Industry Training

Introduction

Welcome to the eighth edition of *Safe Practice in Physical Education and Sport*. The only publication of its kind, this handbook is essential reading for all those involved in the teaching of physical education, physical activity and school sport in all types of educational establishments. The aim of the handbook is to provide a sound framework against which you may analyse and adjust your own practice, and to help you make informed judgements about safe practice in relation to your own circumstances.

Numerous national organisations commend this publication to school staff, parents and other adults working in an educational context. It is also used extensively by the legal profession.

It has been fully updated to reflect recent developments in practice, nationally recognised guidance, statute and case law relevant to physical education, physical activity and school sport. In response to ongoing review and consultation, it has also been extensively restructured and redesigned to ensure that it remains user-friendly. In addition, afPE has reviewed its resources and professional development following the publication of the new teachers' professional standards and the Ofsted inspection framework. The new edition of *Safe Practice in Physical Education and Sport* will support physical education and sport (PES) professionals in achieving effective health and safety procedures as outlined in the aforementioned publications.

Terminology Used in the Handbook

The term **must** is used only where the situation described relates to a statutory requirement. Otherwise, **should** and similar terminology are used to illustrate regular and approved practice.

The term **teacher** is used as a common descriptor of the adult teaching the class, whether a qualified teacher, support staff member, visiting coach or other person contributing to the PES programme.

The term **class teacher** or **QTS** is used to identify the qualified teacher.

The term **lesson** is used to describe both curricular time activities and out of lesson time sports sessions.

The term **parent** is intended to include carers, guardians and other next-of-kin categories.

The term **head teacher** or **leadership team** is used to refer to the overall management of any educational establishment.

A **hazard** is something with the potential to cause harm, and **risk** is the likelihood of injury occurring from a hazard.

The term **accident** describes an event that results in injury.

The term **incident** describes an adverse event resulting in an **undesired situation** or **near miss** where no injury occurred but there was the potential to cause injury.

The principles set out in this handbook are also relevant to other contexts, such as early years, further and higher education, prison services, commercial providers and other countries. All those involved in the delivery of physical activity in such contexts should be able to apply the guidance provided to their own circumstances.

Health and safety legislation applies to all the home countries in the United Kingdom. However, other specific legislation may vary. Although the position in each of the home countries is broadly similar, those involved in the delivery of PES in England, Northern Ireland, Scotland and Wales are recommended to visit the following websites for details of specific legislation and policy:

www.legislation.gov.uk/browse (UK-wide information covering England)

www.legislation.gov.uk/browse/ni

www.legislation.gov.uk/browse/scotland

www.legislation.gov.uk/browse/wales

Navigating this Handbook

Section 1: Basic Principles

Important reading for **all who teach and manage PES**, it sets out the rationale for the book and gives explanations of the models included.

Section 2: Safe Teaching Principles

This section is also important reading for **all who teach PES**. The first part of this section provides a table of the effective teaching principles underpinning the provision of adequate safety standards. The second part provides additional information on each one. You can then use this information according to your needs.

Section 3: Safe Management Principles

Very relevant to **subject leaders, leadership teams and governors**, as well as any teacher seeking detail about specific issues, this section contains a generic policy statement and eight aspects of management including:

- summary lists of issues that may be relevant for inclusion in a school's PES documentation on policy and procedures

- 46 different topics of safe practice that will help structure the subject documentation and provide detailed guidance on current safety standards

- 70 case law summaries that reinforce the topic principles.

Section 4: Essential Learning about Safe Practice

This section is important reading for **all who teach PES**. It emphasises the importance of involving students in their own safety, setting out what students should learn, based on an easily remembered acronym, and some thoughts on how the principles may be easily learnt.

Section 5: Applying the Principles to Specific Areas of Activity

This section gives a summary of principles applied across nine areas of activity and related to specific sports and physical activities.

CD-ROM Appendices

Twenty-five appendices, including exemplar forms and other supplementary information, are available on the CD-ROM. Some can be amended to a school's particular situation.

Section 1:
Basic Principles

This section sets out the rationale for the book and gives explanations of the models included. **It is important reading for all who teach physical education and sport.**

1.1 Overview

1.1.1 An activity is judged to be safe in physical education and sport (PES) where the risks associated with the activity are deemed to be acceptably low. **Risk** is the likelihood – or probability – of harm occurring, and **safety** is a judgement about the acceptability of those risks. Identifying the risks and deciding whether the level of risk is acceptably low, through good teaching and management of a situation, is the day-to-day responsibility of all teachers of physical education. Some feel more comfortable with this than others. In practice, the realisation of risk actually leading to injury is rare in PES.

1.1.2 PES consists of practical activities involving lots of movement, often at speed, with changes in direction, frequently focusing on an object or other people, making rapid decisions, possibly in a relatively confined area and involving relatively large numbers. In such a situation, injuries will happen very occasionally and almost always be of a minor nature, only rarely causing more serious harm. The fact that an occasional accident occurs does not mean there has been a breach of safety standards, particularly where sensible, proportionate and appropriate forethought and planning are evident.

1.1.3 Health and safety statute, supported by civil case law, places ultimate responsibility for health and safety on the **employer** (eg local authority [LA], governors, trustees or proprietor). This includes the duties to:

- have a health and safety policy (including PES)
- initiate procedures to ensure satisfactory implementation of the policy
- provide a safe place of work
- assess and manage the risks of all activities
- inform employees of measures to make situations safe
- provide training and supervision, where appropriate
- monitor implementation of the procedures.

1.1.4 The responsibilities cannot be devolved, but tasks to fulfil the employer's responsibilities can be, and are, devolved to school level. Schools **must apply** the employer's policies and directives – this would include what is often referred to as 'guidance' – though the leadership team and staff may choose to go beyond what the employer requires in order to establish appropriate standards specific to a particular school's context.

1.1.5 The same legal source requires **employees** – those teaching and managing the subject – to:

- take reasonable care of the health and safety of themselves and others
- cooperate with the employer on health and safety issues
- know and apply the employer's policy for health and safety
- report any concerns about health and safety
- do what is within their power to prevent further injury from reported concerns
- not interfere with or misuse items for health and safety, such as fire extinguishers or safety signs
- participate in safety inspections.

1.1.6   The underlying rationale for identifying and applying consistent, safe standards is as follows:

- Students should be able to experience a wide range of activities in which safe-practice measures enable such opportunities rather than prevent them.

- They are entitled to be taught in a safe and healthy environment.

- They should be empowered to manage their own safety in order to progressively become independent in lifelong activity.

- High quality PES involves challenge and progression.

- Safe-practice requirements should be proportionate to the identified risks of an activity.

- Common sense should be used in assessing and managing the risks of any activity.

- Teachers have a legal duty to be proactive in establishing and maintaining a safe learning environment.

- Accident prevention is desirable for health, economic and legal reasons.

- The existence of risk and exposing someone to that risk is sufficient for liability to be established. Injury is not a necessary outcome in health and safety law (though it is for civil claims for compensation).

1.1.7   Schools thus have a **duty** to provide a safe working environment and safe systems of work for the staff, students and other visitors, as well as a responsibility to ensure students are educated about safe practice.

1.1.8   There is an old adage that teachers should 'teach safely and teach safety'. Often, the focus has been on controlling safe standards in teaching situations – **teaching safely** – with sometimes less thought about students learning about safety in order to become independent in their activity – **teaching safety**. Both aspects are important. Applying safe practice in PES is **our** responsibility – every single one of us – those who teach it, those who lead and manage it (subject leaders, leadership teams and network managers) and those who learn about it (students).

1.1.9   This edition of *Safe Practice in Physical Education and Sport* is set out in a format to emphasise these three aspects:

- **Teaching** – good teaching is safe teaching.

- **Managing** – good leadership and management contribute towards a safe learning environment.

- **Learning** – learning about and applying safe practice is fundamental to responsible independent participation in physical activity.

1.1.10   Effective teaching and effective leadership and management are recognised as being significant contributors towards effective learning – a simple but very appropriate model on which to base the development of safe practice.

1.1.11   Dependence on activity-specific checklists does not enhance a clear understanding and application of safety standards to our work. Whether in adventure, aquatic, athletic, dance, games, gymnastic or health-based activities, or physically active play, there are common principles of safe practice that apply. These form generic prompts for ensuring safe standards that need to be understood and applied to a specific situation.

1.1.12   This handbook sets out **generic principles** that may impact on safe practice across the range of activities in PES. Use this handbook to consider the generic principles and select and apply those that are relevant to your particular circumstances and the particular activities you teach. In this way, the issues common to virtually all practical contexts in PES can be applied to specific situations. **All teachers** of PES need to consider and apply these generic principles to their particular situations as needed.

1.1.13 What is necessary to ensure the safe delivery of, and learning from, a broad PES programme? Simply:

- good teaching in lessons

- good leadership and management (organisation) of the subject

- effective, inclusive safety education (what students should know)

- safety standards and procedures plus a risk assessment for PES that are:
  - written
  - comprehensive
  - specific to the school
  - reviewed regularly (typically annually)
  - clearly and regularly communicated
  - applied in practice by all contributing to the PES programme.

1.1.14 This model is based on the requirements established by statute, case law and best practice. With these criteria in place, the teaching and management of PES will be safe and effective in contributing to students becoming independent through challenging but safe experiences in physical activity and sport throughout their lives.

1.1.15 The triangle **risk-management model** (Figure 1 – below and Appendix 1 on the CD-ROM), consistently promoted by afPE, is used within this handbook as it is comprehensive, logical and easy to apply to all physical education and sport situations. It identifies the different issues that may make one situation safe but another, though similar, of greater risk. For example, where all other aspects are common, variations in student behaviour and attitude can make a situation safe where behaviour is good, and unsafe where it is poor, whether in adventure, aquatic, athletic, dance, games, gymnastic, health-based or active play contexts.

1.1.16 Schools need to consider the detail set out in the model and amend it to make it specific to the particular circumstances of the school.

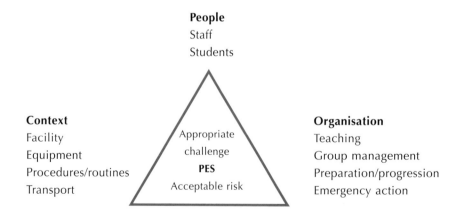

Figure 1: The triangle model for safe practice/managing risk in PES
(courtesy of Beaumont, Eve, Kirkby and Whitlam)

1.1.17   **Managing risk** (safe practice) is simply a process of applying established safety principles, deciding whether these are sufficient for the circumstances and, if necessary, applying further, additional safety measures to ensure the work situation is acceptably safe. In this way, the benefits of appropriate challenge, enjoyment, excitement, progression, achievement and improvement can be provided within a safe learning environment where the benefits outweigh the risk of injury.

1.1.18   A structured way of working through this process is to apply existing procedures and routines to the particular situation then think logically through the session to decide whether the applied procedures are sufficient to make the session safe. This is **forethought** or forward planning and is an essential aspect of effective teaching, effective management and effective learning. Where concerns exist about safety standards, additional procedures need to be applied to alleviate the concerns. When all relevant controls are in place, then the remaining risk is **residual or real risk**, and teachers can determine whether this level of risk is outweighed by the benefits of doing the planned activity. Where the risk still outweighs the benefits of the activity, it should not take place, or be abandoned if it has commenced.

1.1.19   If one considers a continuum from a totally safe context to one that is dangerous (Figure 2), then an increased likelihood of injury occurring can be anticipated as one progresses along the continuum.

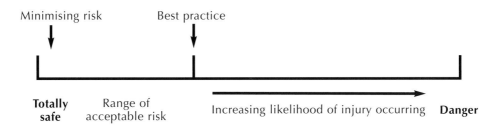

Figure 2: Managing risk*

1.1.20   Teachers are often very good at establishing and maintaining safe learning situations in all aspects of their work, including PES. They **manage risk** effectively. This is evident in the ongoing monitoring and observation of students and the adjustment of situations within a range of acceptable risk where injury is unlikely because the pitch and organisation of the tasks set are within the capabilities of the students involved – ie good teaching and a form of **risk-benefit analysis**. High quality PES, or best practice, may be achieved through pitching the challenge of the students' work on the cusp of this acceptable range of risk. The cusp is not a set point as this will move along the continuum according to the level of challenge and safe organisation of the situation. Events may be extremely challenging but safe because the circumstances are managed efficiently.

1.1.21   There may be occasions when teachers recognise that a situation has progressed along the continuum, beyond the cusp of best and safe practice, to a point where injury is more likely to occur. This is, in effect, a **risk assessment**. They then stop the work, reassess and amend the situation to move back within the range of acceptable risk, where the pitch or organisation of the activity is again challenging but safe. This is an example of **risk control**. Across the profession, this awareness and response are very evident. This is managing risk appropriately in order to achieve high quality learning, progression and development in a safe learning environment. Where the level of risk cannot be brought back under safe control, the activity must be abandoned.

* Whitlam, P. (2004) *Case Law in Physical Education*. Leeds: afPE/Coachwise Ltd. ISBN: 1-902523-77-6.

1.1.22   Some colleagues deployed to deliver PES misunderstand the expected standard of safety required and seek to make situations as safe as possible, rather than as safe as necessary – a very helpful explanation of managing risk by the Royal Society for the Prevention of Accidents (RoSPA). Others may lack the competence and confidence to provide a learning environment where the challenge is appropriate while remaining within a safe context. In order for them to feel safe, they actually **minimise the risk** by limiting the students' work to a level where the demand is insufficient to enable learning to occur; challenge is lacking and progression, excitement and high quality physical education cannot evolve. This is not good practice. It is important that any such lack of confidence and competence by members of staff is recognised and respected, and support provided to enable them to develop the confidence to allow challenging and exciting student activity to occur. In this way, they will progress from minimising risk to managing risk and be better placed to fulfil student entitlement in PES.

1.1.23   This handbook supports the promotion of good practice as simply **teaching safely and teaching safety** through effective teaching and effective management, achieving effective learning about safe practice. Within this, it is recognised that school staff work within a 'range of reasonable options' (as per the Woodbridge School case [2002]), which means there is no single way of organising a learning situation; lessons can include the application of alternative and acceptable strategies other than those included here. The content offered here is general guidance to help achieve successful and safe outcomes.

1.1.24   Inevitably, it is impossible to account for all eventualities, and you may have specific issues or concerns that are not answered by the guidance given here. In these circumstances, you are encouraged to seek further clarification from appropriate sources (eg LA support staff, higher education providers, other school staff, governing body of sport websites, sports coach UK) and/or through afPE's newsletter, website or health and safety team (email, telephone or written correspondence) or the health and safety professional development programme within the National College for Professional Learning (NCPL) programme (contact cpdopportunities@afpe.org.uk).

1.2   Relevant Case Law

1.2.1   R versus Porter (2008):

*A young child fell down some school steps. The Court of Appeal dismissed the allegation of negligence by distinguishing between **real risk and fanciful or hypothetical risk**. One of the criteria for establishing whether real risk exists is whether there is evidence of similar accidents in normal circumstances. No history of accidents in the same context is a strong indicator that real risk is manageable.*

1.2.2   R versus Chargot and Ruttle Contracting (2008):

*This case reinforced the principle that the Health and Safety Executive focus on the **leadership** in relation to safety standards and accidents. The duties set out in the Health and Safety at Work Act 1974 were described by the judge as 'responsibilities imposed on employers as results to be achieved or prevented' and therefore cannot be ignored or dismissed. It also confirmed the **common sense standard** of a reasonable response to health and safety concerns as being 'a material risk to health and safety which any reasonable person would appreciate and take steps to guard against'.*

Section 2:
Safe Teaching Principles

The quality of teaching is recognised as being the greatest influence on students' achievement and attainment.

This section is of particular relevance for everyone delivering physical education and sport sessions.

'Safety is not a gadget but a state of mind.'

Eleanor Everet, American health and safety consultant

2.1 Overview

2.1.1 This section sets out the **fundamental principles** all staff teaching physical education lessons and sport sessions need to consider and build into their planning and teaching as appropriate to the particular circumstances. The content is based on the premise that effective teaching will be safe teaching.

2.1.2 When planning and delivering physical education lessons, staff should consider – and record if appropriate or necessary – whether the following principles are relevant to the particular circumstances in order to ensure students feel safe and are safe during the session.

2.1.3 Those principles considered to be pertinent to the particular circumstances of the teacher should be built into the planning and delivery of the sessions. This will provide a safe and secure learning environment where the **benefits of the activity outweigh the likelihood of injury** occurring. By applying these principles to your normal forethought, you will remember them quickly and put them into practice easily.

2.1.4 Where the relevant principles cannot be applied, the teacher should approach their manager and discuss their concerns.

2.1.5 The first part of this section provides an overview of the effective teaching principles underpinning the provision of adequate safety standards. **The second part provides additional information on each one**. You can then use this information according to your needs, either:

- referring to the first part as a prompt for effective, safe planning and teaching and/or

- using the detail in the second part as a learning tool to develop further your understanding of why these principles are so important and what variations may apply in different circumstances.

2.2 Safe Teaching: A Summary

2.2.1 **All teachers** should consider and apply the following principles relevant to them when planning and teaching physical education and sport (PES); not all will be relevant and appropriate to any single lesson – selection of, and emphasis on, particular aspects will be appropriate for a lesson or series of lessons:

> A version of the following tables that can be amended to be specific to individual needs is included on the CD-ROM as Appendix 2.

People-related principles

The Adult Teaching the Lesson (the 'Teacher') Should:	Further Information (Paragraphs and Page)
• have the **competence** to teach the activity safely – do they have the knowledge, expertise (and qualifications where deemed necessary) to respond to the circumstances that can be reasonably anticipated to occur in relation to the ability levels of the students and the demands of the activity	2.3.7–2.3.11, page 26
• show **forethought** by thinking and planning logically through the lesson – 'This is what I want to do; this is the way I want to do it; is it safe?'	2.3.31–2.3.36, page 28
• have the **observation and analysis skills** necessary to ensure that what is going on is safe and, if it is not, know what to do to make it safe	2.3.40–2.3.43, page 29
• have good **discipline, behaviour control and group-management skills** to organise and maintain a safe learning environment for all involved	2.3.12–2.3.18, page 26
• **know the students** and cater for their individual needs, confidence, previous experience, behaviour, abilities, health and fitness profiles, medical conditions, stage of development, religious and cultural needs, vulnerability and understanding of safety awareness	2.3.37–2.3.39, page 29
• ensure **support staff** involved in the lesson are suitably **managed**, know their **role and responsibilities** and are kept up to date on relevant student and school information	2.3.69–2.3.73, pages 33–34
• **wear suitable footwear and clothing** for practical activities and **remove their personal effects, such as jewellery**, to minimise the likelihood of causing or receiving injury	2.3.19–2.3.30, pages 27–28; 2.3.49–2.3.55, pages 30–31
• check that **student clothing** is appropriate for the activity and the weather conditions	2.3.2–2.3.6, page 25
• check that **student footwear** (including barefoot work) is appropriate for the activity and work surface, and provides traction, and consider any implications of mixed footwear	2.3.19–2.3.30, pages 27–28
• ensure students tie long hair back; fingernails are appropriately short to prevent injury to themselves or others and check that **student personal effects**, including jewellery and cultural or religious adornments, have been removed or the situation adjusted to make it safe for participation with the personal effects if they cannot be removed; where the teacher cannot identify any reasonable alternative organisation strategy to make the situation safe, the student should not take part in the activity aspect of the lesson	2.3.49–2.3.55, pages 30–31
• ensure **personal protection** is worn by the students where it is deemed necessary for safe participation, or the activity is amended to enable safe participation without the personal protection	2.3.56–2.3.60, pages 31–32

21

	Further Information (Paragraphs and Page)
• develop **students' involvement in, and responsibility for, their own safety** relevant to their age, ability, experience and awareness by checking their understanding; providing opportunities to assume appropriate levels of responsibility; regular question and answer; giving clear instructions and demonstrations; and highlighting examples of good practice	2.3.65–2.3.68, page 33
• follow relevant **safeguarding** procedures	2.3.61–2.3.64, page 32
• check **parental consents**, where and if relevant to the activity.	2.3.44–2.3.48, pages 29–30

Context-related principles

The Adult Teaching the Lesson (the 'Teacher') Should:	Further Information (Paragraphs and Page)
• know and apply the employer's and/or school's **policy and procedures** relating to physical education, such as dealing with emergencies or physical contact (touching) with students	2.3.17, page 26; 2.3.45, page 30; 2.3.49, page 30; 2.3.59, page 32; 2.3.107, page 38; 2.3.108–2.3.112, pages 38–39
• maintain a knowledge of how many students and who are present and participating in the lesson, and maintain relevant **registers and records** of non-participation in order to monitor and adjust the programme, where necessary, when students rejoin after injury or absence	2.3.113–2.3.117, page 39
• check the **changing provision** in terms of safety, security, and supervision appropriate for the age and/or development stage of the students	2.3.74–2.3.81, pages 34–35
• ensure orderly movement to the **work area**, whether on or off site	2.3.125–2.3.127, pages 41–42
• be familiar with the facility, whether on or off site, and check the available **space is sufficient** for the group size, nature and demands of the activity and skill levels of the students	2.3.126, page 41
• carry out a **visual check of the working area**, noting any obstacles, damaged areas or leakages for example	2.3.125–2.3.127, pages 41–42
• carry out a visual check of the **fire safety provision** and that evacuation routes are clear as they enter a facility and before the lesson commences	2.3.99–2.3.101, pages 36–37
• know the school's procedures for dealing with **injury, emergency evacuation or critical incidents** as relevant to an on-site or off-site location	2.3.103–2.3.107, pages 37–38

The Adult Teaching the Lesson (the 'Teacher') Should:	Further Information (Paragraphs and Page)
• consider **equipment** practicalities, including storage, accessibility, condition, carrying, positioning, being fit for purpose, using the item only for the purpose it is designed for, retrieval systems (such as necessary in athletics throwing events), and, where appropriate to the activity, ensure that any necessary **safety and rescue equipment** is readily to hand throughout the lesson	2.3.87–2.3.98, pages 35–36
• ensure any **electrical equipment** has been certified as safe to use by the school's system for testing electrical equipment	2.3.82–2.3.86, page 35
• be familiar with any **walking route** taken by students when they go to any off-site event so safety procedures are adequate	2.3.118–2.3.120, page 40
• follow all school procedures for the safe use of any **transport system** when taking groups off site, such as safe embarkation points, legal requirements being met and passenger lists available to ensure immediate emergency contact with parents.	2.3.121–2.3.124, page 40

Organisation-related principles

The Adult Teaching the Lesson (the 'Teacher') Should:	Further Information (Paragraphs and Page)
• use a well structured and differentiated **scheme of work** to set appropriately challenging work	2.3.181–2.3.185, page 48
• establish a consistent **lesson structure** that includes introductory activity (including appropriate warm-up), technical development, consolidation of skills and concluding activity (including appropriate cool-down)	2.3.144–2.3.145, page 43
• identify clear **learning outcomes** and safe strategies to achieve these, whereby the benefits of the experience outweigh the likelihood of injury occurring	2.3.142–2.3.143, page 43
• carefully plan and graduate **progression and pitch** (level of demand) of the activity, checking students are competent, confident and appropriately prepared before moving on to more complex or demanding tasks	2.3.158–2.3.169, pages 45–46
• use **regular and approved practice** (ie that based on local authority [LA], professional association, governing body of sport or other reliable guidance) so any improvisation strategies are rare, used with caution and only after due forethought as to the possible safety factors	2.3.170–2.3.176, pages 46–47
• ensure a safe **learning environment** through a clear explanation of the task, checking understanding, observing the students' initial response for safe standards, and then reinforcing the instructions and amending or developing the task for individuals in order to maintain a safe but challenging learning situation	2.3.65–2.3.68, page 33; 2.3.102, page 37; 2.3.126, page 41; 2.3.146–2.3.150, pages 43–44; 2.3.194, page 49

• monitor particular students closely, such as those with **visual, hearing, cognitive, behavioural, language, confidence or any other individual needs** to check that they understand the task, can learn within an environment that is safe for them and support staff can be guided accordingly	2.3.102, page 37
• consider their **teaching or observation position** to enable frequent scanning of the whole class to ensure safe practice is maintained	2.3.199, page 50
• manage and supervise **group work** while knowing the **number of students** involved in the lesson and take account of any safe-practice implications for the group size in relation to factors such as planned teaching style, ability, confidence, any specified adult:student ratios or a possible need to adjust the organisation of the lesson to accommodate any space restrictions	2.3.138–2.3.141, page 43
• ensure **preparation** for the lesson is sufficient for the weather conditions and demand of the activity; specific to the activity, where appropriate, and performed safely and accurately in order to be effective in preparing the body and mind for the activity	2.3.145, page 43; 2.3.200, page 50
• consider the level, form and procedure for appropriate safe **supervision** according to the gender mix, age, behaviour and experience of the group, including changing provision	2.3.192–2.3.198, pages 49–50
• **match the students** in terms of size, ability, confidence, previous experience in teaching situations and the first stages of competition, particularly where weight bearing, physical contact or 'accelerating projectiles' are applied and also consider any implications of managing **mixed-gender** activities	2.3.146–2.3.150, pages 43–44
• provide accurate **demonstrations** and explanations in a form that enable individual perceptual preferences – visual, aural and kinaesthetic – to be used to develop understanding and competence	2.3.131–2.3.133, page 42
• where games are concerned, **rules are strictly applied**, even where the students have devised their own	2.3.180, page 48
• restrict **staff participation** in student activities such that their role is simply that of enabling increased fluency to a game situation, as in pausing the flow to establish better positions to receive passes, and ensuring where any physical contact between staff and students is necessary, it is conducted in an appropriate manner such that it cannot be misconstrued or misused	2.3.186–2.3.191, pages 48–49
• consider **rehydration** provision, **additional clothing** and **sun protection** being available as a safety factor according to the weather conditions or demand of the activity	2.3.177–2.3.179, page 47
• monitor the group for signs of **fatigue**, adjusting the level of demand and participation accordingly	2.3.134–2.3.137, pages 42–43
• build **contingency planning** into their preparation for on-site and off-site activities in the event that a situation arises whereby the possibility of injury increases	2.3.128–2.3.130, page 42
• maintain a constant **ongoing safety check** – sometimes referred to as a **dynamic risk assessment** – throughout the lesson and consider how the planned activity or organisation can be amended to maintain that safe standard where doubt is established	2.3.153–2.3.157, pages 44–45

Safe Practice in Physical Education and Sport 2012 Edition

• be aware of the relevant aspects of the school PES **risk assessment** or the normal operating procedures (NOP) and emergency action plans (EAP) of off-site facilities.	2.3.152, page 44

Remember

- Consider which of these safe teaching issues are relevant to your circumstances.

- Obtain additional information on each topic later in this chapter and further into the handbook if you need it.

- Apply the relevant principles as appropriate to your planning and delivery of lessons and sport sessions.

- Regularly refer to the full list and review when your teaching situation alters in any way.

- Discuss any concerns with your line manager.

2.3 Safe Teaching: Some Additional Information for the Teacher

2.3.1 To aid easy access to the issue on which further information is sought, the order has been changed to an alphabetical list within the three factors of people, context and organisation. Each provides more detail if you wish to read up on why they are essential to safe teaching.

People-related principles

Clothing for activity

2.3.2 Students should wear clothing that is **fit for purpose** according to the activity, environment and weather conditions.

2.3.3 **Loose clothing** in gymnastics may catch on equipment and cause injury. Any items, including any of cultural significance, need to be relatively close fitting or removed for reasons of safety of the individual. The fabric of clothing for gymnastics needs to be such that it will not cause slipping from equipment, particularly when individuals are working at a height or in an inverted position.

2.3.4 Students should wear sufficient and appropriate clothing according to the **weather conditions** in order to minimise the likelihood of injury in cold conditions or illness in very hot conditions. When participating in hot weather, protection from the sun is advisable; many schools have established policies for wearing caps and loose, light clothing, as well as advising parents to provide suncream protection for their children.

2.3.5 Loose clothing for **swimming** is not advised, other than during skills tests in controlled situations, due to the drag created, which may adversely affect the confidence of weaker swimmers.

2.3.6 When students arrive at a session with clothing deemed to be inappropriate, strategies need to be applied to make their inclusion safe, or to limit the extent of the activity element of their participation.

More information on student clothing can be found in *Section 3: Safe Management Principles, paragraphs 3.5.44-3.5.48, pages 88-89*.

Competence

2.3.7   Anyone teaching physical education lessons needs to be competent to do so safely.

2.3.8   Individual staff feeling they lack the level of competence necessary to safely teach aspects of physical education or to the level of ability and experience of the students should discuss this with their line manager or head teacher.

2.3.9   The same level of competence **applies at all times** whether in lesson time or out, on or off site, in term time or holidays where the activity is part of a school-organised programme.

2.3.10   Competence to **work alone** in teaching physical education includes the ability to: progressively develop techniques and skills; know whether a situation is safe and, if not, make it safe; apply the rules of a sport; control and organise the class; and use knowledge of the students to provide appropriate challenge and support.

2.3.11   An adult who does not have qualified teacher status (QTS) could therefore be considered to be competent to work alone, but they must **always** work under the **supervision and direction** of a qualified teacher.

> More information on the competence of staff to teach alone can be found in *Section 3: Safe Management Principles, paragraphs 3.4.35-3.4.45, pages 62-64.*

Control, discipline, behaviour and group-management skills

2.3.12   Poor discipline, control and behaviour management or inadequate group-management skills on the part of the teacher may adversely affect the standard of safety in any situation.

2.3.13   **Regular scanning** of the whole group and of any sub-groups is important, even when focusing on supporting a particular student or sub-group, in order to maintain an awareness of what is going on generally.

2.3.14   **Positioning** in order to observe the maximum number of students and maximum work area at any time is important.

2.3.15   The ability to recognise a potentially unsafe situation and **halt activity quickly** to prevent the potential being realised is also important. A clear command to stop activity immediately is a key factor. Strategies and reasons for applying this command should be regularly communicated to students.

2.3.16   Teachers need to have thought through any possible safety implications and the efficiency of changing **group sizes** during lessons before initiating the change because of available space, behaviour, mobility and other relevant factors.

2.3.17   The school's **behaviour** policy and procedures should be known and applied.

2.3.18   Those teaching **higher-risk activities**, such as contact sports, aquatics, combat sports, adventure activities and athletics throwing events, have a particular need for effective discipline, control, behaviour-management skills and observation in order to monitor and respond to any potentially unsafe situation arising.

> More information on control, discipline and group management can be found in *Section 3: Safe Management Principles, paragraphs 3.4.67-3.4.77, pages 71-72.*

Footwear – staff and students

2.3.19 The basic principle is the necessity for **secure footing** whatever the surface or activity involved.

2.3.20 All staff need to **change** from fashion footwear into that appropriate to the lesson location, be it indoors or outdoors, on a hard or soft surface.

2.3.21 For student work in dance and gymnastics, **barefoot work** is the safest whether on floor or apparatus because the toes can grip; aesthetics are also improved through better foot extension. Where the floor condition is unsuitable for barefoot work then close-fitting footwear with thin, pliable soles is next best. Hard-soled trainers are less appropriate and may create a hazard.

2.3.22 **Socks** on a wooden floor cause slipping and are dangerous for any activity.

2.3.23 For **trampolining** activities, non-slip socks or trampoline slippers should be worn to prevent slipping, and to prevent students' toes getting caught in the webbing of some beds.

2.3.24 Some form of footwear is preferable for **indoor games** activities due to the higher frequency of sudden stopping and changing direction quickly where toes can be stubbed.

2.3.25 Footwear for **outdoor games** and athletic activities is dependent on the playing surface used. Studded, bladed or ribbed soles are beneficial in sports where the surface is soft or slippery and smooth soles would not provide secure footing.

2.3.26 All footwear should be of the correct **size** and correctly **tied** in the manner of its design to ensure appropriate support for the ankles. As fashion evolves, there are often items of casual or leisure footwear on the market that have the appearance of trainers. It is important that teachers check to ensure footwear has the required specification and provides the necessary support for safe participation.

2.3.27 Students wearing **boots** for outdoor lessons should avoid, wherever possible, walking over hard surfaces to gain access to the playing area. This can result in studs or blades becoming unacceptably rough and sharp, proving hazardous to opponents in competitive games and practices.

2.3.28 Careful thought should be given to an activity where **mixed footwear** is worn by different students. The premise is, again, secure footing, but consideration needs to be given to whether the mixed footwear, such as trainers and studded boots, would create a likely potential for injury being inflicted on some students. In these circumstances, the teacher may need to consider conditioning the activity to make it safe or even grouping according to footwear in order to manage any perceived risk of injury.

Relevant case law

2.3.29   Farmer versus Hampshire County Council (2006):

*A Year 1 class (5–6 years) had been taught by an experienced teacher how to lift, carry and place gymnastic equipment. The class worked in **bare feet**. A girl fractured her toe when a group dropped a low portable beam. A claim for negligence was based on the need for footwear to be worn when carrying equipment. The claim was dismissed on the basis that barefoot work in gymnastics is **normal** where the floor is suitable; the children had been taught how to carry the items; they were closely supervised by the teacher; footwear gives very little protection if a heavy weight is dropped on the foot; and there is an inappropriate time factor for a whole class to put on and remove footwear during a lesson.*

2.3.30   Villella versus North Bedfordshire Borough Council (1983):

A young girl trampolining in bare feet caught her toe in the webbing and fractured her femur. The claim for compensation was upheld.

> More information on footwear can be found in *Section 3: Safe Management Principles, paragraphs 3.5.49-3.5.57, pages 89-90.*

Forethought

2.3.31   Teachers are required to think about what they want the students to learn, how they want to teach to achieve those outcomes, and how to best organise the lesson before actually engaging in the activity in order to anticipate any situations where harm is likely. This is forethought – **forward planning**: anticipation of what may happen.

2.3.32   As well as anticipating what may cause injury in a planned activity, teachers should think beyond the activity itself to the **organisation and logistics** of a whole event. For example, this may include any implications for transporting students and possible external causes that may impact on the event, such as being delayed by heavy traffic or a road traffic accident. Possible illness or injury to participants or staff during the event is another important factor to plan for.

2.3.33   Such **contingency planning** ensures the more-likely incidents that are not part of a planned event can be managed safely and efficiently.

2.3.34   An important aspect of forethought is providing **clear instructions** to students so there is no misunderstanding of what is expected.

2.3.35   Very occasionally, something may occur that could not reasonably be anticipated (eg a sudden change in weather conditions). In such circumstances, the teacher needs to pause the activity, consider if and how the situation can be managed to make it safe once more and, if no additional precautions or controls can be identified to adjust the situation to enable continuing safely, then the activity must be abandoned because the law requires teachers not to knowingly place others in unsafe situations.

Relevant case law

2.3.36   Denbighshire County Council versus McDermott (2005):

*An experienced climber but inexperienced leader gave **unclear instructions** when he told a hesitant group member abseiling down a rock face with two colleagues roping from the top to 'let go of the rope'. The instruction was meant to encourage* *the climber that she was being supported by her colleagues. The two colleagues at the top of the face thought the instruction was to them and let go of the supporting ropes; so did the injured person. All three let go so no control existed over the descent. She fell 10m on to rocks.*

Knowledge of the students

2.3.37   It is important that the teacher has relevant knowledge of the students they teach for reasons of safe practice. Where the teacher is not the usual adult responsible for the students (eg they are a visiting coach or supply teacher), it is essential that that person is provided with key information about individuals within the group being taught.

2.3.38   This knowledge is important for reasons such as enabling full exploration of gymnastic equipment by those who are confident, competent and well behaved, or adjusting the task for those lacking adequate safety awareness so an artificial ceiling of challenge, progression and enjoyment is not imposed unnecessarily on a whole group.

2.3.39   **Key information** any teacher working with a group would benefit from knowing includes:

- medical information – on a need-to-know basis

- behavioural information

- previous experience

- confidence and competence

- any special educational needs and disability (SEND), individual need or any specific personal circumstances that may affect the student's performance, such as a recent bereavement.

Observation and analysis skills

2.3.40   The ability to **analyse and evaluate** student response to particular tasks is essential to safe teaching, as well as improving performance.

2.3.41   Teachers need to constantly check whether what is taking place is safe and, if not, intervene or stop the activity to make it safe. This requires the expertise to know what is safe and what is required to adjust the technique, skill or movement to make it safe.

2.3.42   For example, teachers should be able to confidently establish when the onset of fatigue begins to impact upon concentration levels – particularly important in activities such as swimming, gymnastics, trampolining and sustained running – or whether the space available to a student is sufficient for the safe execution of a movement.

2.3.43   Where teachers feel they do not have this level of expertise, they should discuss the issue with their line manager in order to determine what should be done to maintain safe situations in lessons.

Parental consent

2.3.44   Parents cannot withdraw their child from prescribed curriculum subjects without formal agreement. They can, however, choose whether their child can take part in **optional** activities outside normal lesson times.

2.3.45 Teachers need to know and apply the school system for arranging parental consent for children to participate in such school sport opportunities.

2.3.46 The consent given is for participation in organised activities and, as such, the information provided to parents needs to be as **comprehensive** as possible in order for them to make informed decisions. They should be made fully aware of the itinerary, at which times the school or the parents have duty of care, any particular requirements and where and when the students will be dismissed.

2.3.47 Any student not providing a **signed consent form** should not take part in an optional school sport activity as there is no evidence that parents have given approval. Neither should students take part where the parent has crossed out any part of the consent form or amended the wording in any way as this could create difficulties should an emergency arise.

2.3.48 Consent forms do not indemnify the teacher should a student be injured and thus no offer of **indemnity** by a parent should be accepted. Even though such an arrangement may be made in good faith by the teacher and parent, the student, if injured, can make a claim for compensation retrospectively in their own right within three years of them becoming an adult, thus making the arrangement between the teacher and parent meaningless in law.

> More information on parental consent can be found in *Section 3: Safe Management Principles, paragraphs 3.5.2-3.5.7, pages 78-79.*
>
> Sample consent forms are available in the following appendices on the CD-ROM:
> - *Appendix 6: Department for Education Recommended Annual Consent Form for Participation in Optional School Trips and Other Off-site Activities*
> - *Appendix 7: Sample Consent Form for the Use of Digital Imagery in School*
> - *Appendix 8: Parental Consent Form for a Student to be Transported in Another Adult's Vehicle.*

Personal effects, including jewellery and cultural or religious adornments

2.3.49 There should be a **whole-school** written policy that is clear, unambiguous and fully available to teachers so they can put into practice what the school policy requires.

2.3.50 Staff also need to be mindful of their own adornments and remove them prior to teaching physical education. The wearing of rings and large hooped or drop earrings, for instance, has been responsible for unnecessary injury in the past and represents a hazard to both staff and students involved in the lesson.

2.3.51 The following procedure should be applied at the commencement of every lesson:
- **All personal effects** should be removed. Staff should always give a verbal reminder to students and, where necessary, visually monitor the group and/or individuals. Particular vigilance may be required when dealing with body jewellery.
- If they cannot be removed, staff need to take action to try to **make the situation safe**. In most situations, this may mean adjusting the activity in some way or, where a risk assessment allows, protecting the item (eg a medical bracelet) with

tape, padding or a wristband. Taping over ear studs, for instance, may offer a measure of protection in some physical-activity situations where individuals are required to work within their own personal space. However, the amount of tape used needs to be sufficient to prevent the stud post penetrating the bone behind the ear should an unintentional blow be received from someone or some item of equipment, such as a ball. Where taping is utilised, the teacher supervising the group maintains the legal responsibility to ensure the taping is effective in its purpose. Staff are not required to remove or tape up earrings for students. Students should come ready for the lesson, preferably with earrings removed or adequately taped.

- If the situation cannot be made safe, the individual student(s) concerned should not actively participate. **Alternative involvement** in the lesson should be possible.

2.3.52   Staff should regularly ask whether anyone is wearing **body jewellery**. Should someone disclose that they are, then the procedure above needs to be initiated. Where no disclosure arises, the lesson can begin, but should the teacher see that body jewellery is being worn during activity, they should stop the activity and initiate the procedure above.

2.3.53   The wearing of **sensory aids**, such as spectacles or hearing aids, will usually be determined by the nature of the activity (eg activities involving physical contact may not be appropriate). Where the sensory aid needs to be worn for safe participation by the individual, then the staff, wherever possible, need to **amend** the activity (such as providing more space and time) or the equipment (such as using a soft ball instead of a harder one) in order to seek to make participation with the sensory aid safe for the wearer and others in the group.

2.3.54   **Long hair** worn by both staff and students should always be tied back with a suitably soft item to prevent entanglement in apparatus and to prevent it obscuring vision. **Nails** need to be sufficiently short to prevent injury to self and others.

Relevant case law

2.3.55   R (ex parte Roberts) versus the Chair and Governors of Cwnfelinfach Primary School (2001):

*The judge determined that the school was entitled to **exclude** the student from physical activity when she wore jewellery, which the parents refused to remove. This was on the basis of health and safety. A claim that the exclusion breached the European Convention on Human Rights was rejected.*

> **More information on the management of personal effects can be found in**
> *Section 3: Safe Management Principles, paragraphs 3.5.58–3.5.65,* **pages 90–91.**

Personal protective equipment

2.3.56   Wearing personal protective equipment (PPE) will not guarantee freedom from injury. It can though, in many cases, **mitigate** the severity of injury by reducing a high-risk situation to one of reasonable or acceptable risk.

2.3.57   It is wise for teachers to fully **inform students** about the purpose, function and limitations of PPE in order to counteract any false sense of security that may arise as a consequence of wearing protective gear. In all activities, it is the application of good technique and skill and rigorous adherence to the rules that remain the most important features of safe participation.

2.3.58   It is a **parental responsibility** to provide PPE where the school has advised it is necessary. It is insufficient to tell students and expect them to inform parents. Teachers should check the school has an effective communication system to keep parents informed of such needs.

2.3.59   It is recommended that PPE policy and procedures **strongly advise** the provision of particular items to parents. Where policy is made mandatory, any student participation without the PPE does not absolve the teacher should injury occur as a result of not having the particular item.

2.3.60   Where the teacher believes PPE is necessary but students do not have the necessary item(s), the teacher is required to consider whether PPE is essential and, if so, to **modify** how the activity is carried out in order to enable participation without the item. This may take the form of grouping according to PPE available and conditioning, or otherwise adjusting, the learning situation to make participation reasonably safe without the PPE item. Teachers cannot proceed with what they planned and ignore the lack of PPE if the planning indicates it is necessary to be worn.

> More information on the use of PPE can be found *in Section 3: Safe Management Principles, paragraphs 3.5.66-3.5.92,* pages 91-95.

Safeguarding

2.3.61   All schools are required to have clear safeguarding policies and procedures. Teachers need to know these, apply them and **inform support staff** of the required protocols and who the member of staff responsible for safeguarding is, to whom they should report concerns.

2.3.62   A teacher's duty is to **pass on concerns** about possible abuse to the appropriate person. There is no requirement for that teacher to find evidence to support any concern nor to have to be certain that significant harm may have, or has, occurred in order to report the concern.

2.3.63   Safeguarding in some schools may be limited in scope to protecting students from **deliberate harm**, including physical, emotional or sexual abuse, neglect, bullying, racist abuse, harassment, discrimination and the potential for abuse of trust by adults working with children and young people. All staff need to know about the **indicators** of intentional harm, the school's systems for reporting causes of concern and how to deal with students **disclosing** information about intentional harm to themselves or others.

2.3.64   In addition to the consideration of preventing intentional harm, many schools also address students being safe and feeling safe through protection from **unintentional harm**. Many of these issues are central to safe teaching and form part of relevant school policies and procedures. For example, the following contribute to this topic, and staff need to know and apply any relevant school procedures about:

- health and safety in PES contexts
- the use of physical intervention (such as supporting students in gymnastics)
- meeting the needs of students with medical conditions
- providing first aid
- educational visits (including sports fixtures, festivals and tours)
- fatigue, exhaustion, overplay and overtraining

- responding to weather conditions

- Internet safety/use of digital imagery in learning and sports events

- transporting students

- staff competence to teach PES safely

- progression in competence and skill

- the implications of intimate care in a PES context

- implications for emergency evacuation from the school buildings during PES sessions and inclement weather conditions.

> **More information on safeguarding can be found in *Section 3: Safe Management Principles, paragraphs 3.5.121-3.5.145*, pages 99-106, and *Appendix 9: Aspects Relevant to Safeguarding Within a Physical Education and Sport Context* on the CD-ROM.**

Students' involvement in, and responsibility for, their own safety

2.3.65   If students are to become independent in their activity through their lifetime, then they need to **learn** about safety standards that apply to their chosen activities at the level of performance, officiating or management they will operate at.

2.3.66   Safe practice is something students, as well as the teacher, need to be aware of and apply in all their activity.

2.3.67   This learning should evolve from the earliest educational experiences in schools. The youngest children should be encouraged to look around them to identify whether they perceive anything that could harm them. Continuously, the teacher needs to identify general considerations and question with the students whether a situation is safe and what considerations need to be made. Progressively, the students should organise learning contexts and the teacher monitor whether the necessary safety considerations have been addressed. Ultimately, the students should have had the learning experiences that enable them to plan and manage their own activities in safe contexts, though in a school situation these would be at best remotely managed rather than truly independent because of the continuing duty of care.

2.3.68   Students should be made aware of the importance of **not eating or chewing** during activity.

> **More information on safety education and the importance of students taking responsibility for their own safety can be found in *Section 4: Essential Learning about Safe Practice*, pages 165-173.**

Support staff

2.3.69   Any adult who is not a qualified teacher, licensed teacher or graduate trainee on the school roll who contributes to a student's learning comes under the collective term of 'support staff', sometimes also known as '**adults supporting learning (ASLs)**'.

2.3.70   This will include classroom assistants, teaching assistants, learning mentors, visiting coaches and volunteer parents but **not trainee teachers**.

2.3.71   Such staff can add to the quality of a PES programme through their expertise, encouragement and support. They can also enable teachers to develop their own expertise by the **teacher learning from the support staff**, particularly when the support staff have specific activity expertise. Class teachers should look to develop their own expertise by working alongside support staff with specific activity expertise wherever possible.

2.3.72   **No support staff should operate independently**. They can work alone if competent and have been evaluated but must be managed effectively by the teacher, who remains legally responsible for the students in their care, whether through direct or indirect supervision of the support staff. Such management involves ensuring any support staff are aware of the limits of their role and responsibilities in relation to applying school policies and procedures.

2.3.73   Communication is also essential so support staff are aware of any relevant student medical conditions, behaviour issues, particular abilities and individual needs.

> **More information on the management and deployment of support staff can be found in *Section 3: Safe Management Principles, paragraphs 3.4.50–3.4.66, pages 65–71*, and *Appendix 16: Potential Roles and Responsibilities when Support Staff Lead School Groups Off Site* on the CD-ROM.**

Context-related principles

Changing provision

2.3.74   This principle is about ensuring **dignity, decency and privacy** where needed, be it for reasons of physical development or other individual needs.

2.3.75   Many primary schools lack changing rooms but find spaces where the sexes, individuals or small groups can change separately in the upper years.

2.3.76   There is no statutory requirement for students to be supervised at all times. However, case law provides a clear indication that the incidence of injury is much higher when students are not supervised than when they are.

2.3.77   The degree and method of supervision will vary according to the particular circumstances, but age, behaviour, potential bullying, location of the staff (in relation to organising equipment, changing, fulfilling the usual pre-lesson organisational tasks or using the time as a positive part of the learning experience) and safety aspects of the space itself will contribute to deciding whether constant direct supervision is necessary or intermittent direct supervision is safe.

2.3.78   Subject to a number of factors, such as location of the changing areas, student behaviour, age and ability, in **joint-gender** teaching situations, where only one member of staff is available for changing-room supervision, a suitable **distant-supervision** system may be implemented. This may take the form of tasking a reliable student with reporting any concerns in the changing area to the teacher outside the changing area.

2.3.79   **Direct supervision** of students enables the teacher to intervene at any time. Decisions to supervise less directly should not be taken lightly.

2.3.80   The changing space should be **checked** regularly, before and during use, to see:

- pegs are not broken, exposing sharp edges
- adequate space is available for the number of students changing

- benching and other furniture is fixed to prevent it toppling over during use

- there are no sharp edges to tiling or heaters that could cause injury

- floor surfaces are not slippery when wet

- personal items and clothing do not litter the floor to cause potential tripping hazards.

2.3.81 Where safety standards are compromised, **alternative arrangements** need to be made and faults reported to the school leadership team for decisions to be taken to restore safe standards.

> **More information on changing provision can be found in** *Section 3: Safe Management Principles, paragraph 3.7.2,* **page 120.**

Electrical equipment

2.3.82 It is a statutory safety requirement that individual electrical items in schools and businesses are tested annually. This is known as **PAT testing** – portable appliance testing – usually an annual certification on individual electrical items.

2.3.83 Someone in school should have the responsibility for ensuring this annual check is carried out by an authorised person, usually external to school.

2.3.84 The items tested will have a label identifying the date of their last test. If it is more than 12 months previous, then inform the relevant person on the leadership team.

2.3.85 Teachers providing their **own items** of equipment need to have them PAT certified by the school before using them in their work.

2.3.86 Any portable electrical appliance lacking a current certificate should not be used.

> **More information on electrical equipment can be found in** *Section 3: Safe Management Principles, paragraph 3.6.18,* **page 112.**

Equipment

2.3.87 Equipment used in a lesson should be **visually checked** prior to students using it, to ensure it is safe to use, assembled correctly and not damaged or faulty.

2.3.88 It is a leadership responsibility to ensure **specialised equipment**, including that for fixed play, gymnastics and fixed weight training, is inspected regularly by a competent and reputable specialist company and staff are informed of any adverse implications of that inspection.

2.3.89 All schools should have a system for teachers to report **faulty** equipment and for ensuring that they in turn are made aware of any faulty equipment.

2.3.90 **Students** should become involved in checking and reporting any faulty equipment in relation to their age, ability and previous experience.

2.3.91 Equipment that has been **condemned** by a specialist company must not be used and needs to be removed so it cannot come back into use inadvertently. Such equipment needs to be made readily identifiable by the specialist company so teachers do not continue use in ignorance of the unsafe situation.

2.3.92 **Storage** of equipment should be discussed by staff so all are aware of what equipment is stored where and why. Storage provision may be limited; space needs to be sufficient to allow safe accessibility for students to pick up, transport and site the equipment they are using.

2.3.93 Students should be taught how to **lift and carry** equipment safely from an early age; how many to a particular item, how to carry correctly and to remain focused on the task and not lose attention that may lead to inadvertent actions, such as stumbling over another item.

2.3.94 In **athletics** events, the importance of transporting individual items correctly cannot be overemphasised. All staff should be familiar with the required procedures for carrying and retrieving discus, shot and javelin implements and for the use of rakes and spades in sand jumping pits.

2.3.95 Equipment should be used for the **purpose it is designed for**. Improvisation is rarely necessary due to the range, quality and quantity of equipment available to schools. Where a decision is made to use an item for a purpose it is not actually designed for, the teacher would need to have a very strong justification for deciding to improvise. Staff discussion about the use of particular items for any reason not directly related to design and purpose will be of benefit in eliminating extraordinary use and establishing consistent practice and safety standards throughout the school.

2.3.96 **Safety and rescue** equipment, such as that relevant to swimming lessons, needs to be confirmed as being to hand before lessons begin so, should an incident occur, a rescue can be initiated immediately without the need for the teacher to locate the equipment after the incident arises.

Relevant case law

2.3.97 Hall versus Holker Estate Co Ltd (2008):

See Section 3: Safe Management Principles, paragraph 3.6.46, page 118, for details.

2.3.98 Morrell versus Owen (1993):

*The court determined that the organisers of an indoor athletics event failed to exercise the degree of **organisational care** necessary when the netting in a sports hall was used for discus throwing, but someone the other side of the netting was hurt because the netting billowed out into the adjacent space and failed to absorb the momentum of the discus.*

> More information on equipment can be found in *Section 3: Safe Management Principles, 3.6 Equipment Management*, pages 110-120.

Fire safety provision

2.3.99 It is the responsibility of the **leadership team** to ensure specific fire safety regulations are applied in the school. This should form part of a school's risk assessment or be a separate risk assessment with all staff kept informed of fire safety precautions and required procedures.

2.3.100   In the **physical education context,** this would typically involve teachers visually checking the emergency evacuation signs are in place and illuminated where required; emergency exits are not blocked and are operative; mats are stored in a specific mat store, where provided, or stored away from electrical circuits to minimise the possibility of fire causing toxic fumes; the teacher knowing how many and which students they are responsible for; being familiar with the emergency evacuation procedures; and knowing the quickest routes to safety.

2.3.101   Teachers should also take account of the possibility of **emergency evacuation** taking place in cold or inclement weather and any implications for potential hypothermia when students may need to leave an indoor facility for an extended period of time while wearing minimal clothing. Teachers should be aware of the school's procedure for catering for this without students being required to delay evacuation in order to put on clothing and footwear.

> **More information on fire safety can be found in** *Section 3: Safe Management Principles, paragraphs 3.7.37-3.7.38,* **page 125, and** *3.11.12,* **page 156.**

Individual needs

2.3.102   Teaching a mixed-ability class is more complex than teaching a small group of talented performers. Students are individuals with differing levels of confidence, ability and prior experience. Within the limits of a large group, those individual circumstances should be monitored and catered for through pre-planning and knowledge of the students involved.

> **More information on individual needs can be found in** *Section 3: Safe Management Principles, paragraphs 3.5.13-3.5.35,* **pages 80-87.**

Injuries, emergencies and critical incidents

2.3.103   Teachers need to know and apply the **school's procedures** for dealing with injuries and other emergencies. Where concerns exist about not knowing the whole-school procedures, teachers need to consult the head teacher.

2.3.104   Particular forethought should be given to dealing with injuries that may occur at the **extremities of the school site** and also during off-site activities that frequently extend beyond the normal school day. In such circumstances, effective and efficient communication with the 'office' or leadership team is essential.

2.3.105   Teachers need not be qualified in **first aid** but must be able to manage the initial injury situation. It is important that teachers have a working knowledge of dealing with emergency situations to the extent that they can manage an initial injury situation effectively and summon the appointed person or first-aider to take over management of the injury.

2.3.106   First aid organisations advise that, in the event of an accident, a responsible person should **manage** the situation typically by:

- keeping calm

- reassuring any casualties

- assessing the situation – making any danger safe and not moving any casualty unless in immediate danger

- ensuring the rest of group is safe – stopping all activity
- sending for help – preferably by mobile, walkie-talkie or sending students to the 'office'
- monitoring, treating and managing situations where there is more than one casualty in the order of those:
  - unconscious
  - with severe bleeding
  - with broken bones
  - with other injuries
- regularly checking consciousness and informing the paramedic if consciousness is lost (also informing them of any relevant medical issues)
- not trying to do too much
- getting others to help
- asking the students (according to age and ability) what happened if the full incident was not seen
- recording the details as soon as possible after the incident.

2.3.107   On the very rare occasions a major crisis or **critical incident** occurs, teachers need to know and apply the school's plan for dealing with such instances. School policy should make staff aware of the relevant aspects of such a plan, and teachers of physical education should familiarise themselves with how they would respond, to what would be a small section of the plan, should they ever become involved in a major incident while taking teams to fixtures, festivals or on sports tours.

> **More information on accidents, emergencies and critical incidents can be found in *Section 3: Safe Management Principles, paragraphs 3.9.18–3.9.37, pages 137–140, Section 4: Essential Learning about Safe Practice, paragraph 4.3.5, page 169,* and in the following appendices on the CD-ROM:**
>
> - ***Appendix 3: First Aid Qualifications and First Aid Kits: An Explanation of the Health and Safety Executive Approved Code of Practice (HSE ACOP) on First Aid 1997***
> - ***Appendix 4: School Accident Report Form***
> - ***Appendix 5: Standard Accident Procedures.***

Policies and procedures

2.3.108   Policies and established procedures provide order and a secure learning and work environment for staff and students. They should be clearly **recorded** and frequently **communicated** to the staff.

2.3.109   Very few policies and procedures that relate to PES are physical-education-specific – they are whole-school policies and procedures, such as those for dealing with injury and emergency situations, emergency evacuation, medical information or obtaining consent for optional activities.

2.3.110   All those contributing to or supporting PES sessions need to be aware of the content of whichever school policies impact on PES and ensure that the detail is applied.

2.3.111 Teachers need to **inform support staff** of relevant policies and procedures before leaving them to teach alone.

Relevant case law

2.3.112 Hippolyte versus Bexley London Borough (1994):

An established asthmatic student in a secondary school suffered a degree of brain damage subsequent to an attack developing during a lesson. She refused the teacher's request to report to the first-aider until the teacher's concern was so great that she then took the student to the school office for attention and expert support. The Court of Appeal dismissed the claim for negligence because the school had **clear and detailed procedures and the teacher followed the procedures fully**. *It was also determined that the 16-year-old student, as an established asthmatic, would be fully aware of the implications of her refusal to follow the teacher's request for her to visit the first-aider and had therefore contributed to the tragic outcome.*

> More information on policies and procedures can be found in *Section 3: Safe Management Principles, 3.2 A Generic Policy Statement for PES*, page 54, and *3.3 Guidance to Develop and Manage Safe-practice Procedures in PES*, page 55.

Registers and records

2.3.113 It is a legal requirement that a school records the presence or absence of students.

2.3.114 It is important to maintain evidence of students' **participation** in practical activities by recording their presence or absence from lessons.

2.3.115 Where a student has been absent from practical activity for a period of time, the teacher needs to **reintegrate** that student into the lessons with care. Extra observation is important to ensure that they can cope with the pitch and progressive experience provided to catch up on the progression made during their absence. The same principle applies where a student joins a group part-way through a lesson.

2.3.116 Equally, records of achievement and attainment provide hard evidence of what a student can and cannot do. This then enables the teacher to pitch the **demand of activity** at a level appropriate to the confidence, prior experience, ability or amount of missed work of individual participants.

Relevant case law

2.3.117 Moore versus Hampshire County Council (1981):

A student who was excused physical activity for medical reasons eventually persuaded a teacher to allow her to take part. During her first gymnastics lesson, she fell and broke her ankle while attempting a handstand. The teacher had **not supervised her closely** *in what was her introduction to work the other students had experienced over a series of lessons, thus failing to cater for that student's individual needs and background.*

> More information on registers can be found in *Section 3: Safe Management Principles, paragraph 3.4.72, page 72.*

Transport and walking routes

2.3.118   When taking students off site, the safety implications of any **walking route** should be known to all staff involved in the session so appropriate safety procedures may be ensured.

2.3.119   Where staff are not familiar with walking routes, they should seek guidance and try to check the route personally before embarking on the excursion.

2.3.120   Where staff judge that the route is unsafe for any reason, they should consult the leadership team.

2.3.121   Students may be **transported** to off-site events by car, taxi, bus, minibus, coach, train or aeroplane. Generic safety procedures apply to these, and some specific considerations will also be relevant, such as the need for booster seats in private cars for students less than 12 years of age and less than 135cm in height. Staff need to be aware of any particular **school requirements** relating to any form of transport for students. Where unsure, the leadership team should be consulted.

2.3.122   As well as safety issues relating to the form of transport used, staff also need to have planned, **before the trip commences**, for considerations such as:

- safe embarkation points

- where the staff sit in the mode of transport in order to maintain adequate supervision and control

- where the students sit – leave the rearmost seats empty if possible in case a vehicle runs into the back of the bus, coach or minibus

- knowing the number of students on the vehicle and counting them back on to the vehicle after any break in the journey

- having a secure system in place to contact parents, directly or via the school, in the event of a delay in the return journey or the vehicle being involved in a road traffic accident

- dismissal and dispersal of the group after the event – students should not be dropped off at any point where the teacher has not informed the parents prior to the event unless the parents concerned can be contacted to confirm any change in the process

- how many staff are required for the journey, this being determined by the type of transport, group-management implications at the event, behaviour, discipline, disability, length of journey or driving requirements.

2.3.123   Where the teacher drives a minibus, the school is likely to have detailed procedures that must be followed. It is not a legal requirement that more than one adult accompanies a group on a minibus, but the driver must not be distracted unless in the event of an emergency, and cannot drive and supervise at the same time.

2.3.124   Where unsure, consult your leadership team.

> **More information on transport and walking routes can be found in *Section 3: Safe Management Principles, 3.8 Transport Management pages 127-133*.**

Work area

2.3.125   **Before and during lessons**, the work area needs to be checked to ensure it is safe for student participation. This may include the following:

- The **floor** or other outdoor work surface needs to provide secure footing to prevent tripping, slipping or other injury.

- **Obstructions** should be identified and removed, where possible, or the students made aware and the teacher take account of these throughout the session.

- **Run-off areas** from sport pitches and courts should be adequate for the age, ability and level of performance of the students.

- **Lighting** needs to be adequate for safe participation, and artificial lighting high and protected by grilles or similar covering to prevent sharp particles falling to the floor.

- The **temperature** needs to be adequate for safe activity. There is no upper limit of temperature for activity – where hotter than appropriate, the demand of the activity should be reduced or draught created to reduce the temperature. The minimum temperature for indoor PES activities is technically 15°C, but where any temperature close to or below that exists, either body preparation needs to be extended or the lesson shortened or abandoned.

- **Clarity of water** is essential in swimming, such that the teacher can see the bottom of the pool at all times, being aware of glare and shadow. They should frequently **scan** the bottom of the pool during lessons to ensure no student has inadvertently slipped below the surface.

- **Sand landing areas** for athletics need to be dug before and during the activity and regularly raked as well.

- **Sports pitches and athletics areas** need to be checked for any dog excrement, glass, sharp shards of plastic or metal, stones or even syringes, which could cause cutting injuries, and holes that may cause tripping injuries. In some schools, this poses a significant problem, and teachers need to be guided by the leadership team and governors as to what a safe standard for participation is and how this safe standard is to be maintained.

- **Goalposts** should be checked visually for corrosion or missing bolts that may make them unsafe for use, and portable goalposts are to be adequately anchored to prevent them being pulled over. Nets should be tucked into the bases or pegged to avoid a tripping hazard.

- Additional checks may be necessary, according to the particular school or other facility provider requirements and circumstances.

- Facilities that offer unauthorised access to high-risk environments (such as a pool or climbing wall) or equipment (such as trampolines) need to be made **secure** when not in use.

2.3.126   Where a work area is considered to be too **small** for the safety of the numbers involved, the teacher has to consider ways in which the delivery of the lesson can be adjusted to create a safe working environment, such as reducing the degree of free travel, structuring tasks more tightly to reduce movement or even having half the class work at a time. If safety is judged to remain compromised after having considered and applied such adjustments, then the teacher must approach the leadership team to discuss the implication for safe practice.

Relevant case law

2.3.127 Taylor versus Corby Borough Council (2000):

The council was held responsible for not carrying out adequate risk assessments of the state of some playing fields. The established system was reactive, in that faults were dealt with if noticed, rather than proactive through regular and adequate checks being made.

> **More information on work areas and playing surfaces can be found in *Section 3: Safe Management Principles, paragraphs 3.7.3–3.7.56,* pages 120–127.**

Organisation-related Principles

Contingency planning

2.3.128 Despite careful pre-planning, there are occasions when the planned task, activity or session cannot proceed on grounds of safety. Abandonment or alternative plans need to be applied.

2.3.129 Contingency plans should be identified by a 'what if' question prior to the activity taking place so, at any time and for whatever reason (such as immediate inclement weather, injury or mismatch between student ability and the demand of an activity), safety standards can be maintained by stopping the activity and initiating an alternative strategy.

2.3.130 During the planning stage, staff should think through the following process:

- This is what I want to teach. This is how I plan to teach it. Is it safe?

- If something happened to make the situation unsafe, what would I do to maintain the safety of the students?

- If I cannot introduce a safe alternative, I have no option but to abandon the activity.

Demonstrations

2.3.131 Student perceptual preferences differ – preferring **visual, aural or kinaesthetic** experiences in order to assimilate movements; learning through seeing a movement, hearing how it should be performed or placing the body or relevant part into the desired position(s).

2.3.132 Demonstrations should provide one or more of these experiences so students can understand the movements required.

2.3.133 Staff should be aware of safeguarding procedures with regard to placing parts of a student's body correctly during a demonstration.

Fatigue and exhaustion

2.3.134 Teachers should constantly **monitor** students to check the demand of an activity does not create an unacceptable level of stress on any individual. Increased demand should be progressive and at a rate appropriate for the individual.

2.3.135 Activities and tasks should be appropriate to the age, ability and fitness level of an individual and based on **progressive demand** following a programme of increasing challenge.

2.3.136 Physical signs are evident in students as fatigue and exhaustion occur. These may vary, but a flushed face, wide eyes, frantic or disjointed movements and loss of performance are frequent indicators.

2.3.137 Teachers should familiarise themselves with any additional 'elite level' training that students may be undertaking outside school that may increase fatigue.

Group work

2.3.138 A class may be divided into smaller groups for reasons of safety, opportunity to progress, optimising activity levels or management of the available space.

2.3.139 Group sizes and make-up will also vary according to age, experience, knowledge of the group and behavioural issues.

2.3.140 Teachers need to consider how **group numbers** are established or amended during lessons in order to maintain a safe learning environment. For example, groups using a restricted space, such as a small fitness suite, may need very structured management of movement from one workstation to another.

2.3.141 Where the class is divided into smaller groups, methods of supervision need to be carefully considered.

Learning outcomes

2.3.142 A key aspect of structured learning is through the use of learning outcomes, whereby the student knows what is expected of them and what they should have gained in knowledge and experience by the end of a lesson or series of sessions. This contributes to safe experiences, as well as safety education.

2.3.143 It is important that teachers reflect on, and monitor, whether students demonstrate understanding and application of safe practice in order that they may become progressively more independent in their lifestyle activity.

Lesson structure

2.3.144 Structured lessons contribute to safe learning situations. There is clear evidence that there are more injuries in unstructured situations than structured ones. **Planning** is therefore essential to safe practice – in whatever form the individual teacher needs, prefers or is required to do it.

2.3.145 **Preparation** for activity is important in order to minimise the likelihood of injury. A safe warm-up should be a fundamental aspect of all lessons, whether led by the teacher, student or self-managed.

Matching the students

2.3.146 Individual student levels of confidence, strength, prior experience, size and ability need to be accommodated in teaching contexts and the earliest stages of competition. Grouping and pairing students according to any of these individual characteristics need to be considered in order to establish a safe learning environment.

2.3.147 Such group management is essential where **weight bearing** (such as counterbalancing in gymnastics), **physical contact** (as in tackling in contact sports) or '**accelerating projectiles**' (where a hard ball is thrown or bowled at an opponent) form part of the learning experience.

2.3.148   **Mixed-ability** pairing or grouping, as in peer teaching and learning, is acceptable where the outcome is clearly understood to be assisting and supporting cooperatively, rather than competing.

2.3.149   The factors above apply to all groups, whatever the gender mix. In addition, **mixed-gender** grouping may require consideration of dignity and confidence where mixed-gender groups may participate together. Teachers need to think about physical contact, supporting and differing levels of strength.

Relevant case law

2.3.150   Mountford versus Newlands School (2007):

*A teacher played an **overaged player** in an inter-school rugby match. An opposing player was badly injured when tackled within the rules of the game by this player. The court ruled that the teacher was negligent. In view of the difference in size and physique (178cm [5ft 11in], 82kg versus 155cm [5ft 2in], 45kg), the overage player should not have been allowed to play. Although there is no complete ban on players 'playing down' in age group, and rugby is quite clearly a game designed for players of differing sizes and shapes, the fact that the overage player would cause harm to a far smaller opponent was foreseeable and preventable.*

> **More information on matching students can be found in *Section 3: Safe Management Principles*, paragraphs 3.9.10-3.9.16, pages 136-137.**

Ongoing risk assessments

2.3.151   Risk assessment is simply a judgement as to whether a situation is safe within established practice and procedures or additional precautions are required to make the situation safer. **Risk-benefit analysis** is the act of comparing the benefits of the activity or experience against the level of risk and likelihood of injury occurring. If the risk is greater than the benefit, then the activity either does not take place or is amended to a level where the positive benefit is greater than the risk of injury.

2.3.152   Written risk assessments for physical education should be available in all schools and departments and should be readily available to all who contribute to teaching the programme. Teachers should ask for information about these if they have not been informed of any concerns (or informed that there are none). These risk assessments need to be specific to the school circumstances, reasonably detailed and reviewed regularly (annually is typical or following an incident). It is preferable that all staff, or as many as possible, are involved in the process of completing the written risk assessment as this helps establish consistent safety standards and safe practices. Individual staff should be informed of any significant risks requiring action and advised as to how to manage the risk safely. Where such information is not provided by managers, the individual teacher is advised to ask about the contents of the written risk assessment.

2.3.153   Dynamic (ie **continuous** or ongoing) assessment of risk, anticipating the likelihood of injury occurring, should be part of a teacher's normal planning, teaching and evaluation of a session. Such risk assessments are not in written form but should be evident in the planning and teaching of the activity as an ongoing process. This involves forethought and anticipation of what could go wrong in the planned session and how any such event would be managed effectively. This is not an onerous task – it forms part of a normal planning exercise.

2.3.154   Dynamic management of risk is based on a teacher's **expertise** and previous experience, as well as forethought and anticipation of what could happen as a result of the planning, organisation and delivery of the session.

2.3.155   During any activity or event, staff need to remain **vigilant** and should constantly reassess the precautions they have put in place. They should respond to any changes to the anticipated situation that might impact on student safety and well-being by modifying the activity in order to eliminate unacceptable risk.

2.3.156   **Near misses** – occurrences in which a group member could have suffered harm but fortuitously did not – should be noted and used to inform future risk assessment.

2.3.157   Where a teacher is not confident in their ability to carry out this process, they should consult their employer and discuss additional professional learning in this area.

> **More information on risk assessment can be found in *Section 3: Safe Management Principles, paragraphs 3.11.7-3.11.22,* pages 155-161, and *Appendices 10 and 11 (Welsh versions in Appendices 12 and 13)* on the CD-ROM.**

Progression

2.3.158   Progression is about the **staged development** of expertise according to confidence, ability and successful prior experience.

2.3.159   Carefully planned and graduated progression of activities is fundamental to enabling students to safely improve their experience and expertise in PES. Progressive practices enable young people to develop or proceed in competence and confidence in more complex movement and skills application over time.

2.3.160   Lessons planned from the scheme of work should provide the basis for progressive learning.

2.3.161   Planning provides a basis for teachers to set an appropriate pitch (level of demand) in tasks and student challenges that are based on knowledge of the students' capabilities, their prior learning and the scheme of work, whereby they are capable of achieving the learning outcomes at a level appropriate to their individual abilities.

2.3.162   Intervention in the students' work leads on from sound planning and establishing an appropriate level of challenge. Appropriate **adjustment, modification or conditioning** of activities should then lead to improving understanding and accommodating the ability range, previous experience, confidence or group size in lessons.

2.3.163   Teachers should check students are competent, confident and appropriately prepared before moving on to more complex or demanding tasks.

2.3.164   Established training principles and schedules or age-related factors (such as pitch size or length of events) relevant to the group's capability, fitness and physical development also contribute to safe teaching and setting the challenge of an activity at an appropriate level.

2.3.165 Individual progression within a class situation may be developed through various **strategies**, including safely working from:

- single to combined tasks

- non-contact to contact situations

- simple to more complex tasks

- copying to practising then refining, adapting and varying movements, skills and tasks

- comparing to analysing to judging performance

- familiar to unfamiliar situations

- set to negotiated and possibly self-determined tasks

- individual to pair and small-group activities

- generous spacing to more restricted spacing

- cooperative to competitive tasks

- limited responsibility to remotely supervised activity.

2.3.166 Teachers should assess an individual's mental and physical readiness before teaching a new skill or progressing to greater complexity.

2.3.167 Safety may be compromised where a student or group of students cannot match the demand or pitch of a task or activity. Equally, work that is not sufficiently challenging may lead to boredom and casual application by the student that compromises safe practice. The teacher should look to see whether this situation occurs and, where it does, respond to this by adjusting the demand of the activity, making it easier or more difficult according to the individual circumstances.

2.3.168 **Fatigue and injury** may occur where students are required to use equipment or attempt a task that is inappropriate to their age, stage of development or ability and where they are required to play on pitches and courts inappropriate to their stamina, strength or disability, or where they are required to carry out events over longer distances than those recommended for their age or stage of development. Age-related pitch and court sizes should be made available, either in a permanent or temporary form (such as using marker discs). Information on these are available on governing body of sport websites and home country sport agency technical websites and publications (such as Sport England's 'Comparative Sizes of Sports Pitches and Courts', April 2011). Also, the range, quality and availability of age- and ability-related equipment for most activities should enable schools to satisfy their particular equipment needs.

Relevant case law

2.3.169 Anderson versus Portejolie (2008):

A skier was seriously hurt when taken off-piste during a ski-school lesson. He was successful in claiming negligence on the part of the instructor, arguing that he was ***not experienced*** *enough to have been taken off-piste and that the instructor should have realised the demand of the task was beyond some in the group.*

Regular and approved practice

2.3.170 Regular and approved practice is that which is **common and accepted** as safe practice across a wide geographical area and not simply an idiosyncratic approach to teaching, progression and organisation.

2.3.171   Such practice is deemed to be widely used because it is safe.

2.3.172   Following regular and approved practice is good practice and provides a strong defence against a charge of alleged negligence as the practice is typical of what the profession would utilise in teaching aspects of the physical education programme to students.

2.3.173   **Typical sources** of widely used, established practice include guidelines provided by LA, governing body of sport, government agency, professional association or respected and acknowledged experts in a particular field. For example, sports coach UK produces a *Code of Practice for Sports Coaches*, which can be downloaded from the Resource Bank on its website (www.sportscoachuk.org) or purchased from www.1st4sport.com

2.3.174   **Improvisation** of equipment, or improvised use of equipment for purposes other than those it was designed for, is not widely held to be good practice and should be considered only with great care and forethought. The quality, range, quantity and specificity of equipment today really removes the need to improvise.

Relevant case law

2.3.175   Woodroffe-Hedley versus Cuthbertson (1997):

*An experienced alpine guide caused the death of a client by not following the **established climbing procedure** (regular and approved practice) of providing a strong enough anchor point, by using only a single ice-screw instead of two, in order to save time. A sheet of ice gave way, and the client was swept away as the single ice-screw came loose.*

2.3.176   Shaw versus Redbridge LBC (2005):

*An allegation of negligence was dismissed because the teacher's action was **typical** of what would be seen across the profession – judged to be 'proper professional judgement' – ie regular and approved practice.*

Rehydration and sun protection

2.3.177   It is common practice in schools to encourage parents to provide their children with sun protection in summer. The school policy on the application of creams and lotions, as well as the wearing of caps and other protective clothing, should be known and applied.

2.3.178   Before lessons commence, forethought should be given to the **weather conditions**, the demand of the planned activity and the need for, location and provision of water to rehydrate the body.

2.3.179   During periods of hot weather, teachers should monitor the students for signs of heat exhaustion, manifested by such symptoms as headaches, dizziness, nausea, cramps, muscle weakness or pale skin. Students indicating symptoms of heat exhaustion should be moved into a cool area and rehydrated.

More information on sun protection can be found in *Section 3: Safe Management Principles, paragraph 3.5.91*, page 95.

Rules

2.3.180   All sports have rules. These have evolved to make competition **fair and safe**. Teachers have a duty of care and a duty of control when officiating in competitive games. They need to know the rules relevant to the activity and must **apply** the rules stringently in order to avoid unnecessary, foreseeable injury.

> **More information on rules can be found in** *Section 3: Safe Management Principles, paragraph 3.4.77*, **page 72, and** *3.5.149-3.5.150*, **page 107.**

Scheme of work

2.3.181   Every school should have a detailed scheme of work that provides for safe, **structured progression** in the physical education programme.

2.3.182   Individual students have individual levels of prior experience, ability and confidence. They need provision to make safe progress at individual or small-group rates. No class has a uniform level of ability or need to progress at the same rate, even if grouped according to ability.

2.3.183   All students learn if they are provided with the appropriate learning conditions. Differentiated work, or personalised learning, involves matching the tasks to the students to enable progress at the appropriate pace within lessons, over a series of lessons and throughout a programme of study.

2.3.184   To provide **personalised learning**, the teacher should know:

- ability levels and prior experience
- what is to be achieved
- students' stage of development
- how students prefer to learn
- how to extend a student's response in an appropriate and safe manner
- how to manage groups so individuals can function individually as and when necessary.

2.3.185   Personalised learning can be addressed through enabling or extension activities modifying the general task, setting different tasks for different students; providing different levels of information, support and intervention; providing more teacher time for some students than others; allowing more or less time to complete a task; using modified equipment and resources to promote success; modifying the playing area or work space for some students; modifying the task; modifying the language used; or sometimes responding to an individual's ability, such as in challenging some for more creative or complex responses.

Staff participation and physical contact

2.3.186   All schools should have a clearly stated policy on physical contact between staff and students. Aspects of this will apply to PES contexts.

2.3.187   It is very likely that most students will need some form of support or physical contact during their physical education experience, and it is a school's responsibility to inform parents of this, not an individual teacher's.

2.3.188   In typical circumstances, whatever the context for physical contact between a teacher and student, it is important that the student is made aware of the provision of contact, such as in supporting someone learning a balance or other movement in gymnastics, and what form the contact will take, and the student confirms this will be acceptable.

2.3.189 Contact should be made in a manner that cannot be misconstrued and only for a duration necessary for safe practice.

2.3.190 Full staff participation in student activities is not advised, whether in lesson times or competitive contexts, such as staff versus student matches, because of the likelihood of injury caused by differences in size, strength, previous experience and confidence.

Relevant case law

2.3.191 Affutu-Nartay versus Clark (1994):

*A student was injured during a rugby lesson when the teacher played a **full participative role** in a game. He tackled the student inappropriately 'in the heat of the moment', causing severe injury.*

> **More information on staff participation and physical contact can be found in**
> **Section 3: Safe Management Principles, paragraphs 3.4.92-3.4.100, pages 74-75.**

Supervision

2.3.192 There is no legal requirement to supervise students all of the time, but schools should have a clearly stated position about supervision, both in changing areas and lessons. Teachers need to be aware of the school's requirements and follow them.

2.3.193 Where teachers have flexibility in choosing the degree of supervision, they should take account of the students' behaviour, reliability and safety awareness, the teaching context and location.

2.3.194 Older students may be given less supervision, but they should never be totally independent as the teacher remains legally responsible for their well-being. Such remote supervision may take different forms, such as in expeditionary work, and should be progressively achieved.

Relevant case law

2.3.195 Harris versus Perry (2008):

*A child was injured on a bouncy castle. The parents alleged negligence due to lack of adequate supervision. The claim was dismissed. The court recognised it was 'quite **impractical to keep children under constant surveillance** and it would not be in the public interest for the law to impose a duty to do so'.*

2.3.196 McDougall versus Strathclyde Regional Council (1995):

*A teacher advised his students in a class not to attempt any exercise without his assistance if they were not sure whether it could be performed safely. One of the students was about to perform a vaulting exercise, which he had never performed on his own before, with the teacher in attendance. The teacher then moved to assist another student, but the first student went ahead and was injured. The Appeal Court found that it was not reasonably foreseeable that the student would attempt the exercise without the support of the teacher and the teacher had not deliberately withdrawn support but had found himself in a situation in which he was required to assist someone else. Therefore, there had been **no failure** of supervision.*

2.3.197   Palmer versus Cornwall County Council (2009):

One lunchtime supervisor was responsible for about 200–300 students aged 11–15 in a field during lunch break. An older student was hit in the eye with a stone thrown by another student. The supervisor admitted to concentrating on the younger students with only an occasional glance at the older ones. The main issues were:

- *What should be the **proper ratio** of supervisors to students?*

- *Would the incident have happened irrespective of the number of supervisors present?*

*The Court of Appeal held that if there had been proper supervision, no stone would have been thrown; that one person supervising such a large number was **negligent at a management level**; the purpose of proper supervision is to deter students from dangerous activity and to stop it if it occurs. This highlights the importance of adequate supervision of students in large numbers and thorough risk assessments, guidance, warning and training regarding supervision of students.*

2.3.198   Orchard versus Lee (2009):

*This case shows that the courts remain reluctant to impose liability for accidents in the playground so long as the school has taken **reasonable care** by applying a common sense approach with good risk management, including a risk assessment of supervision levels. A claim for negligence was dismissed when a student collided with, and injured, a lunchtime supervisor during a game of tag. The students were in a play area, playing the game in a typical manner and not breaking any rules. The court said that the student owed the adult a duty of care, but to establish a breach of that duty, the student would need to have been 'playing tag in a way that was to a significant degree **outside the norm** for 13-year-olds', and this was not the case.*

> **More information on supervision can be found in *Section 3: Safe Management Principles*, paragraphs *3.9.2-3.9.9*, pages 135-136, and *3.11.33-3.11.34*, page 162, and *Section 5: Applying the Principles to Specific Areas of Activity*, paragraphs *5.1.15-5.1.16*, page 178.**

Teaching/observation position

2.3.199   Safe student improvement and progress come about in several ways. One key teacher action is being in a position to intervene should it be necessary. This does not mean always being close enough to touch an individual, but rather to be able to attract attention and response from individuals even at a distance.

Warm-up

2.3.200   Preparation for physical activity will vary according to the activity and learning environment. Students need to be taught the principles of **safe exercise** and content of a warm-up appropriate to the activity and conditions.

2.3.201   Progressively, students should take responsibility for warm-up – initially their own and later for the group – as a step towards independent activity in later life. Teachers need to **monitor** warm-up conducted by individuals and led by students in order to ensure it is safe, appropriate and accurately performed.

Section 3:
Safe Management Principles

The quality of leadership and management (ie the organisation of the subject) is recognised as being the second greatest influence on students' achievement and attainment.

This section is of particular relevance for anyone responsible for the leadership and management of physical education and sport in schools and other education establishments and to teachers who want to refer to more detailed guidance.

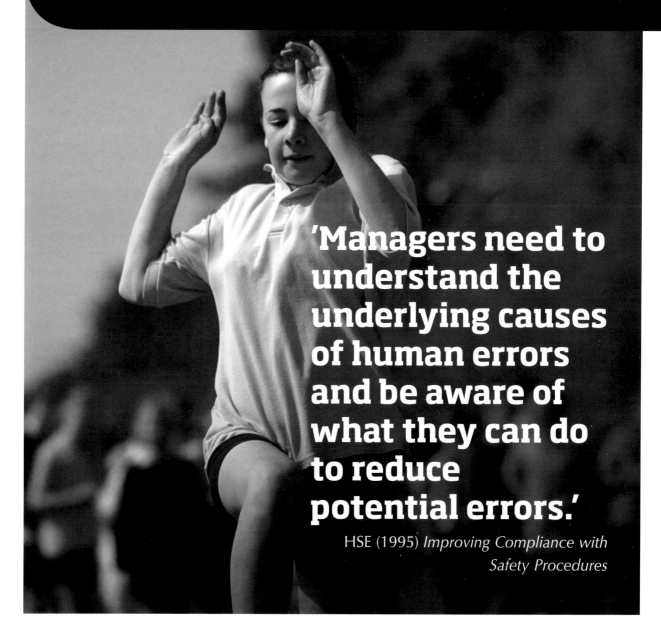

'**Managers need to understand the underlying causes of human errors and be aware of what they can do to reduce potential errors.**'

HSE (1995) *Improving Compliance with Safety Procedures*

3.1　Overview

3.1.1　Accidents happen occasionally in physical education and sport (PES). Many could not be anticipated and are 'no-fault' injuries arising from unforeseen circumstances in fast-moving activities. Some could be foreseen, and lessons learnt from them. When an accident or incident occurs, **analysis** should consider not only the immediate causes but through to the actual causes and whether or not management systems were sufficient. Figure 3 sets out the principle:

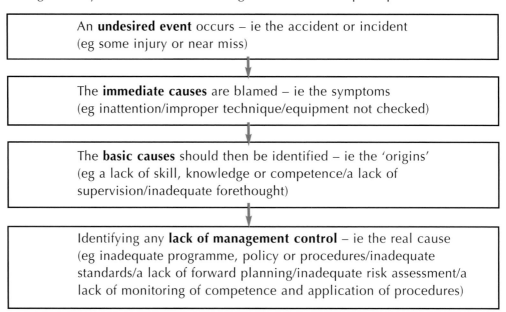

> An **undesired event** occurs – ie the accident or incident
> (eg some injury or near miss)

> The **immediate causes** are blamed – ie the symptoms
> (eg inattention/improper technique/equipment not checked)

> The **basic causes** should then be identified – ie the 'origins'
> (eg a lack of skill, knowledge or competence/a lack of supervision/inadequate forethought)

> Identifying any **lack of management control** – ie the real cause
> (eg inadequate programme, policy or procedures/inadequate standards/a lack of forward planning/inadequate risk assessment/a lack of monitoring of competence and application of procedures)

Figure 3: Why do foreseeable accidents and incidents occur?

3.1.2　All accidents and incidents in PES are **management** issues. By implementing such an analysis, safety standards can be improved through improvement in documented procedures, improved communication, thorough risk assessment and the consistent application of safety standards by all involved in teaching the PES programme. In summary, subject leaders should ask, in relation to safety standards in PES:

- **What do we say we do?**

- **Do we do what we say we do?**

3.1.3　This section sets out the fundamental issues of safe practice all subject leaders of PES need to consider and build into their management and organisation as appropriate to them and the students they work with. The content is based on the premise that effective management will be safe management.

3.1.4　When managing the PES programme, the subject leader should consider whether the following principles are relevant to their particular circumstances in order to ensure students feel safe, are safe and learn how to be safe during any physical education or sport lesson.

3.1.5　The section begins with a framework for a concise **policy** statement setting out **why** a common understanding and consistent application of safety standards are important. Subject leaders and managers should ensure a brief statement setting out such a policy position is made available to, and fully understood by, the leadership team, school staff, visiting staff and governors particularly, as all policies are deemed to be the policies of the governing body.

3.1.6   This policy statement should be supported by more **detailed guidance** as to **how** the policy is put into effective practice through clear and concise procedures. More detailed guidelines relating to a wide range of management issues follow in this section. As well as setting out safe standards of work, the guidance explains why common practices have become established as a professional norm. Subject leaders and school leadership teams may wish to review and possibly develop their existing documentation for PES by drawing on aspects of this guidance appropriate to the particular circumstances.

3.1.7   Schools must implement the **employer's policies** and requirements. These cannot be ignored, but school policies may add to an employer's requirements. Subject leaders need to know what requirements are imposed by the employer and by the school and ensure these are widely understood, adequately cover the PES context and are put into practice in PES.

3.1.8   Where the governing body is the employer, as is the case for academies, free schools, voluntary aided schools, foundation schools and independent schools, the governors have full legal responsibilities to ensure compliance with health and safety law, its related Regulations and insurance provision. Schools where a local authority (LA) is the employer will need to ensure they are aware of any health and safety requirements and that they are provided with any relevant supporting guidance and insurance.

3.1.9   Where additional detailed guidance is not provided by the employer, it would be wise to follow the standards and practice contained in this handbook.

3.1.10   **Case law** indicates that the policy and procedures should be in written form, specific to the school, reasonably comprehensive, regularly reviewed (typically annually), regularly communicated and consistently applied by all staff contributing to the PES programme.

3.1.11   Virtually all the policies, procedures and routines that will apply to safe practice in PES will be **whole-school** policies rather than specific PES policies and procedures, such as those for dealing with first aid and emergency situations. It is the responsibility of PES staff to **ensure the relevant whole-school policies, procedures and routines adequately cover the PES context**, particularly where groups work at the extremities of the school site, off site and outside normal lesson times. Where any concerns about this important scope exist, the subject leader or teacher should discuss their concerns with the leadership team, and produce additional relevant procedures.

3.1.12   Those principles listed in this section that are considered to be pertinent to the particular circumstances of a school may be built into the subject documentation. This will contribute to ensuring a **safe and secure learning environment** where the benefits of the activity outweigh the likelihood of injury occurring. Subject leaders should satisfy themselves that all school and visiting staff contributing to the PES programme are aware of the procedures and standards to be applied.

3.1.13   All policies and supporting documentation relating to safe practice in PES should be **dated** in order to aid a schedule of regular review.

3.1.14   Where safe standards of common practice cannot be assured, the subject leader should approach the leadership team to discuss their concerns.

3.2   A Generic Policy Statement for PES

3.2.1   Safe-practice standards, consistently applied by staff, students and other visitors, across all aspects of the school's PES programme are important.

3.2.2   The **purpose** of documented safe-practice standards in PES is to:

- offer PES within a well-managed, safe and educational context
- set out the responsibilities for health and safety in PES at all levels
- establish common codes of practice for staff and students
- provide common administrative procedures
- ensure statutory and local requirements are followed and other national guidelines, such as codes of practice, are considered
- ensure school health and safety policies and procedures adequately address the PES context of working on and off site and outside normal lesson times
- aid the recording and reporting of accidents and incidents
- audit and achieve consistent safety standards.

3.2.3   The **outcomes** of establishing and applying safe-practice standards in physical education are to:

- enable students to participate in PES that provides appropriate challenge with acceptable risk
- educate students about risk management, and their responsibility in this, in order for them to participate independently in physical activity later in life
- fulfil the provision of a broad, balanced and relevant curriculum for physical education through:
  - an environment that is safe for the activity
  - adequately supervised activities
  - the use of regular and approved practice
  - taking students through progressive stages of learning and challenge
  - building a system of advice and the practice of warning
  - using equipment for the purpose it was intended for
  - providing basic care in the event of an accident
  - the use of forethought and sound preparation
  - involving students in the process of risk management
- ensure clear management responsibilities and organisation provide for safe systems of work
- identify and provide for any professional learning needs the staff are likely to encounter in their work.

An editable version of the policy statement, which can be adapted for individual schools' needs, is available on the CD-ROM as *Appendix 14.*

3.3   Guidance to Develop and Manage Safe-practice Procedures in PES

People-related principles

Staff management

- Duty of care
- Qualifications and competence
- Support staff, volunteers and visiting coaches
- Supervision, control, behaviour management and group management
- Professional learning for staff
- Communication
- Clothing for staff
- Physical contact and staff participation in student activities
- Insurance

Student management

- Consent forms and keeping parents informed
- Codes of conduct
- Individual and special needs
- Medical information and medical needs
- HIV and AIDS
- Clothing for students
- Footwear
- Jewellery, body piercing and personal effects
- Personal protective equipment
- Photography, digital imagery, filming, Internet and mobile phones
- Safeguarding
- Violent play
- Supplements

3.4   Staff Management

3.4.1 According to a school's particular circumstances, **documented procedures** may include reference to:

- duty of care and how this is manifested in PES

- a reminder that the same standard of care applies in all situations whether in or out of lessons, on or off site

- a simple outline of duties imposed by legislation that must be followed

- the importance of keeping parents informed

- induction for all new staff

- any requirements for specific qualifications to teach particular activities, such as trampolining

- the importance of professional learning and maintaining a personal log

- the effective management of all support staff whether on school roll, self-employed or from an agency

- any limitations of role and responsibility of support staff

- information to be provided to visiting staff

- use of cover supervisors

- the management, support and development of trainee teachers

- the restricted responsibility minors can assume in teaching PES activities

- monitoring of safety standards for all staff teaching physical education

- the progressive stages to be followed to progress from direct to remote student supervision and, where relevant, the situations in which it is likely to occur

- expected control, behaviour and group-management standards

- standards for staff clothing, footwear and personal effects when teaching PES

- protocols for physical contact with students in relation to the school's safeguarding procedures

- the limitations imposed on staff, such as performing only static demonstration positions; with the awareness and permission of the student; in a form that cannot be misconstrued and so on

- what to do in the event of a student complaining

- the limits of staff participation in student activities

- duty of care and duty of control as an official in a match

- an outline of insurance cover for school events, in what circumstances any provision is made for staff and students, and how parents are to be made aware of any student insurance provision.

Duty of care

3.4.2   **Everyone** has a duty of care not to cause harm to others. Where the expected professional standards are not met and this results in damage (injury in PES contexts) and this was reasonably foreseeable, an allegation of negligence may apply.

3.4.3   **Negligence** may be defined as: 'careless conduct which injures another and which the law deems liable for compensation' (Frederick Place Chambers, 1995*).

3.4.4   Within education, such allegations are very rare in relation to the number of students being educated and most are rescinded or not found to be valid.

3.4.5   Compensation for injury caused by the careless, unintentional actions of staff, officials or participants in PES is usually obtained through a claim of negligence made by the parents of the student against the employer of the teacher concerned. Significant levels of protection exist against allegations of negligence by staff as individuals.

3.4.6   The **standard of care** expected of school staff originally applied only to qualified class teachers and was described as being **in loco parentis**: in place of a prudent parent. This standard has been modified and updated to the context of a school rather than a home because a class teacher clearly has responsibility for more children at any one time and in a different environment. Modernisation of the school workforce has broadened the scope of this level of professional responsibility even further to include **all adults** who work with young people.

3.4.7   All teachers of physical education are deemed to possess **specialist skills** in the profession of teaching. They are not therefore judged using the general 'reasonably competent person' criteria, but against the common standards of others in the profession. This standard is whether some people in the same profession, working at the same level, would have carried out the same action (ie it is regular and approved practice in the profession).

3.4.8   Within this recognition of whether accepted practice is applied, the courts have also recognised that there is no single answer to a situation. Teachers are expected to operate '**within a range of reasonable options**'. The teaching profession is therefore judged according to what it would be **common** to see across the profession, with no single remedy deemed to be the answer to an issue.

3.4.9   The standard of care has thus been set as that of a reasonably competent person in the same profession working at an acceptable level of expertise and in the same area of activity. A qualified teacher, other member of school staff, visiting coach or volunteer who is inexperienced would be judged by the same standard as more experienced colleagues to avoid **inexperience** being frequently used as a defence against an allegation of negligence. Head teachers, on behalf of the employer, should be aware of this when deploying a varied range of staff.

3.4.10   A fair and realistic view of responsibility is usually taken as not expecting perfection, but requiring a standard appropriate to a competent professional person. There is no distinction in the standard of care expected between teachers and others working with students, other than that set by the level of expertise the individual offers and the circumstances within which they work.

3.4.11   All teachers of physical education have a duty to **work within** a system that anticipates and manages risks. Head teachers must ensure such a system is operable, even by recently appointed staff and any visiting staff.

* Frederick Place Chambers (1995) *Health and Safety at Work: Legislation and Cases*. Welwyn Garden City: CLT Professional Publishing. ISBN: 1-858110-30-0.

3.4.12   All teachers of physical education continue to exercise a duty of care for students aged 18 when under school regulations. This duty of care applies to any school student until they have reached the age of 19, at which stage a young person ceases to have the legal status of being a registered school student.

3.4.13   The duty and standard of care is **continuous** and cannot be diluted or removed by any association with the terms *holiday, abroad, weekend* or similar terms. Whatever the school organises, the school retains a responsibility for. A simple question to establish whether the school holds a responsibility is: 'Who invited the students to participate in the activity?' If the school has played **any part** in that invitation being expressed and accepted, then the school carries some responsibility for the outcomes.

3.4.14   Where a teacher has knowledge and experience that is higher than that expected of a reasonably competent person acting in their position or capacity, they are judged by that enhanced standard of foresight. This defines a **higher duty of care**, in that a teacher with specialist expertise, qualifications or responsibility is expected to have a greater insight and awareness of the consequences of their actions. Thus, 'specialists' in a particular area, those leading higher-risk activities, or those responsible for very young children or young people with limited abilities are deemed to have a higher duty of care (ie a higher level of responsibility) for those in their care. They will be judged as having a greater degree of insight relating to the consequences of their actions.

3.4.15   Injuries will occur in PES simply because of its active nature. These may be 'no-fault' accidents. It is the element of **carelessness** that may impose a liability of negligence. The use of reasonable foresight, anticipation and forward planning is expected, set at the level of guarding against the probable consequences of a failure to take care, to avoid acts or omissions that could be reasonably foreseen as likely to cause injury to other people.

3.4.16   When civil claims for compensation alleging negligence are made, the required level of proof is that of '**probability**' – that the act or omission would probably and foreseeably lead to injury. This standard of the likelihood is much higher than simply 'likely' to occur.

3.4.17   **Defences against a charge of negligence** include the following:

• **Vicarious liability**: An employer is responsible for the acts of an employee when they are acting in the proper course of their employment. This would apply to anything undertaken as part of any contractual or sanctioned voluntary duty. For this reason, those working in PES are expected to:

    – work within guidelines and policies laid down by the employer

    – gain permission for particular activities

    – follow regular and approved practice

    – maintain an up-to-date awareness of the subject through professional learning (PL).

• **Contributory negligence**: Any act or omission by the injured party seeking compensation that contributes to the injury may be taken into account when compensation is determined. The level of compensation may then be reduced according to the claimant's percentage of responsibility for contributing to the injury. The younger the person injured, the less likely they are to be considered to have an awareness of their contribution to the situation. A similar decision is likely to be made for those with some form of learning difficulty.

- **Voluntary assumption of risk**: This principle allows the court to provide no compensation to a claimant whatsoever. It is based on the premise that the participant knowingly **accepts the possibility of injury** through taking part in an activity within the laws, spirit or common practice of that activity. It does **not** allow for the infliction of harm outside the laws and spirit of a game so any intentional or reckless infliction of injury cannot be defended under this principle. It is a concept that applies to adult participation in sport or may apply to voluntary participation by young people but only in very specific circumstances. It would be difficult to apply this defence to a student in physical education lessons that require participation as part of a prescribed curriculum. It would also be difficult to show that young people, particularly, were fully cognisant of the risks involved and legally competent to accept them. The only consent to injury parents have to accept on behalf of their children is that which arises as a result of an unforeseeable accident.

3.4.18   Evidence of the following can also be of great value in **refuting** allegations of negligence:

- policies and guidelines

- schemes of work and lesson plans

- registers of attendance (detailed enough to illustrate what content would have been missed through non-attendance)

- assessment records

- medical information

- risk assessments

- accident logs and analysis of these

- equipment maintenance reports

- minutes of meetings highlighting discussion of safe practice

- professional learning records.

3.4.19   In addition to the common-law duty of care, the Health and Safety at Work Act 1974 imposes particular duties on an employer and its employees, including leadership teams and teachers of physical education.

3.4.20   Health and safety are **integral** to good management. Head teachers have responsibility for everything over which they have control. This includes all day-to-day health and safety issues, whether to do with sessions organised in curriculum time, out of hours, at weekends or even during holidays. Where they do not have direct control, such as in aspects of capital finance, they are expected to take all reasonable measures to minimise a problem. Subject leaders are responsible for health and safety issues within a subject area. Teachers and support staff are expected to know and apply the school policy, report any shortcomings to the leadership team and take reasonable steps to control any existing risks.

3.4.21   Employers cannot transfer their **responsibility** for health and safety, but may delegate, where appropriate, the **tasks** necessary to discharge the responsibility. It is at this level that teachers of physical education are involved in matters of health and safety – in carrying out risk assessments, interpreting the policy within PES, informing others of the risks and taking part in any appropriate professional development.

3.4.22   The **employer's responsibilities** include the requirements to have:

- a written health and safety policy that would include physical education

- detailed procedures that enable the policy to be implemented satisfactorily, and which are reviewed regularly

- systems in place to assess the risks of all activities, manage the risks, inform employees of measures to make situations safe, provide training and supervision, where appropriate, and monitor implementation of the procedures.

3.4.23   All **employees** are required by law to:

- know and apply the employer's policy for health and safety generally and, in this context, also for physical education

- carry out their activities in accordance with any training and instruction from the school leadership team

- report to their line manager any faults and concerns about health and safety

- having reported a concern, then do what is within their power to prevent further injury arising from that concern

- not place themselves or others at risk (such as students and colleagues)

- not interfere with or misuse any items provided for health and safety

- participate in safety inspections.

New case law clarifies duty of care

3.4.24   At the time of publication, new case law was created that altered the common understanding that a school always maintains a duty of care for the students in any activity organised by the school, wherever it occurs and whoever leads the session.

3.4.25   Woodland versus (1) the Swimming Teachers' Association (STA), (2) Stotford (of Direct Swimming Services), (3) Maxwell (a lifeguard), (4) Essex County Council (the school staff employer) and (5) Basildon District Council (the pool owner) (2011):

The complex case title shows that with only one opportunity to make a claim for compensation through the court, the claimant's legal representatives will allege inadequate duty of care against several of the parties involved in the situation at the same time.

During a swimming lesson, a student got into difficulties, lost consciousness and, despite poolside resuscitation, suffered permanent brain damage. How this developed was not observed by the lifeguard.

The school authority claimed it did not have a duty of care to the student because the responsibility had been passed to the swimming tuition company for the lesson.

*The judge agreed and held that the LA did **not** have a duty of care to the student (ie that it was not liable for the student's safety in particular circumstances) because, in activity taking place off the school premises, the level of control the school can apply is less than when on the school site being taught by the school staff or others working to the school staff (such as a visiting coach does in planning, preparation and assessment [PPA] time).*

Provided a school makes careful checks on external agencies and companies about the quality and competence of staff, and proper procedures are in place, the school has fulfilled its responsibility for the care of the students when they are taught off site by the external agency.

The judge:

- *could find no common understanding or interpretation of what a non-delegable duty means*

- *applied his decision only to the specific circumstances before him*

- *was allowing for different interpretations in the future where the circumstances were different by saying that different situations comprise a 'spectrum of liability' and that, within that spectrum, there are a variety of legal obligations that may lead to an employer being liable for the negligence of an independent contractor.*

3.4.26   **The Court of Appeal confirmed the judgement but has left open the possibility that the law might be changed by the Supreme Court.** Meanwhile, afPE advice is as follows:

- The decision does not alter a school's continuous duty of care to students where activities take place on site, whether delivered by a teacher or support staff, such as a visiting coach, because the workforce regulations demand that the coach is managed by the teacher so the teacher maintains responsibility even though someone else teaches the class.

- Where activities take place off site and are delivered by an external agency, the teacher's duty of care to students ends where a clear transfer is made, recognised and accepted and the teacher is not involved in the session.

- The same standard of care applies whether in or out of lessons, on or off site, weekdays, weekends or holidays where the school is involved in the organisation of an activity.

- Parents need to be kept fully informed of who is responsible for their child.

- Clear roles and responsibilities are essential for all adults involved in providing sessions to students.

- Control, behaviour and group-management standards need to be consistent, whoever is teaching or managing a class. Schools should be able to evidence that they have taken this into account.

- Where school staff are present and able to interject if unhappy about the level of safety provision, they should do so.

- Schools need to make careful and considered quality assurance decisions about using particular agencies to contribute to the education of students in their care. This should involve school staff making visits to any premises, facilities or activity centre to be used, and undertaking competence checks to satisfy themselves that the organisation or agency staff they are potentially delegating their duty of care to are sufficiently competent to take that responsibility on. This would require careful checks on competence and control with proper and safe procedures in place. (Many schools already do this as standard practice.)

- Anyone unsure of the situation should contact afPE or an alternative legal source to establish current policy on this decision.

Other relevant case law

3.4.27   Williams versus Eady (1893):

*This described the expected standard of care as that of a **careful parent**.*

3.4.28   Lyes versus Middlesex County Council (1962):

*This case extended the 'careful parent' standard to being in the **context of a school** rather than a home because a teacher clearly has responsibility for more children at any one time and in a different environment than the home.*

3.4.29   Bolam versus Friern Hospital Management Committee (1957):

*This established that a person who possesses **specialist skills in a profession** is not judged by the standard of the reasonable man ('on the street') but by the standard of people within the same profession – ie teachers.*

3.4.30   Gower versus LB of Bromley (1999):

*This ruling broadened the scope of the standard of care to encompass 'a duty to exercise the skill and care of a reasonable member of the teaching profession', thus expanding the standard of **in loco parentis to all adults** involved in teaching young people and not simply QTS teachers.*

3.4.31   Stokes versus Guest, Keen and Nettleford (Bolts and Nuts) Limited (1968):

*This case determined that, where someone has knowledge and experience that is higher than that to be expected of a reasonable person acting in their position or capacity, they are judged by that enhanced standard of foresight, in other words a **higher duty of care** due to specialist skills and experience.*

3.4.32   Woodbridge School versus Chittock (2002):

*This established the principle of a 'range of reasonable options' being acceptable in dealing with issues, recognising that **no single response was the correct way to deal with a situation**; rather that some degree of flexibility according to the circumstances was a more appropriate professional response.*

3.4.33   Shaw versus Redbridge LBC (2005):

See Section 2: Safe Teaching Principles, paragraph 2.3.176, page 47, for details.

3.4.34   Bolton versus Stone (1951) and Harrison versus Wirral MBC (2009):

*These two cases determined that, where it was foreseeable that someone may be injured by an activity but there was **no record of previous injuries** in the same circumstances (making the outcome **rare** rather than probable), there was no negligent liability.*

Qualifications and competence

3.4.35   Staff are not legally required to hold a specific award in order to teach an aspect of physical education **unless** their employer requires such a qualification. LAs and school governing bodies may establish their own policies and insist on certain minimum qualifications before staff are allowed to teach some aspects of physical education, particularly those that involve potentially greater risk. Staff should be aware of these local requirements and ensure they meet the criteria before teaching the activities concerned.

3.4.36   It is wise for staff to be able to demonstrate that they are suitably **trained, experienced and qualified** to undertake the activities in which they engage with students. Examples of potentially **higher-risk** activities include adventurous activities, aquatic activities, athletics throwing events, combat sports, contact sports, aspects of gymnastics, trampolining and free-weights training sessions. Those teaching these activities should hold recognised and current qualifications (eg governing body of sport and other awarding-organisation qualifications, such as those from 1st4sport Qualifications, which also offers the 1st4sport Level 2

Certificate in Supporting Learning in Physical Education and Sport, developed in partnership with afPE; more information is available from www.1st4sportqualifications.com) or significant recent and relevant experience or training to demonstrate their suitability to teach the activities safely.

3.4.37 The **standards** of expertise, discipline, relationships and risk management expected of all adults working with students need to be consistent with providing a safe working environment. This level of competence applies at all times, whether in lesson time or out, on or off site, in term time or holidays, when the activity is part of a school-organised programme and to all who contribute to the programme.

3.4.38 Anyone teaching a physical education lesson should be **competent** to do so safely. This involves having the necessary skills, knowledge, understanding and expertise to plan, deliver and evaluate a physical education programme.

3.4.39 The Health and Safety Executive (HSE) highlights four means of demonstrating competence:

- to hold a relevant qualification

- to hold an equivalent qualification

- to have received appropriate in-house training

- to be competent through experience.

3.4.40 These are not totally discrete alternatives. Qualification, experience and training overlap to produce expertise in a particular field or aspect of PES.

3.4.41 Where someone is not competent to undertake the responsibility placed on them but has been placed in that situation by the employer, or the employer's representative, such as a head teacher, the employer may be **directly liable** for the negligence. A head teacher, as the manager technically deploying staff, must ensure individual teachers of physical education have the competence to fulfil the demands of any tasks to which they have been deployed. Head teachers should recognise that it is unwise for staff to work in areas in which they **lack** the appropriate experience and expertise. They and the employer may be held liable if anyone is deployed in a teaching situation for which they do not have the necessary competence to fulfil the demands of the role. As far as possible, staff should bring any lack of competence to the employer's notice if they feel they are put into a situation they perceive as beyond their ability.

3.4.42 **Class teachers (QTS)** may be required to teach all of the areas of activity in physical education. They should have satisfactorily completed an initial teacher education (ITE) course and, where possible, have attended further professional learning that covered all the activities they will be required to teach.

3.4.43 **ITE providers** accredit new teachers as being competent in all aspects of the professional standards for teachers that 'define the minimum level of practice expected of teachers' (Department for Education [DfE], 2011*). Reference is made within the standards to the teacher being able to establish safe learning environments, provide challenge, adapt teaching to respond to the strengths and needs of individual students and have secure knowledge of the subject. This implies that the individual teacher has experience and has been **assessed** against the framework criteria in the broad range of aspects of physical education. Where such accreditation is given and the new teacher's lack of experience and competence contributes to a foreseeable injury, the ITE provider may be deemed liable for the erroneous accreditation.

*DfE (2011) *Teachers' Standards: Effective from 1 September 2012*. Available on the CD-ROM as *Appendix 15*.

3.4.44   A useful **definition of competence** to work alone in teaching physical education may be that the teacher:

- can teach the relevant techniques, skills, tactics or choreography accurately at a level appropriate to the ability, confidence and previous experience of the students involved

- provides appropriate progressive practices to enable student improvement

- applies the safety issues relevant to the particular activity

- knows and applies the rules if the activity is a sport

- knows the group – their abilities, confidence and particular needs

- has the observation and analytical skills to ensure what is going on is safe and amend anything that is deemed unsafe

- has effective class control.

3.4.45   **Trainee teachers** are placed in schools as a fundamental part of their professional training and are not signed off as competent to teach until the end of the training period. As such, however capable they are in a particular activity, they should not be given full responsibility for any group. They should be supervised, managed and monitored throughout their training period.

Relevant case law

3.4.46   Jones versus Manchester Corporation (1958):

*This case established that, where someone is **not qualified or competent** to undertake the responsibility placed on them but has been placed in that situation by the employer or the employer's representative, such as a head teacher, the employer and manager may be directly liable for negligence.*

3.4.47   R versus Kite (1996):

*Known as the Lyme Bay canoeing tragedy, the managing director of the adventure company was convicted of manslaughter on the basis that he had not established **proper safety standards**, including a failure to appoint staff with adequate experience for the demands of the activity.*

3.4.48   Heffer versus Wiltshire County Council (1996):

*A student was injured in a gymnastics lesson while attempting a straddle vault over a buck. The class had progressed from leapfrog with support to the buck, where support was withdrawn if not requested by students. The student was hesitant and managed initially to successfully clear the buck using a one-foot take-off. In allowing compensation for the claimant's injury, the court judged that the student was supported throughout the leapfrog activity so support should not have been withdrawn on the buck; it should **not** have been left to the student to 'opt in' for support (peer-group pressure may have prevented opting in); reduction in support was judged to be premature and total rather than gradual; and it was deemed that progression to the buck constituted a new activity requiring a continuation of support.*

3.4.49   Kenyon versus Lancashire County Council (2001):

*A student was injured performing a back drop on a trampoline. She claimed **incorrect tuition** and succeeded in the claim. Care needs to be taken when teaching technical skills.*

More information on the competence of staff can be found in *Section 2: Safe Teaching Principles, paragraphs 2.3.7–2.3.11*, page 26.

Support staff, volunteers and visiting coaches

3.4.50   The modernisation of the school workforce and ever-broadening opportunities in programmes offered to students, both on and off site, has led to supervision and teaching responsibilities being given to adults who may not hold a teaching qualification, typically known as support staff or adults supporting learning (ASLs). In these circumstances, the **class teacher always maintains overall responsibility** for what is taught and the conduct, health and well-being of the students involved (though new case law – see *paragraphs 3.4.24–3.4.26*, pages 60–61 – has established possible situations where the duty of care can be fully delegated to an independent third party where the activity is off site and the actions of the adults involved not under the direct control of the school staff).

3.4.51   At no time can support staff **displace** a qualified teacher from the staffing roll. The role of support staff is to complement the qualified teacher timetabled to a class, whether working alongside or at distance from that teacher.

3.4.52   The use of support staff with expertise in aspects of PES can provide opportunities for the professional learning of QTS class teachers, broaden the programme provided to students, increase the quality of learning and challenge to students, and provide greater flexibility in staffing the programme.

3.4.53   The school procedures for engaging support staff, such as coaches, should include answering three essential questions:

- **Is it legal** to engage that person? This will be determined by the requirements of a broad range of legislation that sets out whether particular individuals are prohibited from working with children and young people. The relevant **vetting** and background checks need to be completed carefully.

- **Is it safe** to employ that person? **Safe recruitment** procedures, disclosure certification, possessing a governing body of sport licence to coach, where relevant, confirming qualifications and confirming authenticity of identity are processes involved in determining this.

- **Is it effective** to engage this person? This will be determined by the expertise that person brings to the school, how their expertise may **add** to the professional learning of the school staff, how the quality of student learning experiences will be improved and whether the PES programme will be beneficially broadened.

3.4.54   Adults without QTS working in schools may be on the school staffing roll as support staff or contracted for services, often through an agency. In physical education, all adults in this category **must work under the direction and supervision of a nominated teacher** but may, subject to their competence and the school's policy, work with groups or whole classes alongside or at distance from the supervising class teacher. Head teachers should, on behalf of their employer, ensure support staff are appropriately managed at all times. Guidance on effective recruitment and management of support staff is set out in Table 1.

Table 1: The appointment and management of individual and agency coaches

1 Head teachers and other managers of coaching support staff are strongly advised to ensure safe recruitment by using the following procedure:

a Arrange a face-to-face interview with each coach to confirm their identity using original documents (passport, driving licence, recent service provider bill confirming current home address).

b Vet whether the coach is barred from working with children and check Criminal Records Bureau/Disclosure and Barring Service (CRB/DBS) enhanced disclosure – see original and record number; decide if portability applies and is acceptable; check with original responsible authority and establish whether additional information is on the CRB/DBS form. If so, require a new certificate from the coach to access the additional information. If no response is received to enquiry or information is held, a new disclosure certificate is essential. (This procedure is likely to be changed by the Protection of Freedoms Act 2012).

c Check qualifications – see originals; accept Level 2 award as normal baseline qualification for each activity the coach is expected to teach, diverting from this standard only if the coach is observed prior to acceptance and demonstrates exceptional coaching qualities and is working towards a Level 2 qualification; refer to the higher level teaching assistant (HLTA) standards for your baseline (www.tda.gov.uk/support-staff/developing-progressing/hlta.aspx). Alternatively, check the criteria given in afPE (2010) 'Best Practice Guidance on the Effective Use of Individual and Agency Coaches in Physical Education and Sport', www.afpe.org.uk/images/stories/Use_of_coaches_in_schools.pdf

d Check training undertaken and experience of working with children and young people (eg child protection workshops).

e Explore motivations to work with children and attitudes towards children and young people.

f Checking reference(s) – investigate any gaps in coaching employment and any conditional comments in the reference.

g Check with the relevant governing body of sport that the coach is currently licensed to coach (a qualification cannot be rescinded, but a governing body licence to coach can be if any poor practice or abuse issues have arisen).

h Ensure correct employment status and employment rights are known to the coach – provide a written summary/include in the contract as appropriate.

i Ensure the coach is fully aware of insurance provision and what aspects she needs to provide for herself (according to employment status) re:

1 employers' liability (compulsory) – legal liability for injuries to employees (permanent/temporary/contracted for services) arising in course of employment

2 public liability (essential) – legal responsibility for 'third party' claims against the activities of the individual/group and legal occupation of premises

3 professional liability (desirable) – legal cover against claims for breaches of professional duty by employees acting in the scope of their employment (eg giving poor professional advice)

4 hirers' liability (desirable) – covers individuals or agencies that hire premises against any liability for injury to others or damage to the property while using it

5 libel and slander insurance (optional) – cover against claims for defamation (eg libellous material in publications)

6 personal injury: accidental bodily injury or deliberate assault (desirable) – arranged by the individual or the employer

7 miscellaneous – a variety of types of insurance such as travel (compulsory or desirable) or motor insurance (compulsory – minimum of 'third party') – check personal exclusions and excesses individual carries.

j Set out a clearly defined role, identifying any limits of responsibility, lines of supervision, management and communication, specialist expertise needed (eg children with individual special needs) and ensure they are appropriately qualified/experienced to undertake the role.

k Determine an agreed period of probation and monitor the coach's performance and attitude closely during this period.

l Check that all of the above have been addressed by the agency or school before a self-employed or agency-appointed coach begins work.

m Agree an appropriate induction package that must be fulfilled.

2 Head teachers and other managers of coaching support staff are strongly advised to ensure induction by using the following procedure:

a The head teacher or their representative presents the coach with a summary of relevant school policies and procedures, including: risk assessments; emergency evacuation; referral and incentives; behaviour management; first aid; child protection procedures; and something about the ethos of the school – how staff work with children and young people (such as looking for success in young people, rewarding achievement).

b Identify a member of staff to manage induction into school procedures who will:

1 arrange meeting with special educational needs coordinator (SENCO) and class teacher(s) as appropriate for specific information about students

2 monitor and assess competence of the coach through observations and discussions with students and other staff

3 determine the coach's role in contributing to the overall assessment of students.

3 Head teachers and other managers of coaching support staff are strongly advised to ensure qualifications, experience and qualities necessary for the coach to work alone by using the following procedure:

a Expect a Level 2 award as the normal baseline qualification for each activity the coach is expected to teach. Divert from this standard only if the coach is observed prior to acceptance, demonstrates exceptional coaching qualities and is working towards a Level 2 qualification.

b Check previous experience in working with small/large groups.

c   Check behaviour-management skills.

d   Check:

   1   quality of relationships – the way the coach cares for and respects students, is an appropriate role model and promotes the school's ethos

   2   developing knowledge of the students – their levels of confidence, ability, individual needs, medical needs and behaviour

   3   student management – how they match students' confidence, strength and ability in pair and group tasks, maximise participation, have strategies for effective student control and motivation, apply the school's standard procedures and routines (eg child protection, emergency action, jewellery, handling and carrying of equipment)

   4   knowledge of the activities – appropriate level of expertise to enable learning to take place in the activity or activities being delivered, use of suitable space for the group, differentiated equipment, differentiated practice, evident progression and application of rules

   5   observation and analytical skills – providing a safe working and learning environment, ability to identify faults and establish strategies for improvement.

4   Head teachers and other managers of coaching support staff are strongly advised to ensure day-to-day management of the coach by using the following procedure:

a   Check the coach has received a summary of school and subject procedures and understands what is required (including clear guidelines in relation to handover of responsibility at the start and end of lessons/sessions).

b   Ensure the coach receives relevant information on students/groups (eg illness, family bereavement, behaviour issues).

c   Monitor promptness.

d   Establish regular review and evaluation of coach's work.

e   Determine who assesses students' work.

f   Ensure the coach is supported, valued and accepted as a member of staff.

g   Monitor dialogue and the relationship between the class teacher and coach.

5   Head teachers and other managers of coaching support staff are strongly advised to ensure monitoring quality and effectiveness by using the following procedure:

a   Ensure direct monitoring of the coach for an agreed period – use the criteria set out in 3 above.

b   Set up continual indirect monitoring to ensure students make progress and enjoy lessons/sessions.

c   Ensure students are engaged in consistent high quality learning, using challenging and stimulating activities that support them to achieve their potential, not just activities that keep them 'busy, happy and good'.

6 Head teachers and other managers of coaching support staff are strongly advised to ensure identification and provision of PL by using the following procedure:

a   Evaluate the coach's abilities against HLTA standards.

b   Arrange attendance on an afPE/sports coach UK ASL induction course.

c   Agree essential qualifications and desirable qualifications – plan and provide for a personal development programme beyond governing body of sport coach qualifications to enable the coach to proceed from emerging to established, and advanced rating.

7 Head teachers and other managers of coaching support staff are strongly advised to ensure dealing with inadequate performance by the coach by using the following procedure:

a   Proactively monitor the coach's work as set out in 5 above.

b   Where performance is inadequate and poses a health and safety risk to the students or has the potential to impact on their welfare, intervene immediately. Where performance is technically inadequate, review the situation with the coach after the lesson.

c   Agree and provide supportive PL to improve inadequate aspects of their performance.

d   Monitor for improvement.

e   Where little or no improvement occurs, terminate a short-term contract or initiate competence procedures if it is a longer-term contract.

f   Where necessary, terminate a longer-term contract where competence does not improve.

3.4.55   Employers who use recruitment agencies to provide support staff, such as visiting coaches or supply teachers, are now, under certain conditions, **legally responsible** for what the visiting support staff do so they must be sure the agency and coaches act appropriately and in accordance with the school's standards for competence and safety.

3.4.56   Initially, it is good practice for class teachers to **directly supervise support staff at all times** in order to evaluate their competence. Direct supervision involves support staff working alongside a class teacher so the teacher can intervene at any time, if necessary.

3.4.57   At a later stage, **distant supervision** may be appropriate for support staff, according to their competence and the level of responsibility assigned to them. This would allow them to work at some distance from a class teacher, possibly out of sight, in a different facility or even off site. However, frequent monitoring by the teacher would be part of good management.

3.4.58   It is good practice for schools to keep a **register** of any support staff used who are not on the school roll, including contact details and work undertaken, for future reference.

3.4.59   The level of supervision required for support staff should be determined by a thorough risk assessment. Support staff should be judged on the **national standards** for HLTAs or, alternatively, on competences specific to physical education to determine the eventual level of direct or distant supervision required, as described in Table 2.

3.4.60   Where support staff teach a group during a class teacher's **PPA time**, some other member of staff must pick up the duty to effectively supervise and direct the support staff in question.

3.4.61   Careful thought should be given before **cover supervisors** are allowed to supervise practical lessons for absent physical education staff. Where the competences set out in Table 2 are not evident, the lesson should take place in a classroom with preset, pre-experienced study materials.

Table 2: Competences to determine the level of supervision required by support staff

Quality of Relationships	Knowledge of Students	Student Management	Knowledge of Activities
• Value, care for and respect all children. • Present an appropriate role model (eg use of language, dress, fair play, equality). • Seek to promote the ethos of the school. • Work well with the school staff.	• Identify and respond to individual: – levels of confidence – ability – special educational needs and disability (SEND) – medical needs – behaviour – age/ development stage – specific and circumstantial needs.	• Use regular and approved practice. • Match students' confidence, strength and ability in pair and group tasks. • Maximise participation. • Have strategies for effective student control and motivation. • Apply the school's standard procedures and routines (eg safeguarding, emergency action, including first aid, personal effects, handling and carrying equipment).	• Understand where and how their work fulfils or complements any relevant prescribed curriculum, programme of study and/or wider curriculum activity. • Demonstrate the appropriate level of expertise to enable learning to take place in the activities being delivered. • Demonstrate an understanding of the overall needs of the age group with whom they are working. • Use: – suitable space for the group – differentiated equipment – differentiated practice – effective progression – observation and analytical skills. • Know and apply rules. • Provide a safe working and learning environment. • Identify faults and establish strategies for improvement.

Safe Practice in Physical Education and Sport 2012 Edition

3.4.62   **Trainee teachers** do not come into the category of support staff because their placement in schools is primarily for their professional learning, not to support class teachers. The particular conditions for trainee placements should be clearly set out by the ITE provider through a detailed contract with the placement school. As they are neither qualified nor in a support role, trainee teachers should not work alone.

3.4.63   **Students** on a school roll, whatever their age, are deemed to be minors and can only assist with the delivery of activities (eg junior sports leaders). Regardless of their experience and qualifications, minors cannot be legally responsible for a group of children, and direct supervision by staff is always required. They must therefore always work **alongside** an identified member of staff who is able to monitor them and intervene immediately, if necessary.

3.4.64   Where physical education staff choose to **combine classes** to provide some form of physical activity for classes whose usual teacher is absent, they should carry out a risk analysis to determine that it is safe to proceed in the circumstances.

Relevant case law

3.4.65   Viasystems (Tyneside) Ltd versus Thermal Transfer (Northern) Ltd (2005):

*This case established that two different employers can be liable for the negligence of an employee. The implication from this is that a school, LA, governors or other education employer utilising an external agency to deliver part or all of a physical education programme could be held liable, along with the agency involved, should any member of the agency staff be negligent in carrying out their delegated role. This has a significant **management implication** for head teachers as the ruling is now supported by statute on the employer's responsibilities for agency workers. (See paragraphs 3.4.24–3.4.26 pages 60–61 for an update on case law in particular circumstances.)*

3.4.66   Burton versus Canto Playgroup (1989):

*Adult staffing of a playgroup was supplemented by a **14-year-old helper** who was left alone to supervise a climbing frame. She had been given no training, nor did she have the experience to anticipate the action of a young child who had not been on the apparatus before. The child jumped and injured herself. The playgroup was held responsible for inadequate supervision.*

> **More information on support staff can be found in *Section 2: Safe Teaching Principles, paragraphs 2.3.69–2.3.73*, pages 33–34, and *Appendix 16: Potential Roles and Responsibilities when Support Staff Lead School Groups Off Site* on the CD-ROM.**

Supervision, control, behaviour management and group management

3.4.67   There is no legal requirement to directly supervise students at all times. The level of supervision will be determined by the students' age, behaviour, ability, previous experience, work environment, identified risk and other contextual factors. However, analysis of case law provides a clear indication that the incidence of **injury** is much higher during **unsupervised** activities than supervised ones.

3.4.68   It is wise to supervise more closely all groups in higher-risk situations, such as adventurous activities, aquatic activities, combat sports, contact sports, athletics throwing events, gymnastics, trampolining and free-weights training sessions.

3.4.69   **Direct supervision** of students enables the teacher to intervene at any time. Decisions to supervise less directly should not be taken lightly.

3.4.70   Where a degree of independence is required, progress towards **remote supervision** should be developed by stages and over time. The member of staff involved maintains responsibility for the students, regardless of whether she is present.

3.4.71   Poor control, discipline and behaviour management or inadequate group-management skills by the teacher may adversely affect the standard of safety in any situation. The head teacher technically deploys staff into their teaching commitments and thus carries responsibility on behalf of the employer should a teacher be placed into a situation where they do **not have the skills** to fulfil the requirements of the deployment safely.

3.4.72   Group numbers should be known and checked before, during and at the conclusion of activity. It is a statutory requirement for schools to maintain **registers** for several reasons, including proof that a student was or was not present when some curriculum aspect was taught; whether or not they participated in the lesson is helpful information should a claim be made at a later date, and assessment records should indicate whether a particular student achieved, or otherwise, the intended learning outcomes.

3.4.73   The needs of students with **visual, hearing, motor or cognitive impairment** need to be considered and catered for appropriately to enable them to participate safely. All staff, regular or visiting, need to be fully aware of the implications of the ability and needs of any student in order to provide a worthwhile and safe learning opportunity.

3.4.74   Careful thought should be given to **supervising** changing rooms. While there are a number of organisational tasks to be completed at the beginning of a lesson, it should not be forgotten that changing rooms are part of the area of learning.

3.4.75   Where circumstances prevent full supervision, such as where a single teacher is responsible for a mixed group changing in separate changing areas, a clear management procedure needs to be devised and communicated to the students.

3.4.76   Teachers need to have thought through any possible safety implications and the efficiency of amending **group sizes** during lessons before initiating the change because of available space, behaviour, mobility and other relevant factors.

3.4.77   **Officiating** at a sports event carries a dual role of duty of care and duty of control. The duty of control includes the requirement to know and apply the rules stringently so injury cannot be anticipated through lax application of the rules. The duty of care applies to the safety of the players within the competition and any spectators within the playing area. It is thus important that the official seeks to ensure spectators do not spill on to the playing area and that a suitable run-off area is maintained as a buffer zone between spectators and the playing area for the protection of both groups.

Relevant case law

3.4.78   Porter versus City of Bradford MBC (1985):

*A student was injured during a field-studies event when two students threw rocks from a bridge on to the rest of the group. The teacher, who had not previously taught the group, could **not control or organise** the group adequately. The LA, as employer, was held responsible for the head teacher deploying that teacher into that situation without the skills and training to provide adequate supervision and control.*

3.4.79   Wooldridge versus Sumner (1962):

*This case reinforced the principle that a spectator injured during the normal course of events in a competition cannot claim negligence on the part of the players, officials or organisers, provided the spectator has been made aware of the need to remain **outside the playing area** and any run-off zone.*

3.4.80   Smolden versus Whitworth (1996):

*A player was paralysed during a rugby match when the scrum collapsed. The referee was judged to have been negligent by **not applying the laws** of the game consistently. He allowed 32 scrums to collapse (a potentially dangerous event) without taking action to prevent further occurrences.*

> **More information on supervision can be found in *Section 2: Safe Teaching Principles, paragraphs 2.3.192–2.3.198*, pages 49–50, later in this section, paragraphs 3.11.33–3.11.34, page 162, and *Section 5: Applying the Principles to Specific Areas of Activity, paragraphs 5.1.15–5.1.16*, page 178.**

Professional learning for staff

3.4.81   Health and safety law includes a **requirement** that employees receive the professional learning necessary for them to fulfil the demands of the work they are deployed to do by managers. Professional learning opportunities in safe-practice procedures are therefore a necessity and an entitlement where any lack of confidence or competence is evident.

3.4.82   Changes in common practice also mean those involved in physical education need to undertake professional learning in order to keep abreast of what is acceptable and safe. Such opportunities may be necessary to compensate for omissions in ITE courses.

3.4.83   A rolling programme of professional learning, particularly in relation to safe practice, evidenced through a personal or collective **training log**, would indicate that staff's required qualifications and experience, relevant to the programme being offered to students, remain current.

3.4.84   **Primary teachers** with little or no ITE in physical education may be at risk unless further training opportunities are provided. Such teachers should undertake appropriate professional learning before being allowed to teach a full range of activities. Head teachers must be satisfied that all those who are required to teach physical education are able to do so in a safe manner, with a sound understanding of the needs and stages of development of all the students in their charge.

3.4.85   Some **governing bodies of sport** and other awarding organisations require qualifications to be revalidated periodically. This is not simply to endorse previous requirements, but to inform learners of changes and developments that may have occurred in the interim period. Guidance should be obtained from the relevant governing body of sport, awarding organisation or LA, education and library board in Northern Ireland, or an expert consultant.

Relevant case law

3.4.86   Norfolk County Council versus Kingswood Activity Centre (2007):

*An eight-year-old was injured when he fell 6m from a climbing wall. The investigation established that the screw of a karabiner (metal loop) had not been tightened, allowing the karabiner to open and free the safety rope when a weight was applied. It also found that the **training and supervision** procedures were not sufficient for the activities being carried out and were not being routinely followed on the ground. It was described as 'an accident that could have been prevented had the correct safety procedures been followed and the staff undertaking the activities been trained and supervised'.*

Communication

3.4.87   The consistent application of safety standards is an essential aspect of maintaining a safe learning environment. **Regular discussion** between staff helps achieve such consistency. Staff and departmental meetings tend to be minuted. This provides a good context for the regular reporting and discussion of safe-practice standards and routines with recorded evidence of such professional learning taking place. Safe practice should be a standing item on staff or departmental **meetings** so concerns, clarification and instruction can be ensured.

3.4.88   Circulating minutes of staff meetings to the school leadership, and even the governing body, ensures they are kept informed of professional learning related to safe practice, provides a form of reporting concerns about health and safety, and confirms that school policies and procedures are being appropriately applied in the PES context.

Clothing for staff

3.4.89   Clothing and **correct attire** for a particular activity represent important features of safe practice that apply in equal measure to both staff and students.

3.4.90   Staff should always endeavour to **change** for physical education. On the rare occasions that this proves difficult or impractical, a change of footwear and removal of jewellery, at the very least, should always be undertaken.

3.4.91   **Security of footing** is essential in all situations. Footwear appropriate to the surface conditions is essential for personal and student safety.

General information on clothing can be found in *Section 2: Safe Teaching Principles, paragraphs 2.3.2-2.3.6*, page 25.

General information on footwear can be found in *Section 2: Safe Teaching Principles, paragraphs 2.3.19-2.3.30*, pages 27-28, and later in this section, *paragraphs 3.5.49-3.5.57*, pages 89-90.

Physical contact and staff participation in student activities

3.4.92   Schools should have clear **codes of practice** about physical contact with students as part of their safeguarding policy. Physical contact is defined, in this context, as the 'intentional bodily contact initiated by an adult with a child'.

3.4.93   Teachers of physical education are likely to come into physical contact with students from time to time in the course of their teaching for reasons of safety, support, providing confidence or demonstration. Teachers should be aware of the limits within which such contact should properly take place and ensure decency, dignity and respect are never compromised.

3.4.94   Any physical contact should be in the context of **meeting a student's needs** in order to:

- develop techniques and skills safely
- treat injury
- prevent injury occurring
- meet any disability-specific needs
- prevent harm to himself or others.

3.4.95   Physical contact between a student and a teacher should be carefully considered. There are instances when it is necessary (eg to demonstrate a skill), but such contact should remain **impersonal** so there is no risk of it being misinterpreted or misconstrued by the student, parent or observer. If a student needs support, they should be informed beforehand of what contact this support involves.

3.4.96   Children with a range of special educational needs and disabilities (SEND) may require a greater degree of support and proximity. Physical contact should always be in an open environment with no intimate touching at all, other than for specific care needs.

3.4.97   The teacher should only ever deploy the degree of physical force they genuinely believe to be necessary in order to safeguard a student against hazard and/or for the purpose of restricting injury.

3.4.98   Staff should be aware of the risks associated with **personal participation** while teaching or coaching physical activities, particularly those involving physical contact or in which hard missiles (eg cricket/rounders balls) are used. Staff participation should be restricted to practical demonstrations in a controlled, essentially static setting or to bring increased fluency into a game situation. Such involvement should not compromise any ability to retain acceptable control of the whole group.

3.4.99   Adults should **avoid** playing a full part as a participant in a game with young people due to the differences in strength, weight and experience. It is good practice to take a limited role in a game periodically to set up situations that enable the students to learn from that participation. This would exclude adult involvement in activities such as tackling (other than static demonstrations), shooting with power and bowling or pitching with pace.

3.4.100   Where any complaint is made about a teacher's physical contact with a student, the situation should be reported immediately to the person responsible for safeguarding in school or member of the leadership team to explain the circumstances and obtain guidance and support.

Relevant case law

3.4.101   Affutu-Nartay versus Clark (1994):

See Section 2: Safe Teaching Principles, paragraph 2.3.191, page 49, for details.

> **More information on staff participation and physical contact can be found in**
> ***Section 2: Safe Teaching Principles, paragraphs 2.3.186-2.3.191, pages 48-49.***

Insurance

3.4.102 School status and whether or not an LA retains insurance costs centrally will determine whether the school should make its own insurance arrangements.

3.4.103 Teachers should **check** with their head teacher and/or employer to clarify precisely what insurance cover is provided, under what circumstances the cover applies and whether it is advisable to initiate additional cover for themselves or for any volunteer or visiting staff who may be self-employed. This information needs to be shared with any such volunteers or visiting staff.

3.4.104 Some employers may insure staff for any **extension** in the range of their work outside their normal school role, such as coaching or managing regional representative teams; others may not. Where this extension is not provided by the employer, similar cover will need to be sought through the relevant governing body of sport or established by the individual himself.

3.4.105 There are several aspects of insurance that may apply:

- Employer's liability insurance is a statutory requirement on employers to cover **injuries to employees** that may occur while they work within the remit of their contract, whether they are permanent, temporary or contracted for specific services. LAs are exempt from this requirement, but should either act as the insurers or make other insurance arrangements to cover the potential liabilities of their employees. **Schools not maintained by an LA are not exempt** and must therefore comply with these requirements. This insurance provision does not apply to students in schools as they are visitors to school, rather than employees.

- Public liability (sometimes referred to as third party liability) cover is essential in order to address the legal responsibility for claims made by others concerning the activities of the individual or group. This would include any **negligent act** by students within the scope of the school's provision for their education.

- Professional liability cover for staff is advisable. This provides cover against claims for **breaches of professional duty** by employees acting in the scope of their employment, such as giving poor professional advice. This type of cover is particularly important for anyone working in a self-employed capacity, such as a visiting coach.

- **Personal injury** insurance for staff, against accidental bodily injury or deliberate assault by someone, is desirable. This may be arranged by the employer or may need to be provided by the individual. It is a parental responsibility to provide personal injury insurance for students. Some schools choose to make this facility available collectively to parents, but there is no requirement to do so.

- There may also be a range of **miscellaneous aspects** that require insurance cover according to the particular role of the individual. These may be compulsory or merely advisable and may include travel or motor insurance. Where not provided, it is the responsibility of the individual to ensure adequate provision is made where appropriate to the work circumstances.

3.4.106 The provision and requirements for **transport** insurance vary. Staff need to make the following checks:

- Confirm that commercial transport companies have the appropriate range of insurance cover.

- Ensure the school minibus insurance policy is appropriate for the journey being undertaken. There are additional insurance and licence requirements for travelling abroad. When travelling abroad, staff should be sure to take the insurance certificate (or a copy) on the journey.

- Check the employer's policy on the use of private cars to transport students. Local requirements vary considerably. Some employers do not allow it. Staff intending to use their own or others' private cars should enquire about the licensing, insurance and procedures required and obtain confirmation from other drivers that their insurance covers the risk involved.

> Sample forms dealing with the use of private cars can be found on the CD-ROM in *Appendix 8: Parental Consent Form for a Student to be Transported in Another Adult's Vehicle* and *Appendix 17: Volunteer Driver's Declaration.*

3.4.107   Insurance cover relating to the use of **facilities** is also relevant to the employer or owner of the facility and should also be checked, along with who is financially responsible and under what circumstances, should any claim arise.

3.4.108   It is important that adequate risk assessment of activities and events is made so appropriate insurance cover can be arranged where necessary.

3.4.109   The employer's insurance provision will cover all events organised by the school, whether on or off site, in lesson time or outside, in term time or during holidays, provided the head teacher is fully aware of the events taking place. The head teacher will then determine whether the governors and LA (where appropriate as the employer) need to be informed. Staff should check what documentation needs to be completed and ensure this is in place prior to the event.

3.4.110   All **special events** will need appropriate insurance. Staff should check with the head teacher and employer, if necessary, to clarify what provision is in place and whether any additional cover needs to be arranged. Sports tours arranged wholly by the school are likely to be covered by some aspects of the employer's provision, but need some additional aspects to be arranged specifically.

3.4.111   Sports tours, ski trips and other events arranged as a **package** through a commercial provider usually have a full range of insurance cover built in. Staff need to check the detail carefully, particularly the levels of compensation offered and any particular exclusions to the cover. They also need to provide parents with full details of the cover so parents can make additional arrangements should they wish.

3.4.112   Centrally organised events, such as **sports festivals**, in which students from a variety of schools take part will need appropriate insurance cover. It is important that the organiser for the managing agency, such as a governing body of sport, schools association, schools partnership or LA, clarifies who the employer providing essential insurance is and what schools, or even individual parents, need to consider providing, then informing the relevant parties of this information.

Relevant case law

3.4.113   van Oppen versus the Clerk to the Bedford Charity Trustees (1988):

> *The court established that it is the school's duty to insure against negligence and it is the **parents' responsibility** to consider personal injury insurance for their children because it is a matter of choice or discretion.*

3.4.114   Jones versus Northampton Borough Council (1990):

*A man hired a sports centre for a game of football and was told the floor was wet but failed to tell the other players the floor was unsafe due to a leak in the roof. One player slipped on a wet patch and was injured. The person hiring the facility was held to be negligent for **failing to inform** the other players of the risk even though he was aware of it.*

3.5   Student Management

3.5.1   According to a school's particular circumstances, **documented procedures** may include reference to:

- the frequency and use of consent forms
- keeping parents informed
- student codes of conduct
- determining ratios and group sizes
- supervision protocols
- addressing individual and special needs
- communicating medical information
- dealing with medical situations
- kit preferences and requirements
- footwear appropriate for different aspects of PES
- protocols for jewellery, body piercing, sensory aids and other personal effects
- recommendations for personal protection and staff action if not provided
- the use of goggles in school swimming sessions
- protection against weather conditions
- violent play in sports contexts
- use of digital imagery, social networking, Internet and mobile phones in PES
- safeguarding procedures
- advice on the use of sports supplements to enhance performance.

Consent forms and keeping parents informed

3.5.2   It is a common misconception that consent forms signed by parents **indemnify** the school and employer against any claim for negligence. This is not so. Such disclaimers have no standing in law. The courts would not recognise anyone being absolved of their professional responsibility before an event takes place. Also, under the principles of the Unfair Contract Terms Act 1977, minors have three years after reaching the age of consent (18 years old) to retrospectively file a claim in their own right for any injury suffered as a minor. This clearly sets a parental consent form as a participation agreement only. Such an agreement does not absolve responsibility. It is a signed statement indicating that the parent is willing for their child to take part in certain activities offered by the school, based on the information the parent has received.

3.5.3 As a form of consent, **participation agreements** apply to optional activities only and not to mandatory educational experiences, such as the school's duty to deliver a prescribed curriculum. Technically, there is no requirement for schools to inform parents about how and where the curriculum is delivered, though many do keep parents informed as to where their child is at all times they are under the duty of care of the school and whether any additional safety measures have been implemented.

3.5.4 Practice varies in schools. Some schools require parents to sign a **single consent form** to be effective throughout the student's whole school experience (a recommendation by the DfE in England). It is more common for schools to obtain one at the beginning of each academic year. In some schools, more frequent responses from parents are required. The protocol for consent forms should **not be burdensome** on staff or parents but should fully **inform parents** of the schedules and organisation of any optional activities their child may be involved in.

3.5.5 Effective practice involves keeping parents fully informed about what the student is participating in and has been informed of. They confirm that they understand the risks involved in an activity and agree to comply with the conditions stated or they choose to withdraw their child from any particular school event covered by the consent form.

3.5.6 Parents may be kept informed about generic procedures relating to optional activities through the school's **normal communication systems**, such as the school's prospectus, newsletter or website, provided parents are made aware of this practice. Specific information, possibly relating to dispersal procedures not normal to the school's practice or delays in journeys, needs to be relayed to parents via a reliable system that keeps them informed as to the situation pertaining to their child.

Relevant case law

3.5.7 G (a child) versus Lancashire County Council (2000):

*A student received a serious mouth injury in hockey while not wearing a mouth guard. The judge determined that, while the provision of personal protection is a parental responsibility, it is the responsibility of the school to ensure **parents receive critical information** about personal protective equipment (PPE) and that simply passing on the information via students is insufficient.*

> **More information on parental consent can be found in *Section 2: Safe Teaching Principles, paragraphs 2.3.44–2.3.48*, pages 29–30. Sample consent forms are available in the following appendices on the CD-ROM:**
>
> - *Appendix 6: Department for Education Recommended Annual Consent Form for Participation in Optional School Trips and Other Off-site Activities*
> - *Appendix 7: Sample Consent Form for the Use of Digital Imagery in School*
> - *Appendix 8: Parental Consent Form for a Student to be Transported in Another Adult's Vehicle.*

Codes of conduct

3.5.8 It is good practice for schools to agree a code of conduct with parents and students before students participate in sports activities and other educational visits. Acceptance of a code will provide staff with the necessary authority to carry out their responsibilities.

3.5.9   Codes of conduct set out the **expectations** placed on a student by the school and are useful documents to make clear to students and parents the standards expected of those taking part.

3.5.10   In extreme circumstances, a code of conduct could be used as the basis for the early return of an individual from an event, such as a sports tour, if their behaviour causes concern, the parents are aware of acceptable behaviour being a condition of taking part and they have been made aware of the school's prerogative to impose an early return at the parents' cost.

3.5.11   An agreed code of conduct should be formalised and sent to parents, with the consent and medical forms, for them and their child to sign.

3.5.12   Typical behavioural standards in a code of conduct include requirements for students to:

- observe normal school rules
- cooperate fully with all staff at all times
- consult with school staff if in doubt about any issues
- fulfil any tasks or duties set prior to and during the event
- participate fully in all activities and sessions during the event
- be punctual at all times
- not leave group sessions or accommodation without permission
- always return to the meeting point or accommodation at agreed times
- be in groups of not less than three students if granted indirectly supervised time
- avoid behaviour that may inconvenience others
- be considerate to others at all times
- not participate in social networking communication other than any specifically allowed by the school
- behave at all times in a manner that reflects positively on themselves, the party and the school
- abide by the rules, regulations and laws of the school, venue or countries visited
- comply with customs and duty-free regulations if the event involves travelling abroad
- not purchase or consume alcohol, tobacco products or purchase dangerous articles, such as explosives and knives, during a school excursion
- accept that a full written report of any misconduct will be forwarded to the school governors, leadership team and their parents.

For a sample code of conduct, see *Appendix 18: Exemplar Code of Conduct for Students* on the CD-ROM.

Individual and special needs

3.5.13   All students, irrespective of any special need, have an **entitlement** to a meaningful and fulfilling experience of PES. Not only can it provide enjoyment, involvement and participation in a range of physical activities, it can also bring about significant and long-lasting gains to psychomotor and sensory development, physical health and well-being and, through the successful achievement of well-matched challenges, improve social and emotional stability.

3.5.14   With appropriate management, students with special needs should have access to a full and rewarding experience of, and participation in, physical activity at all levels. **Inclusion** is an entitlement supported by significant statute and regulation. Anyone with a disability should not be treated less favourably, should be enabled to participate in PES as far as is reasonably practicable and, as such, reasonable adjustments to enable this must be made.

3.5.15   The development of '**can do contracts**', devised through discussion between teachers, support staff, parents and, where relevant, specialist medical staff, enables students to participate appropriately in activity lessons.

3.5.16   Teachers working with students who have individual needs will benefit from being made aware of a range of teaching and learning strategies that will help ensure all students, whatever their particular needs, obtain full benefit from PES provision. Specialist support can be obtained from a range of experts in specific fields.

3.5.17   Special needs can be broadly, though not exclusively, categorised as:

- speech and language

- sensory

- physical

- behavioural

- cognitive

- a combination of two, or more, of the above.

3.5.18   It is important to remember that all special needs tend to exist on a continuum from very mild to very severe. Thus, while the needs of some students may be very clear, others' needs may not have been previously diagnosed. Even where there is a diagnosis, it cannot be taken for granted that all students with a similar diagnosis or 'label' have exactly the same needs and require the same response to meet those needs. Further, some special needs may be intermittent or degenerative in nature, and these need to be taken into account in teaching situations. Thus, it is important that individual needs are recognised and responded to in an individual and specific manner.

3.5.19   **Speech and language difficulties** cover a wide range of needs, which may include students with general receptive or expressive language difficulties, dyspraxia, dysphasia, autism or autistic spectrum disorder (ASD). Many of these will be towards the very mild end of the continuum of difficulty and thus it is likely their needs will not have been identified. Where needs are not taken into account, the students are likely to misunderstand or not understand what is required of them. As a consequence of this, they may not be able to carry out tasks as expected or at all, and this can result in poor and disruptive behaviour as they become frustrated. They may respond poorly to criticism of their poor performance from staff. This can result in staff responding to their behaviour, rather than attending to the root cause of their difficulty, which can further exacerbate the situation.

3.5.20   Some students develop **coping strategies**. These can sometimes be identified and may be characterised by the time spent watching other students before starting the activity or being last 'in the queue', thereby allowing themselves time to assess what is required of them.

3.5.21   **Sensory difficulties** largely cover the areas of vision, hearing and dual impairment. Where the impairments are significant enough for them to have been diagnosed, specialist advice should be sought. Staff should ensure this advice is followed and used in developing risk assessments. This may include the provision of specialist equipment or support. It may involve ensuring students use their spectacles or hearing aids.

3.5.22   Some students develop coping strategies similar to those described above for children with speech and language difficulties.

3.5.23   **Physical disabilities** can manifest in different ways. Some students may appear 'clumsy' in their movements. This may be associated with a specific learning difficulty, such as dyslexia, a lack of early childhood motor experience or one of a range of other difficulties. The condition may not be formally diagnosed and, as such, no support may be directly available. It is important, as with all children with SEND, to praise effort and progress. This maintains and promotes self-esteem and reduces the risk of the real difficulty being masked and behavioural difficulties arising from the frustration of failure.

3.5.24   Many schools will have students diagnosed with some form of **physical dyspraxia**. In these situations, it is likely some support or advice from a physiotherapist or occupational therapist (OT) will be available to those working with such students. This can take the form of an exercise programme that can be included as part of a normal physical education lesson. Staff working with dyspraxic children have found that including such specific exercises in warm-ups for all students can additionally have a positive impact on the motor development of the whole class.

3.5.25   **Behavioural difficulties** are many and often complex. They may mask other, undiagnosed difficulties that, when left unaddressed, lead to frustration from failure, resulting in low levels of self-esteem, unwillingness to take part and disruptive behaviour. Among possible causes, difficult behaviours may arise from a particular condition such as attention deficit hyperactivity disorder (ADHD), a mental health condition and/or poor early childhood experiences.

3.5.26   Those working with students exhibiting difficult behaviours should look for signs of the **possible causes** of the difficulties and take the necessary action to respond to these. One fundamental approach is to ensure the student's confidence is developed by providing a carefully graded programme using a small-steps approach that ensures success. Each element of success should be praised. As levels of self-esteem increase, the level of disruptive behaviour often falls.

3.5.27   It is not always possible to identify the root causes of behavioural difficulties as the outside signs of difficulty may be the same across a number of causes. Thus, a student's aversion to an activity may arise from a previous traumatic experience, such as an accident in water in early childhood that has left the child fearful of swimming. The school may be unaware of this. Students may also have experienced significant pressure to take part in activities from a young age in which they experienced a lack of success and so have become demotivated. They may be reluctant to change for an activity due to a medical condition such as psoriasis. These are a few of many circumstances that can lead students to refuse, or be reluctant, to carry out a task. Such situations need to be handled sensitively and may require further investigation in order to promote an environment where students will take part and levels of disruption be reduced.

3.5.28 **Cognitive difficulties** can also be many and varied. Students with cognitive difficulties typically have problems in grasping concepts quickly; thus, staff need to take extra care in explaining the requirements of a task. This should be done in small steps, often using demonstration and personal support, to ensure all students understand each step before moving on to the next. Each step should be rewarded with praise and encouragement.

3.5.29 Those working with students with special needs should acknowledge that whatever the origins or cause of particular needs, activities should be of **equal worth, challenge and relevance** to those provided for other students. The aim should be to maximise everyone's participation in physical activity and sport. To this end, those providing physical activity and sport for students with special needs should:

- take account of the specific individual needs and the risks that may be attached to them for the students when taking part in a range of physical activity

- liaise with the school's SENCO (or the learning support service in Scottish schools) and other specialist support (eg speech and language therapist [SALT], OT, physiotherapist or school nurse) to ensure students with special needs are never placed at unnecessary risk and, where appropriate, a healthcare plan is developed

- liaise with parents to establish whether they or any other external agencies are supporting the student in physical activities in order to assess how their experiences of the student may be used to promote her physical activity in the school

- carefully risk assess each student with special needs for each planned activity; it should be remembered that, while special needs may require that significant support is in place to allow a student access to an activity, or an alternative activity be provided, there may be other activities where the student is capable of taking part at his own level of expertise.

3.5.30 Staff working with students in a special needs environment should be suitably trained or accredited to manage their physical needs. When working in an integrated setting, mainstream staff should be supplied with details of the students' prior learning ability, and supported by additional expertise in order to effectively plan and manage a range of appropriate physical challenges for those students diagnosed as having additional difficulties within their right to a differentiated curriculum.

3.5.31 Staff responsible for a student with SEND should:

- know the nature of the learning difficulty, disability, or emotional or behavioural disorder

- be aware of any constraints on physical activities as a result of the disability or regime of medication

- be able to provide the emergency treatment necessary if physical activities exacerbate the disability

- have determined that they:

  – have sufficient background knowledge about the student

  – are confident in their approach to teaching students with SEND

  – have the knowledge and techniques necessary for safe teaching.

3.5.32   When planning an activity, careful attention should be paid to each **student's needs** in terms of the location, clothing, physical surroundings, equipment and general organisation of the session.

Table 3: A checklist for planning an activity for students with SEND

Location	Clothing	Physical Surroundings	Equipment
✓ Risk assess all locations both on and off site. ✓ Check access and egress for safety, especially where a student or students may be at risk of absconding.	✓ Ensure all students are appropriately dressed and that any special clothing (eg helmets for some students with epilepsy) have not been left unworn following the changing process.	✓ Assess the acoustics of the location. Where this is an issue (eg prone to echo), ensure all are able to hear instructions and support staff are well briefed to support those who may not hear distinctly. ✓ Assess the lighting of the location. Where there are dark areas or areas prone to bright light, ensure any student with a visual impairment carries out their activities in a place of optimum light for that individual. **Note**: Different visual impairments have different optimum lighting levels. ✓ Ensure floors and flooring are suitable for activities involving those who may have motor difficulties.	✓ Ensure all equipment is safe for use by all students. Where this may not be the case for those with special needs, ensure access to alternative activities. ✓ Ensure specialised equipment is available as necessary (eg sound balls for visually impaired students, a range of balls of different sizes and textures to support those with motor difficulties). **Note**: Specific guidance should be sought from specialists in the field of specific difficulty.

84

Table 4: Things to remember when giving instructions

When Giving Instructions

- Make sure to gain the attention of all students, especially those with special needs, before the explanation of a task commences.

- Ensure there is little, if any, background noise as this can distract some students, and others may find it difficult to hear all your instructions.

- Stand so all students can see your face, with the light on your face, not behind it. This has a number of benefits, including providing a focus for students who are easily distracted, such as those with speech and language difficulties or ADHD, while making it easier for those who lip-read.

- Provide opportunities for those who lip-read to understand instructions. Remember that students with conditions such as glue ear may have an intermittent hearing loss that can affect either ear or both ears. Thus, to reduce any risks, the positioning of such students during physical activities is crucial so instructions are clear and of a volume they can hear. Clearly, for those who are profoundly deaf and do not lip-read, arrangements will need to be made for alternative communication (eg signing).

- Work in small steps. Many students with special needs cannot process large chunks of information easily, and these need to be broken down and supported by regular reinforcement during the activity. A variety of resources (eg pictures or written instructions) may aid the student as they can constantly check themselves and thus move towards independent learning.

- Speak clearly and maintain a normal rhythm without shouting.

- Create a climate in which students feel confident to ask for the instructions to be repeated as some with special needs can feel awkward about this. A buddy system often proves to be useful.

- Use high levels of praise for small gains in performance. This is important for all students, but especially those with social, emotional and behavioural difficulties (SEBD) as they tend to have low levels of self-esteem and confidence.

Table 5: Things to remember in sessions for students with SEND

When Preparing a Session	During a Session	At the End of a Session

• Plan for it to be student- and activity-specific. Do not assume one risk assessment will do for all those with a particular special need involved in a particular activity.
 	
• Build in the necessary control measures to allow students access to activities that might otherwise have been closed to those with special needs.
 	
• Seek specialist support and advice, where appropriate, to ensure the efficacy of the risk assessment. Discussion should result in the development of a medical profile/healthcare plan for the student concerned, covering issues such as:
 	
  – personal healthcare equipment (eg inhalers, syringes, incontinence pads)
 	
  – body splints and aids
 	
  – valves and shunts
 	
  – administration of drugs
 	
  – mobility aids
 	
  – range of physical movement
 	
  – daily living aid
 	
  – care assistance
 	
  – any activities identified as contraindicative by the medical profession.
	• Ensure support staff are fully briefed and clear about the activity and their role in supporting the students who are taking part in it.
	
	• Ensure the necessary equipment is readily available to those who will require it (eg balls with bells inside for some students with a visual impairment).
	
	• Ensure each task is preceded by a demonstration, as some students learn better by observing rather than listening to instructions, and that there are strategies in place for the students to be able to self-check to remind themselves of the expectations of the task.
	
	• Regularly change the activity. Some students, such as those with SEBD, can become easily bored or frustrated, and this can lead to disruption of the whole session.
	
	• Offer regular support, feedback and praise to students. Many with special needs have low self-esteem and respond well to knowing they are improving and doing well, and that this is recognised by peers and staff.
	
	• Encourage public acclaim by getting all students to recognise each other's successes. This aids the process of inclusion.
		• Review progress and encourage all students to assess their own performance and how it might be further improved.
		
		• Ensure that, where additional support has been provided, the support staff have:
		
		  – kept a record of progress
		
		  – recorded any information to be reported to other staff, parents or other professionals
		
		  – noted any further practice to take place before the next session
		
		  – understood their role in any necessary preparation for the next session.

3.5.33 The use of strategies sometimes commercially known as special needs trampolining, simple trampolining, rebound therapy, sen-move trampolining, trampoline therapy and similar titles has become common to provide **stimulus and therapeutic benefit** for students with a range of impairments. This involves the use of a trampoline bed to provide simple stimulus to promote balance, movement, fitness and sensory awareness but does not extend to the skills that form part of trampolining as known in the gymnastic context. These forms of therapy do not constitute trampolining, and the usual qualification requirements for trampolining would not apply, though teachers should be **trained in the particular therapeutic discipline** and fully up to date with procedures such as the safe assembly and folding of the trampoline.

3.5.34 Also, the requirements in trampolining for safety matting and end decks may continue to apply with **ambulant students**. However, with non-ambulant students, the teacher or therapist may need to make an assessment as to whether or not the potential benefit of floor mats would be outweighed by the tripping hazard and the restriction of access for mobile hoists and wheelchairs. Similarly, with the use of end decks, the teacher or therapist may need to make an assessment as to whether or not the potential benefit would be outweighed by the fact that their use may restrict the scope of relevant work.

3.5.35 **Wheelchair users** take a full part in PES situations for groups that are made up of disabled students and mixed groups of able-bodied and disabled students. A risk assessment should be carried out to establish the normal routines for the class to ensure the safety of both the wheelchair users and the ambulant students. This would include consideration about the stability of wheelchairs in activities, who can push a wheelchair and particular conditions during activities.

> More information on special and individual needs can be found on the CD-ROM in *Appendix 19: Students with Special Educational Needs and Disability.*

Medical information and medical needs

3.5.36 It is standard practice for schools to request student medical information from parents and update this information regularly. The onus is on the **parents** to provide adequate information and inform the school when any medical conditions change.

3.5.37 Schools should have a secure system to inform and **regularly update teachers** about student medical conditions and associated risks in order for them to take account of such information in teaching the lesson and maintaining a safe learning environment. This may involve adjusting particular tasks for particular students, such as not asking a student who has epileptic seizures to work at a height in case a seizure occurs with little or no notice while that student happens to be at the top of high fixed equipment.

3.5.38 Class teachers must also **inform any support staff**, whether on or off site, on a need-to-know basis of any medical conditions the visiting staff are likely to be presented with in any group they teach during their visit so the student's needs can be accommodated within the lesson. This second phase of communication is not always effective in schools.

3.5.39 Teachers are not compelled to administer **medicines** to students nor to supervise the administration of medicines. The school will have a policy on this, and staff should follow that policy unless particular circumstances exist where discussion with the leadership team of the school is necessary. Arrangements will differ in practice from one school to another.

3.5.40 There are now many students in schools recognised as having asthma, epilepsy, diabetes or conditions that may cause anaphylactic shock. These conditions can be severe and long-lasting and can, therefore, become **disabilities**. Within equality legislation, schools are required to take this into account. Schools, through the head teacher, have to ensure the requisite duty of care is exercised and instruct staff on what to do if confronted by a medical situation.

HIV and AIDS

3.5.41 The following extract outlines the view of the DfE on children with the human immunodeficiency virus (HIV) or acquired immune deficiency syndrome (AIDS) attending school:

Children with HIV and AIDS

Since on all present evidence, the risk of transmitting HIV in the school setting is minimal, and since the benefits to a child with HIV or AIDS of attending school and enjoying normal social relationships far outweigh the risks of him or her acquiring harmful infections, such children should be allowed to attend school freely and be treated in the same way as other students.

It follows from this that the fact of HIV infection or AIDS should not, in the Department's view, be a factor taken into account by local education authorities, governing bodies and head teachers in discharging either their various duties concerning school admissions, transfers and attendance (in respect of an infected child or otherwise), or their powers of exclusion from school.

DfE (1991) *HIV and AIDS: A Guide for the Education Service*

3.5.42 School staff should consider the following points in relation to students with HIV or AIDS:

- Students may take part in physical education, sport and outdoor and adventurous activities, providing they do not have any other medical condition that prevents them from participating.

- Swimming pools and splash pools should be chlorinated or suitably treated according to standard practice. Normal precautions should be taken.

- Barefoot work presents no risks.

- Bleeding resulting from accidents should be dealt with immediately. First-aiders should wear disposable waterproof gloves and rinse wounds with water only.

3.5.43 **No cases** have been recorded of HIV being transmitted as a result of direct mouth-to-mouth resuscitation, although there is a theoretical risk when there are bleeding cuts or sores in the mouth. In an emergency, direct mouth-to-mouth resuscitation should not, therefore, be withheld. A mask or face shield may be used where concern exists. Rigid airways for resuscitation may only be used by first-aiders who have received appropriate specialist training.

Clothing for students

3.5.44 Students, from the earliest ages, should change into suitable physical education clothing in order that they may participate safely and securely. Although vest and pants were, in the past, an acceptable option for the youngest children, contemporary views on safeguarding, personal development and hygiene mean this is no longer advisable practice.

3.5.45   Clothing for PES should be well suited to its function. It should be light and allow good freedom of movement, without being baggy or loose, for work indoors. Consideration should be given as to whether the fabric may reduce friction on apparatus and cause slipping, particularly if working at height or in inverted positions.

3.5.46   In specific activity situations, adjustments to normal clothing guidelines may need to apply, such as a need for a long-sleeved top to prevent friction burns to the forearms when performing front drops in trampolining.

3.5.47   Loose clothing for swimming is not advised, other than during skills tests in controlled situations, due to the drag created, which may adversely affect the confidence of weaker swimmers.

3.5.48   Clothing for outdoor lessons should again allow good freedom of movement, but will also need to offer some insulation from cold weather in the winter months. Additional layers of clothing during cold weather are advisable. It should be remembered that students who are insufficiently warm and experiencing discomfort will not be appropriately focused, may lack concentration and may be injured because of inadequate attire.

> More information on student clothing can be found in *Section 2: Safe Teaching Principles, paragraphs 2.3.2-2.3.6*, page 25.

Footwear

3.5.49   Footwear that is **fit for purpose** is essential. It should demonstrate effective grip, support and reasonable protection for outside work and games, contrasting with lightness and flexibility for indoor activities such as gymnastics and dance.

3.5.50   Suitable indoor footwear is crucial to safe participation by students and safe supervision by staff. **Security of footing** is essential. Staff may need to respond quickly to prevent a potential injury to a student, making effective mobility essential. Students need footwear that is capable of transmitting feel for the movement and the surface they are working on.

3.5.51   Neither staff nor students should ever participate in **socks** on polished wooden or tiled surfaces as the level of grip is so poor. Well-fitting socks may be acceptable on a carpet surface if traction is not affected and transfer between carpeted and wooden surfaces, such as benches, is not required.

3.5.52   For **trampolining**, non-slip socks or trampolining slippers are necessary to prevent toes entering the gaps in the webbing. Cotton and wool socks are suitable, but nylon socks on a webbed nylon bed are unlikely to provide adequate traction.

3.5.53   **Training shoes**, on which the soles provide good traction, will often prove effective for a range of indoor games, but should not be worn for gymnastics activities for the reasons of 'feel' described above.

3.5.54   Some form of footwear is preferable for **indoor games** activities due to the higher frequency of sudden stopping and changing direction quickly where toes can be stubbed. Staff should try to avoid situations often found in games lessons when organising wet-weather indoor alternative activity in which some students wear training shoes and others are obliged to resort to bare feet.

3.5.55   **Outdoor footwear** for games and athletics may be varied according to the playing surface, and mixed according to the availability of particular footwear to some students. Security of footing is again an essential requirement, along with consideration as to whether the outdoor footwear presents any foreseeable risk to other participants.

3.5.56   Systems need to be in place whereby staff, officials and students regularly check the safety of their footwear. Procedures also need to be applied whereby students avoid, wherever possible, walking over hard surfaces to gain access to the playing area. This can result in studs and other traction devices becoming unacceptably rough and sharp, proving hazardous to opponents in competitive games and practices. Whatever the type of footwear, the need for some form of maintenance is likely, so as not to cause a hazard to anyone.

3.5.57   Where a group presents a **variety of footwear** for outdoor lessons, the teacher with the group has to determine whether the lesson can proceed as planned or whether some conditions need to be applied to enable maximum participation in safety.

> More information on footwear can be found in *Section 2: Safe Teaching Principles, paragraphs 2.3.19-2.3.30*, pages 27-28.

Jewellery, body piercing and personal effects

3.5.58   Personal effects, such as jewellery, religious artefacts, watches, hair slides, sensory aids and so forth, continue to pose difficulties in many schools since such items should, ideally, always be **removed** to establish a safe working environment.

3.5.59   Staff have a duty of care to ensure students are able to actively participate without unnecessarily endangering themselves or those working around them. Systems and procedures need to be in place within the changing area to check students fulfil this obligation prior to participation.

3.5.60   Any exception to this recommendation of complete removal needs to be carefully considered and always comply with a suitable risk assessment.

3.5.61   The use of **retainers** (flat studs that retain the piercing when earrings or studs are removed) is becoming more common as a form of acceptable substitution rather than removal. Provided these are flat and cannot cause damage if a blow or ball hits the side of the head, the level of risk is clearly reduced.

3.5.62   Recent developments in the manufacture of **medical-aid wristbands** have resulted in products with an acceptably low risk factor (soft materials, Velcro fastenings). Such items should be acceptable for physical participation in most activities, largely avoiding the need for removal, provided there are no hard or sharp edges that may cause injury.

3.5.63   Clear expectations should be established throughout the school, and with parents, about the management of personal effects by means of a clear and unambiguous written policy.

3.5.64   The school should have in place a routine for the removal of jewellery and other personal effects, strategies to enable participation by adjusting the teaching situation where removal or safe substitution is not possible, and not allowing a full participative role where removal or adjustment is not feasible.

Safe Practice in Physical Education and Sport 2012 Edition

3.5.65   **Disclaimers** from parents alleging the removal of responsibility from teachers in the event of an injury occurring while their child takes part wearing jewellery should be declined. Such indemnities have no legal status. The duty of care remains firmly with the school on such matters, and the student may take out independent action for compensation when they become an adult, thus nullifying any agreement made in good faith. Schools should work with parents to achieve a solution that does not compromise the safety of the student and others nor the employer's duty of care.

More information on the management of personal effects can be found in *Section 2: Safe Teaching Principles, paragraphs 2.3.49-2.3.55*, pages 30-31.

Personal protective equipment

3.5.66   Injury in physical activity most commonly occurs through physical contact with another player, or contact of some part of the body with:

- a hard ball

- an implement

- a rough surface or chemically affected environment.

3.5.67   The use of PPE is increasingly common for participating in a wide range of physical activities and sports in order to reduce any likelihood of injury. PPE may be defined as any device to be worn or held by an individual for protection against one or more health and safety hazards. The most common forms of PPE used in schools include mouth guards, shin pads, helmets, padding and swimming goggles.

3.5.68   In some sports, the legal principle of *res ipsi loquitor* – 'the thing speaks for itself' – applies. This is clearly relevant to sports such as fencing, boxing or taekwondo in which the wearing of protective items is inherent in the activity itself. This need, however, is not always so obvious in other activities.

3.5.69   A number of governing bodies of sport have introduced their own regulations, which impose the **mandatory** wearing of certain items of protective gear with a view to minimising injury. Whenever students become involved in competition regulated by a governing body of sport, any ruling relating to PPE must be complied with.

3.5.70   Specific governing bodies of sport will provide regulations for the use of PPE in their sports on their websites or on request. The table overleaf summarises the requirements of a number of leading governing bodies of sport relating to PPE.

Table 6: Governing body of sport requirements and recommendations relating to PPE

Governing Body of Sport	PPE Requirements
England and Wales Cricket Board	• Helmets (and boxes for boys) are mandatory when batting using a hard ball and also when fielding close to the bat.
England Hockey	• Mouth guards and shin/ankle pads are recommended at all levels of participation. • Specialist protection for goalkeepers is mandatory.
England Lacrosse	• Mouth guards are mandatory at representative level. • Specialist protection for goalkeepers is mandatory.
Football Association	• Shin pads are mandatory at all levels of participation.
Rugby Football League	• Mouth guards are recommended. • Shoulder pads are permitted at all levels of participation. • Padded helmets are permitted.
Rugby Football Union	• Mouth guards are mandatory for representative matches above school level; otherwise, they are recommended. • Padded helmets are permitted. • Soft shoulder padding is permitted.

3.5.71   It will often be the case that governing body of sport rulings relating to the wearing of PPE are also directly adopted within an educational setting. However, a risk assessment of the activity can bring some **flexibility** to achieving optimum levels of participation and involvement in the taught curriculum, usually through modification of the activity in question (eg using a soft ball and plastic implements available in a number of mini versions of sports, non-contact versions of physical-contact games and practices or wearing light footwear instead of studded boots).

3.5.72   Where students do not have PPE that has been advised, it remains the duty of the teacher to **ensure the safety** of the students. This places a duty on the teacher to consider whether the lesson can proceed as planned – and that injury from the lack of PPE is unlikely – or there is a need to consider ways of amending a planned session to maintain a safe context. This may require grouping according to footwear or according to those with the particular PPE and those without.

3.5.73   Staff should ensure students and parents are kept well informed about the value of wearing PPE and the school policy in relation to its use. A policy strongly recommending the use of PPE is advised as provision is a parental responsibility, not a school responsibility. Should schools decide to adopt a policy of mandatory usage of any PPE in physical-contact situations, their duty of care obliges them to ensure all participants always have access to it.

3.5.74 **Specialist protective equipment,** such as that required for a hockey goalkeeper, may often be provided by the school unless the student elects to participate to a high level in that position, when they may choose to obtain their own.

3.5.75 Protective equipment should be **fit for purpose**, and regulation is extensive. Manufacturers are encouraged to ensure their products conform to specified standards, where they exist. For example, head protectors for cricket should comply with BS 7928:1998 (a British Standard), whereas helmets for pedal cyclists, skateboarders and roller skaters should comply with BS EN 1078:1997 (a European Standard).

3.5.76 PPE works by dissipating direct force relative to both time and impact, thereby offering a measure of protection to parts of the body.

3.5.77 In the case of **mouth guards**, as well as protecting teeth and gums, additional benefits arise in reducing lacerations inside the mouth of the wearer while mitigating injury caused by teeth to an opponent in the event of unforeseen collision. As well as potentially minimising oral/facial injury, there is also some evidence that mouth guards can reduce incidences of concussion, but this is less certain, and only then in situations where a bespoke, personally fitted mouth guard is worn.

3.5.78 Clearly, a bespoke mouth guard, properly fitted by a dentist or dental technician, is the most effective, but cost may be prohibitive. Less effective, but relatively cheap, 'boil-and-bite' versions are now available, which should carry a European Conformity (CE) marking. This indicates that the product has been subject to some quality assurance in assessing its fitness for purpose. There is currently no British Standard available.

3.5.79 **Shin pads** offer protection to the lower leg and should be worn for competitive matches and whenever there is a risk of injury. Better protection is provided where the pad covers much of the length of the leg between knee and ankle while at the same time not hindering performance. Some provide ankle as well as shin protection, particularly useful in hockey.

3.5.80 Protective helmets, or **head guards**, are most commonly used in rugby, cricket and skiing. The soft rugby type provides protection for the head against soft tissue injuries, which are most likely to be sustained when taking the ball into contact situations. They can provide a sense of comfort and protection, with the contoured soft padding usually made of impact-resistant foam, but the guards offer little added protection against concussion and do need to fit comfortably. The rigid outer shell cricket version provides protection against higher-impact forces and usually has some form of grille or visor to protect the face. National cricket associations have made them compulsory in under-19 cricket for all batsmen and any fielder within 14m of the bat. Ski helmets are becoming mandatory in several countries and, where they are still a personal option, schools are advised to build provision for them into the required kit list, whether through hire or purchase.

3.5.81 Padding, or **body armour**, has developed from the traditional shoulder pads. It provides some protection to the shoulders, chest and back from the physical impact when tackling or being tackled in rugby.

3.5.82   **Swimming goggles** are recommended when swimming at competition level, and for extended, regular training sessions. They can help maintain the required body position and improve vision through the water. In contrast, within short curriculum swimming lessons (typically 20–25 minutes' water time) for beginners, or for single, short races in school galas, goggles are not considered to be essential.

3.5.83   Students learning to swim or improving their ability often do not swim in straight lines, become close together and clash heads or hit each other with arms while swimming, causing possibly more severe eye injuries if goggles are worn. Dependency on goggles for underwater swimming is not a factor in being judged to be safe in water, neither are goggles designed for such activity as the eye pressure cannot be relieved.

3.5.84   When goggles are used, they should be made of unbreakable plastic or rubber materials. The British Standard for the manufacture of goggles includes the requirement that the packaging should contain instructions regarding their putting on and removal. Students should be taught to remove them by slipping them off the head and not by stretching the retaining band as wet plastic is slippery and may cause injury to the eye area. Where goggles are not properly fitted, they may mist up and adversely affect visibility.

3.5.85   Given the potential for injury, the teacher responsible for the group should have the prerogative to require any student to remove their goggles for reasons of safety if they constantly adjust or remove and replace them. The teacher is not responsible for fitting or adjusting a student's goggles. Where a student does wear goggles, he needs to be able to carry out the task of fitting them independently.

3.5.86   As with the management of all risk in PES, all aspects of the situation should be taken into consideration before the school, along with the provider (if lessons are taken externally), makes a decision on how to proceed. Where any LA or governors' policies regarding water safety exist, they should be adhered to. Having considered these, schools should fully inform parents of the points raised in the guidance, and the decision of the school in light of this.

3.5.87   In some cases, according to the stage and ability of the student, the use of goggles may be permitted. The reasons for the decisions either way should be fully explained in the risk assessment for that activity.

3.5.88   When students complain of eye irritation in such contexts, the cause, in almost all instances, is an incorrect chemical balance in the water. This imbalance can be eradicated. In other situations, from hospital records, the cause is found to be irritation arising from a reaction to the chemicals used to clean the lenses of the goggles at home. In the case of frequent swimmers training daily, the eyes would be exposed for long periods to the effects of the chemicals in the water. Additionally, in some cases, the tissue around the eyes does not dry out between training sessions and thus becomes more susceptible to infection.

3.5.89   In the rare instances where an individual has particularly sensitive eyes or wears lenses, schools should require a parental letter stating that the student has particular needs to warrant the use of goggles. Such a letter would have the status of simply being informative and would not constitute any form of indemnity should injury arise later through the misuse of the goggles. Additional medical certification of such particular needs is costly and should not be sought as this information is likely to have been previously set down in the student's records.

3.5.90   When parents request the wearing of goggles because of their child's particular need, the school should inform them that the teacher in charge retains the prerogative to require the removal of the goggles for reasons of safety.

94   *Safe Practice* in Physical Education and Sport 2012 Edition

3.5.91   **Exposure to the sun** is an aspect of personal protection that is increasingly important. The risks associated with overexposure to the two bands of ultraviolet light from the sun are well documented, and staff need to be mindful of a range of necessary precautions in ensuring the well-being of students:

- Lengthy periods in direct sunlight, particularly around midday when the sun is at its hottest, should be avoided whenever possible.

- Students should be taught how to screen themselves from the harmful effects of the sun through wearing light clothing and using sunscreen products. Parental approval will be required to use sunscreen products, which parents should provide.

- Sunglasses and hats can provide effective screening in selected activities where they pose no danger to the wearer or other participants in terms of the quality of the items and the nature of the activity.

3.5.92   Documented policy and procedures on the use of PPE should include reference to the range of PPE relevant to the physical education programme, the process for informing parents about recommendations to provide it, how staff are to manage situations and the need for staff to determine whether it is safe to continue a planned session where students lack the necessary PPE or amend it to accommodate the lack of it.

> **More information on the use of PPE can be found in *Section 2: Safe Teaching Principles*, *paragraphs 2.3.56-2.3.60*, pages 31-32.**

Photography, digital imagery, filming, social networking abuses, Internet and mobile phones

3.5.93   Confusion exists as to whether, and under what conditions, students can be **photographed in schools**. Head teachers and governing bodies sometimes forbid photography at school events on the misconception that it is contrary to the Data Protection Act 1998. The Information Commissioner's Office has confirmed that parents can take photos at school events as the Data Protection Act does not apply to such situations. Personal data processed by an individual only for the purposes of that individual's personal, family or household affairs, including recreational purposes, are exempt from the Act. This would include photographs taken by family members of their children at school events. Similarly, events where there will be large groups of participants and/or spectators are deemed to take place in public areas so the permission of those in shot is not required.

3.5.94   However, with concerns about the abuse and **manipulation** of photographs of children, it is wise to inform and involve parents in decisions that affect their child. Also, while it remains within the school's prerogative to create a policy banning photography, school use of photography for educational purposes but no parental allowance for photography at school events could be challenged.

3.5.95   In circumstances where the Data Protection Act does apply, the **key obligation** of schools is to ensure consent from parents and students is obtained for that photography or filming. A common sense approach to obtaining permission has been described in the approved code of practice* as the photographer asking for permission to take the photograph. This will usually be enough to ensure **compliance**. Photographs taken for official school use may be covered by the Act, and parents and students should be advised of why they are being taken. If, after being notified by the school that a student will be photographed or filmed

---

* Information Commissioner's Office (2011) 'Data Sharing Code of Practice',
  www.ico.gov.uk/for_organisations/data_protection/topic_guides/data_sharing.aspx

(stating the reasons for the photographs or film), the student or parent does not notify the school that they object, implied consent can be assumed. It naturally follows that if a student or parent does object, the school should not take photographs or films of the relevant student on that occasion.

3.5.96   Parents should be informed, therefore, and permissions obtained, where relevant, prior to filming or photographing students. It is good practice to include relevant details on school admission forms to inform parents that digital imagery is used in education to **support learning**, and to reassure them it will only be used in specific circumstances about which they will be advised. This information to parents should not be regarded as wholesale permission. Prior to an activity, seeking consent for taking images keeps parents informed and often diminishes concerns. Where consent is sought (eg if digital photography is to be used in a GCSE), permission could be requested for the whole course, rather than for each individual session.

3.5.97   The development of digital technology (eg digital cameras, camcorders and analysis software programs) has opened up an exciting and highly effective way of enhancing learning in schools. PES and other physical activity are areas in which a great deal of visual learning takes place. Digital photographs and video clips can provide students with clear images of performances and specific techniques, as well as immediate visual feedback on their own movements. New software enables this process to be managed easily during physical education sessions, school sport and off-site activities.

3.5.98   Non-digital photography should also adhere to these guidelines, where applicable.

3.5.99   However, certain procedural and protocol issues need to be addressed to ensure **digital images** are managed effectively and securely. This is particularly important since images can now be transmitted and manipulated easily. Great care should be taken to safeguard students when storing and using digital images in an educational context.

3.5.100   In-house use of digital imagery may occur within a school or group of schools as part of a defined educational project or partnership (eg between a secondary school and its feeder primary schools). The way the images are used should be controlled by the school or project manager at all times.

3.5.101   Access to the images should be controlled by **authentication mechanisms** (eg password protection and/or identification of specific computers).

3.5.102   Manipulation of the images needs to be restricted to appropriate formatting and display purposes (eg to enhance the content for educational use).

3.5.103   Staff should be aware of the dangers of distributing the images via email or CD-ROM. This leads to a loss of control of the images by the user group.

3.5.104   The following **filming guidelines** could be followed:

- Arrange clutter-free backgrounds to focus students' attention on the specific performance issues.

- Care should be taken over the angles chosen for filming in particularly sensitive sporting situations (ie swimming, gymnastics, trampolining, some athletics events).

- Profile shots of students (side on) are generally more informative and less prone to risk of misuse.

- Filming students on poolsides should be avoided where possible. Where necessary, general or profile shots should be taken.

- Some specialist sports clothing (eg swimming costumes, gymnastic leotards) can create added risk, and care should be taken to ensure images cannot be misinterpreted.

- Names of students should not appear in images used on websites. If this is not possible, the images should not be used.

3.5.105 **Publishing** images occurs when they are distributed beyond a defined group via videotape, DVD, CD-ROM or a website/the Internet. Publishing images has obvious associated risks, particularly for students in physical education and sport environments.

3.5.106 When publishing video clips, associated risks will be reduced where staff follow the guidelines below:

- Use general-view shots to establish the theme.

- Shots held for a maximum of three seconds reduce risks (this makes the clip very difficult to manipulate).

- Children and young people shown in a video or film clip should not be identified by name and, where possible, not by school or club (ie a logo/badge on PES kit/uniform).

- Interviews should only show the head and shoulders of the children and young people involved. They should not be identified by name (this includes voice-overs and text-overs).

- Group shots should be in wide vision.

3.5.107 Master photographic materials and digital photographs should be stored in a secure environment since these are more readily manipulated if they fall into the wrong hands. Video copies, still photographs and compressed digital videos (eg Windows Media files) are less of a risk since manipulation is more difficult.

3.5.108 Libraries of photographic materials should be managed with care. Unnecessary storage of material should be avoided. Materials should be stored in a locked cabinet and saved for a maximum of five years.

3.5.109 The reuse of DVDs or tapes that have not been erased first can increase the risk of unwanted images being used inappropriately.

3.5.110 The use of **CCTV** for security has become fairly common in facilities that have shared community use. Schools need to consider whether these cameras should run during the school day. If they do, extreme vigilance should be taken, as above, when storing and securing tapes.

3.5.111 Staff using **mobile telephones** during lessons, training sessions or at competitions, for the purposes of either making or receiving calls, is not good practice. The primary responsibility of staff is the supervision and safety of the students. Anything that compromises the teacher's ability to maintain a safe environment and give their full attention to the supervision and coaching of the students should be actively discouraged.

3.5.112 There are situations where access to a mobile phone will make a positive contribution to the safety and welfare of students, and possibly staff, particularly when an emergency occurs. Therefore, a blanket ban on the use of mobile phones by staff is not advised.

3.5.113   Commercial systems are available whereby staff can contact parents of students collectively in the event of an emergency or change in published arrangements. While some cost is involved, such systems contribute to good practice in keeping parents informed about events, training, delays and other relevant information.

3.5.114   While staff should not **email** children and young people directly as individuals, they may do so as part of a disclosed list (having received prior permission from parents to disclose in a group email) where they are disseminating information in relation to training or competitions. Sports clubs may also wish to use disclosed lists for sending club information via a designated and suitably trained adult (because of their position, this person should also have been subject to appropriate selection and vetting processes). Group emails should also give individuals the opportunity to have their contact details removed from the list by including a statement such as: 'If you wish to be removed from this email list, please contact the administrator'.

3.5.115   Staff should be aware of the increasing practice of **cyber-bullying**, which includes posting upsetting or defamatory remarks about an individual online and name calling or harassment using mobile phones. These may be general insults or prejudice-based bullying. Cyber-bullies use their mobile phones or emails to send sexist, homophobic or racist messages, or they attack other kinds of differences, such as physical or mental disability, cultural or religious background, appearance or socio-economic circumstances. In other circumstances, bullies may physically assault other children or young people and post images of the bullying or fights online, or send recordings via text messages to other people. Such pernicious behaviour is wholly unacceptable and, where staff become aware of it, they must inform the school leadership team immediately.

3.5.116   Students' use of the **Internet** is common in education and can be extremely beneficial to learning. There is debate about whether students should be self-regulated in their use of the Internet in schools. Staff need to be fully aware of the school policy and protocols about this and ensure requirements are followed in PES situations.

3.5.117   Where students utilise **computers** on PES courses, the standard health, safety and welfare protocols should form part of their education, including:

- an adjustable sitting position, setting the eye level at mid-screen height

- regular short breaks to rest the eyes and loosen the body

- appropriate positioning of the keyboard in relation to the screen

- no loose wiring that could cause tripping incidents

- bags and other items placed away from the work area to prevent tripping incidents.

3.5.118   **Social networking** sites are popular and commonly used by students, as well as adults. An approach needs to be taken by schools to balance the popularity with the possible adverse consequences, such as the potential for the instantaneous circulation of mobile phone video clips taken in changing rooms while students are in a state of undress or the tweeting of messages, often automatically, into the public domain. Several local safeguarding children boards (LSCBs) and governing bodies of sport provide advice on good practice.

3.5.119   Schools need to impose **strict protocols** about any use of social networking sites in any school context and include reference to this in the school's required code of conduct for students and staff. Staff must report any concerns within the school's safeguarding procedures.

3.5.120   Other than within the school's published protocols, staff should not communicate with students via social networking sites and, where such communication occurs, should include a third person (a member of staff) for monitoring and evidential purposes. Neither should staff allow any student to be a named friend unless the school protocols allow that via limited contexts, strict guidelines and parental approvals.

> **More information on digital imagery and Internet safety can be found later in this section, *paragraph 3.5.129, Table 7: Some aspects relevant to safeguarding within a PES context, Context column, section 4*, pages 103-104.**
>
> **A sample digital imagery consent form can be found on the CD-ROM in *Appendix 7: Sample Consent Form for the Use of Digital Imagery in School.***

Safeguarding

3.5.121   The concept of safeguarding is enshrined in statute based on the principle that the welfare of the child is paramount. All who work with students have a duty to ensure the health, safety and well-being of children in their care and, within the law, may do what is reasonable in all circumstances for the safeguarding or promotion of the student's welfare.

3.5.122   School appointment procedures, including those for visiting coaches and other volunteers, must include **vetting** to ensure the person appointed is not barred from working with children and young people. Currently, all adults who work regularly with students must obtain an **enhanced CRB/DBS disclosure**, or home country equivalent, including regular volunteers. Further detail on the appointment and management of support staff is set out in Table 1, page 66, including the need for necessary checks to ensure the identity of the person, their actual qualifications, relevant courses attended and current licensing to coach from a governing body of sport, where relevant to the activity and required by the governing body of sport.

3.5.123   Enactment of the Protection of Freedoms Act in 2012 will remove the entitlement of an employer to seek to obtain CRB/DBS disclosures. It will become the **responsibility of the individual** to produce the certification to potential employers, thus removing the problems of 'portability' from one teaching or coaching situation to another. The DBS will also take responsibility for vetting and disclosures.

3.5.124   There is no legal requirement for **under-18s** to have disclosure clearance.

3.5.125   All schools are required to have clear safeguarding **policies and procedures**. Subject leaders need to ensure teachers are aware of and apply the necessary policies and procedures relating to the prevention of **intentional and unintentional harm** in the PES context. They also need to ensure the relevant school policies and procedures adequately cover the PES context and, where they do not, inform the school leadership team.

3.5.126   Safeguarding in some schools may be limited in scope to protecting students from deliberate harm, including physical, emotional, and sexual abuse, neglect, bullying, and racist abuse, harassment and discrimination. It is important that teachers of physical education are aware of the general **signs and symptoms** of intentional harm, such as non-accidental bruising, and also consider PES contextual aspects such as intentionally:

- overplaying and overtraining talented students, using inappropriate training methods and imposing physical punishment for not carrying out a task or for being last to complete a task as **forms of physical abuse**

- depriving students of rehydration during physical activity in hot weather or adequate clothing during cold weather as forms of **neglect**.

3.5.127   As well as awareness of observing signs of possible intentional harm, staff also need to be familiar with the school's procedures for dealing with students **disclosing** instances of abuse to themselves or their friends.

3.5.128   In addition to intentional abuse, other, related procedures contributing to students being safe and feeling safe are often included in a school's consideration of safeguarding. For example, in the PES context, this may include several aspects relating to possible **unintentional harm** that are addressed in this handbook, including:

- student health and safety

- meeting the needs of students with medical conditions

- providing first aid

- educational visits (including sports fixtures, festivals and tours)

- Internet safety/use of digital imagery in learning and sports events

- transporting students

- the use of physical intervention (such as supporting students in gymnastics)

- overplay and overtraining

- recognising and responding to signs of fatigue and exhaustion

- responding to weather conditions

- lack of staff competence to teach PES safely

- progression in competence and skill

- the implications of intimate care in a PES context for students with particular needs.

3.5.129   All these issues have particular or potential relevance to PES and are addressed within this handbook. Good practice indicates that brief references to these issues should be contained in a school's documented PES procedures and risk assessments (summarised in Table 7). The essential outcome is to ensure students **feel safe and are safe** within the broader consideration of safeguarding.

Table 7: Some aspects relevant to safeguarding within a PES context

People	Context	Organisation
1 Students • Feel knowledgeable, comfortable and confident in PES (ie caring ethos, safeguarding context and staff relationships). • Group/team sizes match ability, size, age, maturation, demand of activity, space. • Consideration given to specific situations as to whether anyone is likely to feel intimidated, threatened or harmed by others during activity. • Organisation of teaching groups where students lead aspects of session. • Clothing and footwear appropriate for activity and conditions. • Jewellery and other personal effects removed/made safe. • PPE adequate for activity demands. • Equality Act requirements re access and involvement in PES addressed for those with cognitive, visual, hearing or motor impairment. • Students with English as an additional language (EAL) supported to understand safety procedures. • Knowledgeable about procedures and routines. **2 Staff** • Safe recruitment procedures followed for all PES appointments. • Competence to teach activity to level of student ability checked and monitored. • Licence to coach, required by some governing bodies of sport/LAs, checked before employment	**1 Protecting children from deliberate harm** • School safeguarding procedures adequately address PES situations. • School procedures and codes of conduct known and consistently applied by all staff and students. • Checks made with all club links/outdoor activity centres/other organisations used by school/signposted to students, with protocols known and monitored. • Staff have good awareness of bullying/racist incidents, contexts and opportunities in PES and sports trips (including cyber-bullying) and monitor closely. • General and PES-specific indicators of neglect, and physical, emotional and sexual abuse known and regularly monitored by all staff. • Staff responses to disclosure of abusive experiences/knowledge consistent with school reporting policy. **2 Medical conditions** • Staff know administration of medicines is a voluntary activity and cannot be enforced. • Parents asked for relevant medical information. • Information known and regularly updated to class teacher. • Information always communicated to other adults teaching group. • PES-related individual healthcare plans, where appropriate. • Student medications available to use in different PES locations.	**1 Health and safety** • Good teaching standards applied. • Good organisation (management) of lessons by teacher and of subject by subject leader. • Consistent safety standards applied across team delivering PES programme. • School policies, procedures and standards applied in PES. • Risk assessments and documentation in written form, specific to school, reasonably comprehensive and reviewed regularly. • Documents accessible to all staff. • Students involved in their own safety in line with age and ability. • Safe use of resistance equipment in multi-gyms. **2 Use of physical intervention/ contact/supporting** • Extra laps/press-ups etc not used as physical punishment. • Stage/age/physical size/experience matched in contact sports and in dance when lifting/weight bearing. • No adult takes full participation in contact sports or where 'accelerating projectiles' are used or in weight-bearing activities. • Support (eg in dance or gymnastics) only given using appropriate techniques, with student informed and consent given. • Spotters in trampolining well trained, effective and limited in number. **3 Overplay and overtraining** • Awareness of governing body of sport requirements/guidance.

People	Context	Organisation
commences, where relevant. • Observation and analysis skills effective to ensure safe practice. • Control, discipline and organisational skills adequate. • Positive, encouraging, educational manner, appropriate relationships with, and respect for, students evident in all staff. • Enhanced CRB/DBS disclosure confirmed and acceptable by school where any adult works with same group of students three or more times per month. • Coaches need to be thoroughly vetted before starting work in schools to ensure they are not barred from working with children and young people. • Jewellery and personal effects removed/made safe. • Professional development needs identified and supported with regular training. • School procedures to deal with observation or disclosure of possible abuse known and applied consistently. • Young sports leaders always supervised by adult staff. • All PES staff avoid 1:1 situations with students wherever possible. • Senior staff with designated safeguarding responsibility known to all contributing to PES programme.	• Policy on removal/wearing of medical bracelets known and applied. • School policy on medication management followed. • Staff trained in specific medical situations as necessary (eg epi-pens). • School-parent agreements on administration of medicines checked and applied to individuals. **3 First aid provision** • Provision for students available at all times on and off site. • School has clear, detailed and effective procedures for managing first aid/emergency situations. • Time implications for illness/injury at extremes of school site considered and addressed. • Staff know and apply school procedures for management of first aid/emergency situations. • Emergency contact system effective. • Travelling first aid kit taken on all off-site visits. • First-aider or appointed person with any group going off site. • Reciprocal arrangements agreed for use of host school's equipment and facilities when injury occurs at away fixtures/off-site events. • Injury records kept according to school procedures. • Near misses discussed to improve safety standards. • School procedures followed for informing parents and follow-up.	• Appropriate size of court, pitch, hall and equipment for each age group carefully considered. • Matching of students/teams in terms of comparable age, standard, ability and confidence in early stages of competition. • Any significant imbalance in any of these areas (eg size, age, ability, capability), fixture should be stopped and rearranged to reflect better balance and matching of participants. • Appropriateness considered of activities where boys and girls compete or take part together in fixtures or competition. • Programming and scheduling ensures participation in not more than one full sports fixture in any given day **or** where likely that students will participate in more than one game, attention given to programming and scheduling to match preparation by training and levels of skill and fitness to ensure safe involvement. **4 Intimate care issues within PES** • School policy addresses PES context adequately. • Staff trained and assessed as relevant (eg manual handling, administration of specific medicines). • Gender staffing implications considered where intimate care applied. • Dignity, decency and respect consistently evident. **5 Responding to weather conditions** • Avoidance of overexposure to sun effective. • Rehydration systems in place.

People	Context	Organisation
	• Community users aware of limitations of first aid provision by school. **4 Digital imagery, Internet safety, electronic communications** • School policy and strategy on Internet safety applied consistently in PES. • All PES staff trained in Internet safety. • Students reminded about Internet safety during PES sessions. • School policy on staff contacting students by phone, email or text known and applied by all. • Parents involved in any electronic communication about fixtures/visit arrangements, and only via disclosed list. • Photography and filming used only within a clear learning context, and parents made aware of such use within school policy. • Procedures and protocols to ensure ethics and security of digital imagery known by all PES staff, applied consistently and communicated to parents. • Access to images held by school controlled by password/ authentication process. • Clear procedures and agreement where imagery used across groups of schools. • Staff apply general safeguarding considerations in use of imagery (eg students cannot be identified, consideration of filming angles, general shots, particular care in swimming and gymnastics contexts).	• Staff teaching position avoids students looking directly into sun. • Appropriate additional clothing allowed for cold conditions. • Security of footing on playing surface considered. • Students taught safe response if caught in sudden thunderstorm.

Table 7: Some aspects relevant to safeguarding within a PES context (continued)

Context

- School policy applied on parental consent for digital imagery in education contexts.

5 School/department security

- All adults involved in PES programme wear identification/are known to students.
- Facilities not in use locked wherever possible to prevent unauthorised access.
- Facilities checked before locking to ensure nobody locked in.
- High risk equipment disabled/locked/prohibition signs in place to prevent unauthorised use.
- Equipment and facilities checked periodically for continued safe use.
- Routes to outside areas safe, lit at night.

6 Drug and substance misuse

- Staff trained in recognising symptoms of drug misuse.
- School strategies to identify and support students with drug problems known and applied.
- Check club links include anti-doping education and strict application of policies in written and practical procedures.
- Implications of doping to enhance performance communicated to students and monitored by staff.
- School policy on advising about sports supplements is followed.

7 Transporting students

- Clear school/employer policies on use of cars, taxis, coaches and minibuses for PES activities.
- Seat belts always worn in any vehicle where belts are provided.
- Child restraints made available and used where required.
- Roadworthiness of any vehicle used is checked.
- Appropriate insurance, MOT, certification etc in place.
- Requirement for driver to have CRB/DBS clearance checked and approved by school/LA.
- No adult alone in any vehicle with single child other than their own unless an emergency.
- Emergency contact information either carried by group leader or access ensured at any time if information held at school.
- Safe embarkation/disembarkation points identified and used.
- No distraction of driver of any vehicle other than emergency.
- Adult supervision ratios considered pre-journey.
- Reciprocal arrangements in place.
- Accredited/well-known taxi, bus and coach companies used.
- Parents informed where their child is to be carried in another parent's car and agreement obtained.
- Section 19 permit displayed in minibus if any form of charge made by school.
- School/employer requirements for driving minibus fully met.
- Minibus driver's legal responsibilities known and met.
- School system for management of minibuses compliant, effective and ensures safe use.
- Trailer towing regulations met.
- Passenger unobstructed access/exit ensured when luggage/equipment carried.

An editable version of Table 7 that can be made specific to schools' circumstances is provided in *Appendix 9: Aspects Relevant to Safeguarding Within a Physical Education and Sport Context* on the CD-ROM.

Students staying with host families for sporting events abroad

3.5.130   Whatever the event, the well-being of the student remains paramount in law. It cannot be assumed that similar checks will be made in other countries to those made by the CRB/DBS in the UK. Safeguarding systems, policies and procedures and the culture of safeguarding young people may therefore be very different.

3.5.131   Staff need to establish what control is possible over decisions made in the foreign country prior to and during the visit, then confirm with the host school whether there is an equivalent CRB/DBS system in the host country. If there is, the host school should confirm in writing the checking process and that it has **carried out checks** for the host families.

3.5.132   Many LAs and governing bodies of sport have established guidance on developing event **welfare plans** that will cover the welfare and duty-of-care requirements for taking children away.

3.5.133   If the host foreign school or sports club has no specific child-protection policy, the host school or commercial organising agency should be asked to ensure they adhere to the following safeguarding procedures at all times when working with the students:

- They ensure the UK minimum standards (ie the operating standards within the UK school) will not be compromised.

- Hosting arrangements should be made prior to departure.

- They ensure the students share placements in families with same-sex children.

- Where possible, two students should stay with the same host family. If this is possible, two same-gender and similar-age students should share a room.

- The UK school receives confirmation in writing from the host school of the arrangements and approves the host family.

- They provide to the host family a key point of contact and a clear means of communicating any concerns that might arise.

- They make arrangements for the host family to be informed of any special information about the placed student with regard to dietary and medical needs, and acceptable levels of supervision, free time and disciplinary sanctions.

3.5.134   The status of any members of the party who may not be a British national, or who may be in the process of obtaining that status, or who are not members of a European Union member state needs to be checked, including reference to the Home Office UK Border Agency, concerning the right of re-entry.

3.5.135   Arrangements should enable students to **speak to a member of the school staff** confidentially, should they feel uncomfortable in the host-family home. A contingency fund may be advisable should an urgent need to re-accommodate a student arise.

Residential events in the UK

3.5.136   Procedures should be the same as for existing in-school arrangements, and minimum operating standards should be applied in the same way. If a central residential venue is used, then accreditation, safeguarding policies, procedures and good-practice guidance should be in place, but it is wise never to make assumptions.

3.5.137   The vetting of host families in the UK has been seen as good practice for some time. Requirements within the Safeguarding Vulnerable Groups Act 2006 make the vetting of host families in the UK mandatory.

Relevant case law

3.5.138   R versus Church (2008):

A cricket coach was jailed for six months for downloading child pornography films showing children being sexually abused.

3.5.139   All of the following cases were brought under the principle of **'abuse of a position of trust'.** (It is an offence under the Sexual Offences Act 2003 for a person over the age of 18, such as a teacher, to have a sexual relationship of any kind with a child under 18 where that person is in a position of trust in respect of that child, such as in teaching, even if the relationship is consensual.)

3.5.140   R versus Drake (2011):

A physical education teacher who was also a deputy head teacher was sentenced to six years' imprisonment for maintaining sexual relationships with two 14-year-old students and one 16-year-old student.

3.5.141   R versus Thompson (2008):

A physical education teacher groomed a 17-year-old student through texts and telephone calls. He was sentenced to a nine-month prison sentence, to be listed on the Sex Offenders Register for 10 years and is not allowed any unsupervised access to a child under 18.

3.5.142   R versus Walsh (2007):

A physical education teacher was sentenced to 14 months' imprisonment for sending students pornographic Christmas cards.

3.5.143   R versus Brooks (2007):

A physical education teacher received a five-year prison term for having an affair with a 14-year-old student.

3.5.144   R versus Lister (2005):

A physical education teacher was jailed for 15 months for using mobile-phone calls and texts to groom young girls.

3.5.145   R versus Unsworth (2000):

This physical education teacher received a 12-month custodial sentence for having an affair with a 14-year-old student.

More information on safeguarding can be found in *Section 2: Safe Teaching Principles, paragraphs 2.3.61–2.3.64*, page 32.

Violent play

3.5.146 Injuries occur in sport because of bad luck, careless acts or unacceptable violence on the pitch. Violence in sport may cause injury inflicted **outside the laws and spirit of the game**. This is assault: the fear of or actual infliction of force. Dangerous play in sport represents unacceptable risk.

3.5.147 Violence in sport is not confined to adult participation. It is thus relevant to staff, coaches and managers in school situations because they have a **secondary, vicarious liability** for the actions and behaviour of the students on the pitch as they are the final adult to place the students in a competitive situation.

3.5.148 There is, as yet, no reported case of such criminal vicarious liability in PES in the UK, but it could occur where a team manager has knowledge of a student's proven violent sporting offences and fails to apply sanctions such that continued selection is evidence of condoning violent play.

3.5.149 Staff who teach, encourage or accept **over-aggressive play** may be held liable if their players go beyond the rules and spirit of the game. Failure to exercise control of a team is the responsibility of the team manager; one they cannot afford to ignore.

3.5.150 It is therefore important that schools have a brief procedure about the monitoring of students' fair play in competition and that, where violent or reckless play occurs outside the rules and spirit of the game, immediate corrective action during the game becomes necessary. For example, if the official does not remove the player from the game, then the team manager should ensure the player takes no further part in the game because the likelihood of a similar incident occurring becomes foreseeable, and the team manager could be deemed to have condoned the violence and be held vicariously criminally responsible for it. Staff should also encourage students to report any occasion where they feel threatened or intimidated as a result of violence or reckless play.

3.5.151 Further investigation is then needed to establish whether the player has a propensity towards violence or reckless play or it is deemed to have been an isolated incident. This will determine whether that player is selected in future. Where there is the probability of repetition, the team manager selecting the player may be judged to condone violent play and be criminally prosecuted should there be any repetition of reckless or violent play causing injury.

Relevant case law

3.5.152 Dickinson versus Cornwall County Council (1999):

This case has nothing to do with violent play but is relevant in that the judgement established that knowledge or experience of something that was not a foreseeable possibility **becomes a foreseeable event once it has occurred** *and therefore needs to be taken into account with appropriate corrective action part of the planning and management of similar future events.*

3.5.153 R versus Calton (1998):

A student kicked an opponent in an incident off the ball, breaking the opponent's jaw. He admitted grievous bodily harm. He received 12 months' detention in a young offenders' institution. The judge said: 'Any sportsman, adult or boy, who **deliberately assaults another will face immediate custody** *to prevent others from doing the same.'*

3.5.154   Hattingh versus Roux (2011, South Africa):

A hooker in the front row of a rugby scrum received a severe neck injury in a school match. The opposing hooker and prop both intentionally placed their heads together in the same gap when engaging in a scrum, instead of interlocking, to exert increased pressure on the opposing hooker. This is **illegal and dangerous**. *The judge confirmed that players could not seek to deliberately injure opponents.*

3.5.155   Gravil versus Carroll (1) and Redruth RFU Club (2) (2008):

A player admitted punching the claimant in an off-the-ball incident following a scrum during a semi-professional rugby match. The injured party needed facial surgery and was out of the game for six months. The offending player was suspended for eight weeks. The injured player alleged that the club (the second defendant) had encouraged aggressive play through a results-based bonus system. The Appeal Court ruled that it was 'fair and just' to hold semi-professional and professional clubs liable for their players' illegal or violent actions, establishing **'a vicarious responsibility for the injury'**.

3.5.156   R versus Stafford (2009):

A golfer was jailed for nine months for causing actual bodily harm when he hit another player about the head in a 'golf rage'.

Supplements

3.5.157   Talented students may seek advice from staff about the use of sports supplements, such as creatine and other products, to promote body development and, subsequently, enhance sports performance.

3.5.158   Such supplements have not been tested on young people. Studies on adults indicate that many supplements provide no benefit to improvement, with some being contaminated and dangerous to health. Students should be made aware that supplements can place them at risk and cause serious health problems. Nutrition, well-constructed personal training programmes and sensible life management are preferable.

3.5.159   For additional information, see UK Sport (2006) 'Sports Supplements and the Associated Risks'.

Context-related principles

Equipment management

- Storerooms and storage
- Purchase, maintenance, disposal and movement of equipment
- Mats

Facility management

- Changing provision
- Work areas and playing surfaces

Transport management

- Preparation
- Walking routes
- Minibuses
- Cars
- Buses and coaches
- Public transport

3.6 Equipment Management

3.6.1 According to a school's particular circumstances, **documented procedures** may include reference to:

- how equipment is to be stored in order to maintain safe access for staff and students
- how and when staff should monitor the condition of equipment, and the procedures for dealing with defective items
- how to use equipment correctly and deviate from its design purpose, to improvise or adapt for purpose, with care and forethought
- ensuring all electrical equipment used carries a current portable appliance test (PAT) certificate
- the use of mats, clarifying which types of mat are to be used in specific activity contexts, how and where the mats are to be stored, and how they should be carried to maximise their condition and period of use and avoid injury to the carrier
- the use of condemned equipment being strictly forbidden
- any specific qualifications teachers must hold to allow use of specialist items of equipment such as trampoline spotting rigs
- how students need to be involved in the safe handling and movement of apparatus and equipment
- the storage, movement and anchoring of portable goalposts
- procedures for reporting faulty equipment
- specialist annual inspection implications of fixed and large portable equipment in school halls, gymnasia, sports halls and fitness suites, and fixed outdoor play equipment.

Storerooms and storage of equipment

3.6.2 All storage areas should be **kept tidy** in order to minimise the potential for tripping.

3.6.3 Storage areas need to be of **sufficient size** so as not to create hazards. Access should be as **wide** as possible to prevent bottlenecks. Where a separate fire-rated mat store is provided, it should be used, though most schools store mats with other equipment. In such circumstances, the mats should be stored well away from heating sources.

3.6.4 Where equipment is stored around an indoor facility, it should be stored in a safe manner so as to encroach on the work area minimally and, where possible, close to where it is generally used, to minimise carrying distances.

3.6.5 Working at Height Regulations address situations where anyone could fall a distance liable to cause personal injury. Where equipment is **stored above reach height**, the appropriate steps, ladders or platforms should be used in order to comply with the Regulations.

3.6.6 Storage for equipment used outdoors should be secured, to **prevent unauthorised access** to potentially dangerous items. Heavy items are best stored at waist height to minimise the likelihood of back injury through lifting a heavy weight from the floor or it being dropped on to feet if over-reaching above.

Purchase, maintenance, disposal and movement of equipment

3.6.7 Teachers need to be confident that the equipment they plan to use is of **acceptable quality** in terms of its design, manufacture and durability. Such assurance is often obtained through reference to British and European Standards (kitemarked BS and BS EN respectively) and best purchased from a reputable and reliable company that assures such a quality standard, where relevant (not all equipment has provision for a BS EN standard). Where there is no quality standard, teachers need to seek alternative confirmation that the products they intend to purchase and use with students are safe and well made.

3.6.8 Reference to a particular BS or BS EN standard is a means of ensuring the consistency and fitness for purpose of certain products and procedures. However, compliance with a British Standard does not in itself confer legal immunity, although it will strengthen any defence against accusations of negligence in activities involving the use of equipment.

3.6.9 Some employers do not recommend the use of certain items of equipment in **primary schools**. Examples include rebound jumping equipment (eg trampettes and trampolines), which require very specialised knowledge and teaching to be used safely. Head teachers should be aware of, implement and monitor all such policies.

3.6.10 Equipment needs to be **fit for purpose**. Students of differing ages and abilities will benefit from different sizes and types of equipment. Students' individual needs may require adapted equipment in order to allow safe participation.

3.6.11 Accepting **used play items** from parents and other charitable sources, or purchasing from Internet sites, should be done only after careful consideration of the quality and condition of the items.

3.6.12 The Provision and Use of Work Equipment Regulations 1998 (PUWER) require that all equipment should be subject to **systematic and regular inspection** to identify any signs of damage or wear and tear that may cause injury. Some equipment requires specialist attention (such as fixed play, gymnastic and fitness equipment) resulting in a written report, while the requirements for other items may be satisfied through an internal system (such as checking small sports and athletic equipment). Any damaged equipment needs to be taken out of use until repaired or condemned by the specialist company.

3.6.13 Guidance on the selection and use of **specialist companies** for annual maintenance contracts is set out in *Appendix 20* on the CD-ROM. Such specialist inspection does not negate the obligation on teachers to visually inspect all equipment prior to each use.

3.6.14 Criteria associated with competent inspection and maintenance provision would include the following:

- Appropriate insurance should be held by the contractor and made available for scrutiny if necessary.

- Human resources, tools and materials should match the agreed schedule of work.

- The maintenance and inspection work should seek to disrupt teaching as little as possible but be open to observation and monitoring.

- An opportunity should be given to school staff to identify any equipment/apparatus concerns prior to the inspection/maintenance work commencing and, where feasible, for a member of the physical education staff to be present during the inspection.

3.6.15   In order to achieve appropriate safe-practice standards for equipment and facility maintenance, **contracts** should include reference to the scope of the work, the quality and standards of work, the identification of hazards and risks to be managed, and the maintenance tasks to be carried out. The school leadership team has a responsibility to ensure agreed maintenance requirements are achieved.

3.6.16   The **inspection and maintenance process** should identify:

- exactly what apparatus/equipment has been inspected (the inspection specification)

- any apparatus/equipment that is judged no longer safe through damage or deterioration

- any maintenance or repair that has been undertaken to restore faulty apparatus/equipment to safe usage.

3.6.17   The inspection process should have the following outcomes:

- a written, signed, dated report, identifying all work undertaken

- recommendations relating to any item of apparatus/equipment that merits repair but falls outside the scope of the contract in terms of cost

- the immediate and safe disposal or decommissioning of any apparatus/equipment judged to be beyond reasonable repair, with **clear identification** of any items not removed immediately but **condemned** and judged to be beyond safe and economical use.

3.6.18   **PAT testing** assists the identification of safe and tested electrical equipment, eases the tracing of such equipment and provides an audit trail, as well as protecting staff and students against the increased likelihood of harm caused by equipment used in a variety of environments, whether outdoors or in swimming pools or other PES facilities and during the movement of such items. All portable electrical appliances, such as broadcasting equipment, musical equipment, timers, whiteboards or kettles, must be inspected for safety every year and a small PAT certificate attached to each individual item, including any personal items taken into school for use in lessons. Any portable electrical appliance lacking a current certificate should not be used. It is a whole-school responsibility so it is important that the leadership team is kept informed of all portable appliances that need to be registered for PES.

3.6.19   **Outdoor goalposts** need to be correctly located, securely fixed to the ground and have protective padding applied, where relevant, taking note of governing body of sport guidelines. Regular inspection should ensure bolts remain in place, corrosion has not caused the posts to become a risk to participants, and net fixings are suitable and secure.

3.6.20   Larger items of **unfixed equipment**, such as netball posts or portable football posts, that cannot be stored inside a building need to be secured at all times.

3.6.21   **Portable goalposts** are increasingly used for soccer and hockey at all levels. They provide a useful option when storage, portability and flexibility in the use of playing areas need to be considered. Such posts are made from metal or heavy-duty plastic and are light enough to carry. Governing bodies of sport and some commercial companies provide useful guidance on the handling and placing of portable goalposts.

3.6.22   Because of their relative lightness, it is essential that portable goalposts, of whatever size or type, are made secure by the use of chain anchors or appropriate anchor weights when in use or stored, whether indoors or outside. In the event of impact from the ball, unintentional collision by a player or being pulled over by a student, the goalposts need to offer a stable structure. Anchor systems need to be appropriate to the floor or ground conditions, to ensure stability and that they do not become an additional hazard.

3.6.23   Portable goalposts should be:

- obtained from a reputable manufacturer and comply with British Standard Publicly Available Specification (PAS) 36:2000

- assembled in accordance with the manufacturer's instructions

- regularly checked for wear and tear and, where practical, any damage made good by a suitably qualified person

- smooth in construction, with no sharp edges

- equipped with a safe stabilising device that presents no hazard to players or spectators

- of lightweight construction and with integral wheels, where appropriate, in order to limit the lifting required.

3.6.24   Any **netting** should be well fitted and not extend beyond the area covered by the base of the posts. It needs to be secured by plastic hooks or tape. Metal cup hooks should not be used – they have been banned since 2007.

3.6.25   Home-made goalposts or any altered from their original specification should not be used.

3.6.26   Teachers and officials should check the condition and stability of all goalposts before use.

3.6.27   Staff or students with responsibility for moving and positioning the posts should apply safe lifting and carrying techniques, using an appropriate number of people who are strong enough and trained in manual handling techniques, and pull or push the posts backwards according to the design.

3.6.28   Clear guidance needs to be given to students about the dangers arising from misuse (eg climbing or swinging on the uprights and crossbars) of both fixed and portable goalposts. Reported accidents and resulting injuries (in some cases fatal) have had their origins in such activity.

3.6.29   **Playing area markers** are useful in identifying clearly designated playing areas, essential to safe practice whether participating outdoors (eg on a field or hard play area) or indoors (eg in a school hall or sports hall). Brightly coloured games discs provide the safest alternative to goalposts or for the reinforcement of line marking and are also relatively easy to carry to the working area.

3.6.30   Although suitable for 'run-around' relay-type activities, **cones and skittles** should not be used as playing-area markers, particularly in fast-moving games activities where a fall is foreseeable. **Cricket stumps or other low posts** should not be used as markers or substitute goalposts as a fall on to one could cause serious eye or facial injury. **No sharp-ended items** should be used as markers for any reason as a slip may cause impaling on to the sharp point. **Beanbags** are not recommended as markers for indoor work and are particularly hazardous to participants on a shiny floor.

3.6.31   Portable games posts, such as **netball posts**, may create safety issues both in transit to and from the working area and when positioned on the court/playing surface. It is essential that staff and, where appropriate, students who are given responsibility for moving and assembling such equipment are given a suitable induction into safe lifting techniques. It will be necessary for staff to supervise students given such responsibility, and this is particularly important where heavy weights are utilised to stabilise the posts. If made of metal, regular checks should be made for rough edges and signs of rust or other corrosion. When in place, the bases must not intrude into the playing area.

3.6.32 Adapting equipment for use may occasionally be appropriate, such as the use of cones to create mini goals, but this requires careful risk assessment. Some adaptations may be required when modifying the activity for a particular playing surface or space, possibly involving the use of lighter-weight balls for hockey on a hard court space.

3.6.33 **Gymnastics apparatus** falls into two categories. In primary schools, it generally consists of fixed and portable apparatus, such as climbing frames, ropes, benches, movement platforms, nesting tables, boxes, planks and trestles. In secondary schools, many items associated with competitive gymnastics and more formal vaulting and agility activities will additionally be found.

3.6.34 Whatever the function of gymnastics apparatus, staff should ensure the following:

- Only apparatus that has been officially provided, approved and/or kitemarked is used, and staff need to be very wary of improvising beyond its design specification.

- Apparatus is assembled and dismantled systematically and students are taught to do this, wherever possible. It needs to be checked by staff to ensure correct assembly before activity commences, and students should be encouraged to remain alert to, and report, any unintended adjustment as work proceeds.

- Apparatus is age-appropriate such that students are able to manage lifting, carrying and placing it in a safe manner. Students should have a straight back, chin tucked in, be close to the load, have feet apart with one foot in front of the other and be facing in the intended direction of travel with no twisting and with arms bent to bring the load close to the body. They should lift with knees bent, using the legs as the lifting power. Everyone should have a good grip on the load before lifting and should not change their grip once carrying it. The load should not obstruct fields of view. Students should set the load down gently with their backs straight and knees bent.

- Sufficient space is left between apparatus to allow safe movement around it. Dismount points and planned landing areas need to be free from obstruction and always well away from walls.

- After use, apparatus is returned to its designated storage space and left in a stable position.

- Apparatus is regularly inspected and repaired, where necessary, by qualified maintenance engineers, at least on an annual basis.

3.6.35 Apparatus deemed unsafe but repairable should be moved well away from the working area and clearly labelled as unsafe until made good.

3.6.36 Because the annual cycle of apparatus inspection by specialist engineers usually extends to a 12-month period, teachers need to **constantly monitor** the condition of apparatus on a day-to-day and lesson-by-lesson basis, and encourage and equip students to do the same. The following table identifies a number of features related to the safety of key items of gymnastics apparatus.

Table 8: Gymnastics apparatus checklist

	Check that:
Wooden rebound/ take-off boards	✓ the board is stable on impact ✓ the surface is non-slip and free from splinters
Benches and planks	✓ the construction is not warped and is free from splinters ✓ rubber buffers on the supporting feet are secure and the bench is stable ✓ the surface is clean and smooth ✓ fixing hooks are intact and covered with leather or plastic ✓ rubber pads on the top surface are in place if the bench is intended for use in an inverted position
Ropes and suspended apparatus	✓ ropes are not frayed or damaged ✓ pull-out lines are not worn and their securing wall cleats are secure ✓ the runway operates smoothly ✓ ropes are knot-free and the leather end caps are intact ✓ rope ladder floor fixings are intact ✓ knots are not tied into the ends of the ropes
Hinged apparatus fixed to a wall	✓ bracing wires are taut with no visible fraying at any point ✓ castors run smoothly ✓ floor sockets are clean and free from obstruction ✓ securing bolts are firmly fixed and engage properly with their floor and wall sockets ✓ wooden components are free from cracks or splinters ✓ painted components are well maintained, with no evidence of flaking ✓ consideration is given to replacing traditional bare metal tension clamps with padded, boxed-in versions
Single and double beams	✓ hauling cables are free running ✓ trackways are well maintained, enabling smooth movement of the upright ✓ there are sufficient pins and wedges ✓ beam surfaces are clean and smooth ✓ beams run smoothly when lowered and raised ✓ floor sockets are clean
Vaulting apparatus and movement platforms	✓ all wooden components are splinter-free ✓ all covers – vinyl, material or hide – are free from tears, clean and, in the case of hide, suitably textured ✓ construction is stable and solid with no weakness allowing dangerous movement on impact ✓ wheeling mechanisms work efficiently.

3.6.37   Positioning, assembling and **folding a trampoline** should always be undertaken by at least two trained staff. Where older students, sufficiently mature and strong enough, have been trained, they may carry out the folding and unfolding of trampolines under the close supervision of qualified staff ready to give immediate hands-on assistance if needed. There have been several accidents where younger students, lacking the necessary strength and physique, have been left to carry out this task without direct staff involvement. It is important that, in circumstances with such students, qualified staff are directly physically involved as part of the process. Training shoes should be worn when folding or unfolding a trampoline. Clear communication, awareness and a responsible attitude are essential, particularly in the phase where the end of the trampoline has been opened, to ensure it is held with sufficient force to counter the tension of the springs. Elbows and forearms should be kept away from the gap between the folding ends and frame while lowering under control.

3.6.38   The procedures used need to be clearly understood by all involved. The guidance below will promote safe practice:

- Trampolines should be placed well away from any overhead obstruction such as hanging beams or lights. There should be an overhead clearance of at least 5m from the floor to the lowest hanging object for club activities and 8m for the highest levels of competition.

- Once removed, wheel units should be placed carefully in a storage position well clear of the working area.

- The space under and around trampolines should be clear and free from obstructions.

- When unfolding a trampoline, care should be taken to ensure that:

  - training shoes are worn to protect the feet

  - feet are kept well away from the wheels

  - the trampoline is angled and lowered carefully, and the lower leg section held firmly so it does not crash to the floor

  - the frame sections are opened with a firm, continuous movement, with steady force applied and maintained to prevent them from springing back

  - fingers, forearms and wrists are kept clear of all hinges.

3.6.39   Before allowing a trampoline or trampette to be used, staff should check that:

- all the leg braces have been properly fitted and the hinge units are securely housed

- all adjustments are tight

- the hooks of the springs/rubber cables are properly attached, with the hooks pointing down

- the springs/cables are all in good condition

- the safety pads are fitted and entirely cover the springs/cables

- Allen screws are tight (if present)

- the bed is clean and free from damage of any kind

- the wheeling devices are operating smoothly and the pivotal housing on the frame holds the hub of the wheeling mechanism at right angles without any movement of the hub and the housing (trampoline only)

- the floor surround has 25mm matting 2m wide along the sides of the trampoline, and the ends have end decks with appropriate weight-absorbing mattresses of a sufficient size and weight absorbency to meet the requirements of body impact in the event of pitching forwards or backwards. Where trampolines are located in line, weight-absorbing mattresses should be placed on the frame and springs between each trampoline.

3.6.40 When folding a trampoline, care should be taken to ensure that:

- training shoes are worn to protect the feet

- the wheels are securely housed

- adult support and supervision is directly to hand to step in if needed

- the frame sections are closed using a firm, continuous movement, with steady force applied and maintained to resist the tension of the springs or cables

- fingers, forearms and wrists are kept clear of all hinges

- feet are kept well away from the wheels

- the lower frame and leg sections are positioned inside the upper frame and leg sections as the trampoline is rotated from the horizontal to the vertical.

3.6.41 Once folded, trampolines should be locked to prevent unauthorised use. This can be done by locking together two links of one of the leg chains. Trampettes should also be disabled in some way when not in use or kept in secure storage.

3.6.42 When provided, overhead support rigs should be supplied and fitted by recognised specialist manufacturers and engineers. On no account should improvised rigs be used. Training in the correct use of rigs is essential.

> **More information on setting up trampolines can be found in *Section 5: Applying the Principles to Specific Areas of Activity, paragraphs 5.7.30–5.7.31*, page 245.**

Relevant case law

3.6.43 Beaumont versus Surrey County Council (1968):

*This ruling held the LA responsible for the teacher **not disposing** of old trampette elastics **adequately**. A student picked the elastics out of a waste bin and, while playing with them, caused another student to lose an eye.*

3.6.44 Steed versus Cheltenham Borough Council (2000):

*The crossbar of some rugby posts collapsed and fell on to a boy. It was judged that the posts were **rusty and deteriorating** and that the council did not carry out sufficiently frequent inspections of the condition of the posts.*

3.6.45 Greenwood versus Dorset County Council (2008):

*A group of students were involved in folding away a trampoline. One student's arm was fractured when the folding end trapped it. The teacher was judged to have **complied with the established code of practice** in that she had:*

- *supervised adequately*

- *taught the correct process*

- *regularly reminded the students of the correct process*

- *provided step-by-step monitoring of the process*

- *involved sufficient students in the folding process.*

3.6.46   Hall versus Holker Estate Co Ltd (2008):

*An adult was injured during a game of football when he caught his foot in the **net of a portable goalpost that should have been pegged into the ground**. The goalposts collapsed and hit him, causing facial damage. He claimed the owner of the site should have checked the pegs regularly to ensure the facility and equipment were safe. At appeal, it was held that there was no evidence of a suitable inspection system and negligence was evident. This illustrates the importance of ensuring **equipment is regularly inspected**. This is particularly important where it is clear the equipment needs to be regularly maintained and properly assembled for safe use and where it is likely parts of the equipment are occasionally misplaced or removed, rendering it unsafe.*

> **More information on equipment maintenance can be found on the CD-ROM in Appendix 20: Quality Assurance and Quality Standards on the Inspection and Maintenance of Gymnastics, Fixed Play, Sports and Fitness Equipment.**

Mats

3.6.47   It is essential that both staff and students understand the structure, function, capabilities and limitations of mats when used within the physical education programme.

3.6.48   Mats are primarily designed to **absorb impact** for landings on the feet. Their construction dissipates force, thereby reducing reaction to what would otherwise constitute a hard and unyielding surface.

3.6.49   Over the years, considerable improvements have been made to the design and specification of mats, enhancing safety. However, it is important to recognise that mats, whatever their construction and size, **should never be seen as fail-safe protection** systems that supersede effective technique. Students need to be aware that a correctly performed landing contributes most to preventing injury. This technique needs to be taught and re-emphasised regularly.

3.6.50   The guidance below relating to the **maintenance of mats** will promote safe practice:

- When buying new mats, care should be taken that they meet any current standard, where available, and that they fully comply with fire regulations. Assurance should be sought from manufacturers on both these requirements.

- Mats should be covered with material that is **easy to clean**. In order to minimise slippage, the underside will need to be cleaned from time to time and the top surface periodically, according to the extent of use. They should be checked regularly for any embedded objects, such as stones or pins.

- Mats should be **stable and lie flat** to the floor. Wherever practical, mats should be stored in a horizontal position to prevent warping of closed-cell polyethylene foam and disintegration of foam padding.

- Mats should remain free from holes and tears.

- Mats should be **light enough for students to handle easily**, preferably in pairs if the mats are lightweight. Four students may need to carry mats according to their size and strength in relation to the size and weight of the mat.

- Mats should be subject to regular inspection. Damaged mats should be immediately taken out of service until repaired by a specialist maintenance firm or replaced.

3.6.51   In gymnastics, mats should **never** be indiscriminately placed around the working area. Each mat should be placed with a specific purpose in mind. **Mats are typically used to:**

- provide a comfortable, cushioned area for aspects of floor work (eg developing rolling activities)

- identify suitable landing areas to students as they work around apparatus

- provide confidence in feet-first landings from mobile apparatus such as beams and items used for vaulting and balancing (though it is the efficiency of technique in landing from a height that minimises injury, not dependence on a mat absorbing the momentum)

- extending sequence work by providing choice for changes of direction, level and mode of travel.

3.6.52   General-purpose mats (approximately 25mm thick) are generally suitable for curriculum work in gymnastics. Thicker mats (eg 200mm) may be necessary for more specialised, advanced gymnastic activity in which the performer generates high levels of momentum.

3.6.53   Teachers need to exercise **caution** when using thick weight-absorbing mattresses ('crash mats' or 'safety mats') as landing areas. Too much absorption may compromise safe dismounts on to feet by creating rotation on landing. In such situations, they are advised to 'firm up' the landing surface by overlaying the mattress with general gymnastic mats where necessary.

3.6.54   If more than one weight-absorbing safety mat is used to create a longer area (eg for landing from a vaulting horse), the mats should be secured together by placing a longer agility mat roll on the surface of the mats to lessen the risks associated with a student landing on the line where two mats meet.

3.6.55   Mats should never be used to protect against the foreseeable outcomes of poorly developed skill, such as anticipating that students will fall while suspended from a horizontal ladder or similar work situation. In such situations, it is better that apparatus and task are modified to accurately reflect student need and capability, thereby minimising the risk of falling and poorly controlled dismounts.

3.6.56   **Athletics landing modules** are necessary for the safe performance of high-jump technique in which the transference of weight moves from feet to some other body part (eg the Fosbury Flop and related progressions). It is strongly recommended that staff using specialised high-jump facilities have undergone **appropriate training** through the governing body of sport – UK Athletics – or as part of a specialist physical education training programme.

3.6.57   When using landing modules, teachers should ensure that:

- multiple modules, where used, are firmly locked together and a coverall pad used to prevent slippage

- the landing area is sufficiently large and deep enough to accommodate the abilities of the students involved and probable variations in landing position, extending beyond both uprights

- the density of the landing module is sufficient to avoid any bottoming out.

3.6.58   Mats used in **martial arts** activities need to be specific to the activity to minimise the risk of injury from high-impact falls and throws, complying with BS EN 12503-3, in order to provide adequate shock-absorbing properties with a strong base to prevent sliding during activity. General-purpose gymnastics mats should not be used as their density is inadequate for martial arts purposes.

3.6.59   Canvas covers should not be used to cover or secure martial arts arenas. Frames can be constructed to secure mat areas permanently, but they should be covered if they present a hazard.

> More information on equipment can be found in *Section 2: Safe Teaching Principles, paragraphs 2.3.87–2.3.98, pages 35–36.*

3.7   Facility Management

3.7.1   According to a school's particular circumstances, **documented procedures** may include reference to:

- changing provision and routines
- facility provision and any particular safety implications, routines, precautions and restrictions
- action in the event of extremely cold or hot temperatures
- fire safety and emergency evacuation
- cleaning regimes and safe standards of cleanliness
- requirements for regular visual checks by staff and students
- reporting any faults in facilities
- required safe-practice protocols during lessons.

Changing provision

3.7.2   Changing accommodation should be of **sufficient area** to allow space for all students to change safely and keep their clothes in a tidy and clean state. Non-slip floors are essential. Pegs should not be broken, with sharp edges that may cause injury. Shower water mixer valves should be regulated by one control key, which should be positioned out of reach of students to reduce any risk of scalding. Broken wall tiles in shower areas can cause serious injury and should be replaced as soon as possible.

> More information on changing provision can be found in *Section 2: Safe Teaching Principles, paragraphs 2.3.74–2.3.81, pages 34–35.*

Work areas and playing surfaces

3.7.3   Facility provision has moved towards **flexible learning spaces** to meet learning outcomes. Schools will no longer have common provision though generic aspects of health and safety in relation to facilities will remain the same as before. Whatever facilities are available for use, risk assessments will need to be specific to a particular school's use of the facilities.

3.7.4   Adaptable facilities require a risk assessment that considers the variable use of the facility, the implications of converting the facility (particularly where students may be involved), the particular usage the school intends and any guidelines manufacturers provide.

3.7.5   Where schools **share facilities** within a network, it is good practice to establish an understanding that the host school develops normal operating procedures and emergency action plans. These should be made available to other user groups, and they in turn should accommodate these within their risk assessments for the overall experience that may include travel, shared use or other logistical issues that need to be planned for.

3.7.6   The use of facilities **new to a group** will need to take account of health and safety issues such as:

- access and transport implications, such as a safe embarkation/ disembarkation area

- multi-use and the implications of provision for other purposes, including additional equipment, impacting on the safe work area for physical activity

- security of footing, whether on poolsides, outdoor surfaces or indoor surfaces

- storage and the management of movement in and around storage areas

- court/pitch dimensions, including location and the amount of run-off area provided

- safe access and use for those with disabilities

- sufficient space for the planned activity – freedom of movement requires more space than an activity based on restricted movement

- sources of liquid to maintain hydration where necessary.

3.7.7   **Security** of facilities is essential. Where possible, physical education facilities should be locked when not in use to prevent unauthorised access.

3.7.8   The floor area necessary for safe practical work depends on the number of participants normally taking part, their age and mobility, and the type of activity planned. The National Dance Teachers Association (NDTA) recommends a minimum of $3m^2$ per student for primary **dance** and $5m^2$ per student for secondary dance. **Gymnastics** would thus require more space than this per student in order to allow for safe movement and the use of apparatus. Historically, approximately $8m^2$ per student was the standard for a then-typical class size of 30 in a typical secondary-school gymnasium where a range of activities would be taught.

3.7.9   Class and group sizes have tended to increase in recent years. Where this constraint applies, those leading a lesson need to consider **how** the activity can be presented in order to allow safe movement. For example, some types of dance require limited movement, but others are based on significant freedom to move. Without sufficient space, some variation in choreography or style may be necessary. Gymnastics sequences and apparatus arrangements may need to be planned in more compact forms. In games activities, less freedom of movement may be needed, with some form of conditioning applied to the organisation of the activity.

3.7.10   **Indoor floors** should be kept clean and swept regularly. Economies in floor-cleaning arrangements can make planning a safe physical education programme difficult as significant levels of dust increase the likelihood of slipping. Whenever possible, school staff should be involved in decisions about cleaning schedules. Any cleaning and/or polishing of floors should not leave a slippery finish. Loose boards, splintering, cracking and lifting edges sometimes occur with heavy use, creating an irregular surface that can affect the security of footing. Patches of condensation and residual wet mopping after school meals should be dried before activity begins. Sprung or semi-sprung floors are most beneficial to physical education programmes generally in order to protect lower limbs from damage by the absorption of impact energy. Where floors are not sprung, care should be taken with high-impact landings. Where facilities are used for other purposes, such as dining, examinations and assemblies, safe use of the floor in physical education lessons may become compromised, and schools should seek to avoid this practice wherever possible.

3.7.11 **Ceiling height** needs to be sufficient so as not to restrict movements such as lifts in dance, vaults in gymnastics, throws in combat sports and clearance for trampolining at school or higher competitive levels.

3.7.12 **Fixed equipment** such as dance-training barres or folding gymnastics frames should be stable, substantial in design and able to accommodate participants of different ages and abilities. Where mirrors are installed, they should be of strengthened glass.

3.7.13 There should be sufficient space for the safe use of equipment and **adequate electrical points and Internet connections** around the facility so trailing wires or ill-placed or unstable items do not present a hazard.

3.7.14 **Lighting** should be uniform wherever possible. Any risk of being dazzled by sunlight coming through windows, or directly into students' eyes, or glare reflected from water needs to be managed by the considered placement of apparatus, direction of play or movement, frequent changing of teaching position or a more permanent resolution, such as tinting the glass. Artificial lighting should be made from unbreakable materials or set in protective cages. Strip lighting that produces a flickering or stroboscopic effect should be avoided as this could impair visual focus, induce disorientation and trigger seizures.

3.7.15 **Walls** should be smooth to avoid friction injury if body contact occurs, with rounded corners where the possibility of impact is likely and to facilitate safe ball-rebound activities. Background colours and the need for the safe sighting of accelerating projectiles (such as balls) should be considered. Essential features other than physical education apparatus should be positioned well above working height, wherever possible, or recessed where this requirement cannot be met.

3.7.16 **Doors and door frames** should be flush wherever possible. Main access doors should open outwards and have some system of closure control. This is especially important on exposed or windy sites to minimise the risk of doors opening or slamming unexpectedly. **Fire exits** must remain clear at all times, and it must be possible to open fire doors from the inside of the facility. Where possible, they should have flush mounted push pads to minimise the likelihood of injury. **Glass doors** can be hazardous. Where they are necessary, the glass should be smoked or coloured for visibility, unbreakable, reinforced and resistant to impact fracture. If a pane is cracked, it should be replaced as soon as possible. Door glazing should be at a height to accommodate wheelchair users. Where doors are glazed around hand-pushing height, there should be push battens across the door on both sides. It should not be assumed that all glass in a school is toughened in case someone falls into it or seeks to push off from it. This needs to be confirmed, where necessary, or systems in place to minimise the likelihood of injury occurring.

3.7.17 **Heating systems** should provide an adequate working temperature, adjustable to accommodate varying conditions, and be designed so there is no danger of any student being adversely affected by burns, fumes or other hazards to health. A regular inspection and maintenance programme should be established. An even temperature should be maintained throughout the facility. Current building regulations indicate a minimum temperature of 15°C for physical education. Where this temperature is not met, there are implications for extended warm-up, pace and whether lessons can continue with reasonable safety. There is no statutory maximum working temperature. Staff will need to be sensitive to the impact of significantly high temperature on active sessions and plan accordingly.

3.7.18 **Fitness rooms** should provide for:

- sufficient space between and behind items of equipment
- adequate visual supervision across the area
- firm and stable working surfaces
- accommodating free weights, weight stations and multi-gyms, preferably in separate areas
- access to emergency exits
- regular inspection and repair programmes by recognised specialists
- clearly posted safe weight-training procedures in the work areas
- protecting the floor area with mats in areas where free weights are used
- storing free weights on purpose-built stands
- locking collars on free weights when in use
- fixed or sufficiently weighted wedge-shaped floor bases to be used for leg squat exercises
- a consistent temperature; Sport England recommends an air temperature of 12–18°C and adequate ventilation where heat gains are likely.

3.7.19 The water environment of **swimming pools** may be seen as high risk. It is reasonable to expect owners of public swimming facilities to provide a safe working environment for users under the terms of the Occupiers' Liability Acts 1957 and 1984. However, school staff accompanying students, together with specialist swimming staff, should ensure they know and implement the normal operating procedures and emergency action plan for the facility being used.

3.7.20 Particular care should be taken on poolside surrounds where wet surfaces may contribute to slipping injuries.

3.7.21 **Glare** across the water surface, from natural or artificial lighting, may restrict sight to the bottom of the pool across large areas. In such circumstances, frequent movement by supervisory staff and school staff, or some other appropriate action, may become necessary to maintain maximum visual awareness. Glare may also trigger an adverse reaction in students with identified special needs or medical conditions.

3.7.22 Pools should not be used where the water clarity is such that the bottom of the pool cannot be seen at all depths.

3.7.23 The depth and **extent of shallow or deep water** areas should be clearly marked and noted by those responsible for safety. A pool divider, usually a rope, should normally be positioned to delineate shallow from deep water whenever non-swimmers are present though this is not always feasible during mixed sessions. It is particularly important that any sudden changes in pool depth are highlighted.

3.7.24 **Signs** should identify potential risks and be positioned so pool users can see them clearly and interpret them easily. School staff should explain their significance, especially to beginners. All signs should conform to the appropriate British Standards/British Standard European Norm.

3.7.25   Entry from the changing rooms on to the poolside is safest where the water is shallow. Where pool design precludes this precaution, students should be made aware of the hazard, care should be taken when entering on to the poolside and strict behaviour standards applied.

3.7.26   The design of steps and rails should be such as to prevent any part of the body becoming trapped. Where this risk exists, warning signs and regular verbal reminders to pool users should be provided.

3.7.27   The Amateur Swimming Association (ASA) recommends that the temperature of the water should be about 29°C to enable young people to be comfortable and not become unduly cold during the period of time allocated to swimming. Water temperatures for disabled swimmers may be set much higher (as high as 36°C). The ambient air temperature should be slightly above that of the water, to avoid condensation, typically 1–4°C greater.

3.7.28   Those responsible for the management of pools should ensure outlet pipes at the bottom of pools have grilles in place that are securely fastened. Holes in grilles should not be large enough for fingers to become trapped.

3.7.29   Leisure pools, many with special water features and irregular shapes, may cause potential supervisory blind spots that need to be checked regularly.

3.7.30   Pool surround, pool depth, the implications of any protruding ladders or steps and the use of electrical equipment are key considerations when determining whether the facility is suitable for other aquatic sporting activities, such as competitive swimming, water polo or synchronised swimming.

3.7.31   All pools need to operate swimming pool cleaning systems that meet acceptable hygiene standards.

3.7.32   Chemical levels should be monitored at the beginning of the day and at regular times throughout the day. At no time should chemicals be added to water directly when swimmers are present.

3.7.33   Swimming pool surrounds should be kept clear at all times. Pool equipment (eg floatation aids, emergency equipment, lane markers) should be stored appropriately, taking into account the need for safe access to and from the pool.

3.7.34   Adequate, well-maintained **lifesaving equipment** must be readily available in known locations and staff (and students as appropriate) must be trained in its use.

> **General safe-practice guidance on aquatic activities can be found in *Section 5: Applying the Principles to Specific Areas of Activity*, paragraphs 5.2.1-5.2.45, pages 202-208.**

3.7.35   In **sports halls**, the space required for games depends on the standard of play: the higher the standard, the larger the space needed due to greater run-off areas and clearance heights. Netting should not foul footing at any time.

3.7.36   Technical guidance about the design and use of all sports facilities is available from governing bodies of sport, commercial companies, such as Continental Sports (www.continentalsports.co.uk) and national sport associations, particularly the Sport England website: www.sportengland.org/facilities__planning.aspx

3.7.37   Schools are now responsible for determining their own assessment of **fire safety**. Fire precaution procedures must be known and applied by all school staff. Particular consideration needs to be given to regular checking that emergency signs are in place and illuminated where necessary, fire safety equipment is in place and not misused, and emergency exit routes are not locked nor blocked when the facility is in use, such as where trampolines or other equipment are placed across emergency exits. The implications of emergency evacuation by students wearing little clothing in practical sessions into potentially very inclement weather needs to be considered and planned for as do any implications for the mobility of students and staff, such as where wheelchair users may form part of the group. Discussion with students will inform them of their role in an emergency evacuation.

3.7.38   The head teacher is the 'senior manager on site' directly responsible for fire safety in law. If they are not on site, then the next most senior person on site temporarily becomes the responsible person.

3.7.39   **Playgrounds** and other **hard play areas** should be sited to prevent the risk of running into walls or other obstacles, and the surfaces should be maintained in good condition, with no loose materials present in the playing area. Loose grit, accumulation of silt, the absence of post socket covers and any uneven surface caused by frost damage or in the laying of the hard surface all constitute hazards that need to be addressed through regular maintenance and repair.

3.7.40   Wherever possible, **pedestrians and vehicular traffic** should be kept separate. Where this is not possible, adequate signage restricting vehicle speed and routes, as well as pedestrian-priority areas, should be provided.

3.7.41   Reasonable measures should be taken to avoid allowing vehicles on to playgrounds. Where this is not possible, close and careful monitoring by school staff is essential. Wherever possible, car-parking areas should be separate from those used for student play.

3.7.42   The presence of oil on playground surfaces needs to be prevented. It makes surfaces slippery, can cause them to deteriorate prematurely and is therefore a potential hazard.

3.7.43   **Playing surfaces** need to be suitable for activity and in sound condition. They should be routinely and regularly checked to ensure security of footing is not compromised by damage such as holes. Where concerns exist, an effective reporting system needs to be in place.

3.7.44   Safety on **playing fields** can be adversely affected by the aftermath of trespass. Broken glass, cans and other rubbish generally deposited on these sites create serious risks to students.

3.7.45   Deposits of dog faeces infected by toxocara (roundworm) can cause toxocariasis in humans, with symptoms that include blindness, asthma, epilepsy and general aches and pains. All practical measures should be taken to keep animals off playing surfaces and encourage owners to remove any offending deposits immediately.

3.7.46   Where playing fields are used as multi-purpose play areas, litter may be a problem that needs to be controlled. Gang mowers can shred plastic and metal containers into sharp shards that create significant risk.

3.7.47 Pitches should be **marked out** safely so playing surfaces are, and remain, level (corrosive substances should not be used). Regular maintenance is essential. Holes (including rabbit scrapes) should be filled as soon as possible after identification. Adequate run-off areas at the sides and ends of pitches should be provided.

3.7.48 Pitches should be suitable in **size for the ages and abilities** of those using them. Technical guidance is available from commercial companies, governing bodies of sport and national sport associations.

3.7.49 There should be a suitable distance between the playing area and the perimeter of the working space in which it is located, particularly if other students are working in adjacent areas, and proximity to hazardous fixtures and fittings should be avoided. There needs to be a sufficiently clear space to **run off** the pitch or court without danger of collision with objects or people (typically a minimum of 2m, but reference to Sport England's publication 'Comparative Sizes of Sports Pitches and Courts' (available from www.sportengland.org) should be made. It is important to ensure the distance between the playing surface and features such as boundary fences, roads and windows is sufficient to avoid accident or injury and that directions of play account for this.

3.7.50 **Remote facilities** require additional consideration. Staff who are working away from the main building on fields, courts or other play areas should be equipped with radios or alternative reliable communication devices in order to make immediate contact with colleagues if necessary. Some emergencies necessitate immediate support, often including access to first aid.

Relevant case law

3.7.51 Jones versus Monmouthshire County Council (2011):

*Compensation for injury was awarded when a student tripped over a kerb while retrieving a ball from the area surrounding an AstroTurf pitch. The difference in the height of the kerb and pitch was described as being 'borderline' as a **tripping hazard**. The judge determined that if it was recognised as a tripping hazard, something should have been done to manage the hazard. A common sense solution would have been to remind participants about the difference in height and monitor that they were paying attention to the task of retrieving the ball sensibly by looking where they were going.*

3.7.52 Young versus Plymouth City Council (2010):

*A woman regularly walked her dog in a park. On one occasion, she injured her foot, catching it on a 30cm-high wooden marker that had been in situ for several years as part of an orienteering course. She alleged this was unsafe as the marker was partially concealed by grass, difficult to see due to its colour and created a trap for walkers. The council argued the woman knew of the marker and should have looked where she was going. She admitted to probably being aware of the marker at the time of the accident and had known of it on previous visits. There had been **no previous accidents** of this nature in the preceding 10 years. The claim was dismissed – the marker did not present a danger to visitors.*

3.7.53 Bassie versus Merseyside Fire and Civil Defence Authority (2005):

*This determined that it was foreseeable that, where a floor was not kept clean, it could lead to **slipping injuries**.*

3.7.54   Douch versus Reading Borough Council (2000):

A player stumbled and injured himself while running to retrieve a ball during a cricket match, blaming grass-covered humps in the outfield. The judge dismissed the claim on the basis that they were 'minor undulations', with only a remote likelihood of someone falling because of them. However, it was stated that playing areas need to be checked regularly to ensure they are safe to use. This suggests **minor undulations** *can be expected on playing fields.*

3.7.55   Taylor versus Corby Borough Council (2000):

While playing a ball game on a grassed recreation area, an adult was injured because his foot went down a 10cm hole. No regular inspection of the playing surface was carried out, with the repair of defects being reactive, rather than based on risk assessment and regular checks. It was judged that some system of regularly checking playing surfaces is necessary and it is foreseeable that **holes** *in playing surfaces are likely to cause serious injury.*

3.7.56   Futcher versus Hertfordshire LA (1997):

A long-jump participant was awarded damages when injured by landing on **compacted sand**. *The area had been raked, but not dug over before or during the competition.*

> **More information on work areas can be found in *Section 2: Safe Teaching Principles, paragraphs 2.3.125–2.3.127*, pages 41–42.**

3.8   Transport Management

3.8.1	According to a school's particular circumstances, **documented procedures** may include reference to:
	• the need for good group-management skills when taking groups off site
	• the need for risk assessments to include journey implications
	• the inclusion of relevant aspects of the school's critical incident plan in the organisation and risk assessment of the event
	• when parental consent forms are required and the fact that no student participates in a journey where a required consent form has not been received
	• general safe embarkation and disembarkation practices
	• communication with parents if students are delayed on a journey
	• who can drive a school or hired minibus and under what conditions
	• the management system for school minibuses – reporting faults, bookings and so on
	• the checklist minibus drivers should follow before commencing journeys
	• who to consult for information if driving a minibus abroad
	• conditions for the use of staff and volunteers' cars
	• whether booster seats need to be available and used
	• the organisation of groups where taxis are used
	• the procedures where buses, coaches or public transport are used
	• how supervision ratios are determined
	• the benefits of dividing large groups into smaller groups managed by specified adults for ease of management and control.

Preparation

3.8.2 Staff taking groups off site should be **competent** in discipline, control, organisation and dealing with any crisis that may arise. They should ensure there is an effective **emergency contact system**, such as via a mobile phone, or an alternative arrangement if a mobile is not available.

3.8.3 A **risk assessment** for regular activities should be carried out, as well as additional assessments for each special event involving travel. Effective management and control, particularly with younger students, are more easily achieved where large groups are subdivided into smaller groups with a designated adult responsible for each sub-group.

3.8.4 Consideration of the school's **crisis management plan** (sometimes referred to as a critical incident plan or disaster plan) should be built into the risk assessment in the very unlikely event of the transport used being involved in a major road traffic accident that the individual member of staff cannot deal with alone.

3.8.5 Parental **consent forms** are not required when students are transported off site for curriculum experiences where the mode of transport is other than by volunteers' private vehicles though parents do need to be kept informed of where their children are at all times.

Walking routes

3.8.6 Where movement off site involves walking, the route should be **familiar** to the staff involved, with potentially hazardous points identified and precautionary strategies known by the staff and, in an appropriate way, the students. **Ratios** of accompanying adults need to be calculated according to the various factors of the students' age, safety awareness, behaviour and familiarity with the route; and staff competence in relation to group management, knowledge of the group, familiarity with the route and the distance and safety demands of the route. Immediate **communication** with the school base should form part of the planning and organisation of the trip. LA guidance (where applicable) may present further requirements that would need to be adhered to by LA schools.

More information on walking routes can be found in *Section 2: Safe Teaching Principles, paragraphs 2.3.118-2.3.120*, page 40.

Minibuses

The minimum statutory requirements for driving minibuses

3.8.7 School minibuses are usually operated with what is called a **Section 19 permit**. Section 19 of the Transport Act 1985 allows non-profit-making organisations, such as schools, to make a charge to passengers for providing transport. Without this permit, the school would need to have a public service vehicle (PSV) operator's licence, and drivers would need a passenger-carrying vehicle (PCV) entitlement on their driving licence (a full category D addition).

3.8.8 If **no charge** is made for the use of the bus at all, then no permit is required. However, any payment that gives a person a right to be carried on a vehicle (the legal term for this is 'for hire or reward') would require the operator to hold either a Section 19 permit or PSV operator's licence.

3.8.9 It is the school governors' responsibility, as the **operator** of the minibus, to apply for a Section 19 permit. To obtain such a permit, the minibus cannot be run with a view to making a profit. In other words, the minibus is used for voluntary purposes only, but a charge can be made to cover running costs and so forth, directly as a fare or indirectly as a general contribution to school.

3.8.10 The Section 19 permit must be **displayed** in the windscreen of the minibus.

3.8.11 **Drivers** of a minibus with a Section 19 permit must at least:

- be aged 21 or over

- have held a category B licence for at least two years

- receive no payment or consideration for driving the vehicle, other than out-of-pocket expenses.

3.8.12 Without the driver having a **D1 licence**, the minibus weight must not exceed 3.5 tonnes (4.25 tonnes including any specialised equipment for the carriage of disabled passengers) and a trailer cannot be towed.

3.8.13 Thus, where the school offers the minibus to students for a charge, but on a non-profit basis under a Section 19 permit, the driver is exempt from the D1 requirement. This is because the Section 19 permit exempts the employer from holding a PSV operator's licence and exempts the driver from the D1 requirement, providing they receive no payment for driving the minibus.

3.8.14 Drivers who passed their test on or after 1 January 1997 are no longer granted a D1 (not for hire or reward) entitlement. However, they may still drive a 9–16-seat minibus under a permit, provided the conditions set out above are met.

3.8.15 Drivers who passed their car test before 1 January 1997 were automatically granted additional entitlement to drive minibuses with 9–16 passenger seats (category D1) not used for hire or reward. For as long as they hold a D1(not for hire or reward) entitlement, these drivers may drive a 9–16-seat minibus of any weight used under a permit and may receive remuneration for this.

3.8.16 Anyone who has obtained a driving licence abroad is not usually entitled to drive a vehicle with more than eight seats.

Employers may make additional requirements

3.8.17 There is no national standard other than that set out in the Transport Act 1985. However, employers may make whatever additional conditions they wish as to who drives a minibus. Some employers choose to demand a D1 addition; others do not, but, as recommended by the Vehicle and Operator Services Agency (VOSA), they may require some additional training, such as the Minibus Driver Awareness Scheme (MiDAS), Royal Society for the Prevention of Accidents (RoSPA) or local driving course/test (hence schools having their own minibus driving tests) for what is a 'small bus'.

Driving a minibus abroad

3.8.18 Driving a minibus under a Section 19 permit is acceptable only within the UK.

3.8.19 The governing body, as the operator of the minibus, should ensure the requirements set out in EEC Directive 91/439/EU Directive 2006/126 are applied when using a minibus abroad. The requirements of this Regulation include the following:

- A specific **PCV licence** is required; Section 19 permits are not recognised abroad.

- Higher **medical criteria** are applied; for example, insulin-dependent diabetics cannot drive a minibus.

- The **tachograph** is to be completed and used. This is not a requirement in the UK.

- Familiarity with the driving requirements and regulations in the countries to be visited is required.

- Maximum **driving hours** and minimum rest requirements are imposed that are more stringent than in the UK.

- Vehicle **documentation** must be carried at all times. For example, passenger lists are to be carried with the vehicle.

Management of the minibus

3.8.20 The Public Passenger Vehicles Act 1981 identifies the operator as the person for whom the driver drives the vehicle. If the driver is driving the bus on authorised school business, then the operator is the governing body or LA, according to the type of school, who will be responsible for the lawful use of the vehicle.

3.8.21 Best practice is where someone on the school staff has responsibility for ensuring maintenance, confirmation of roadworthiness, scheduling, record keeping and driver management are organised effectively.

3.8.22 Only minibuses with **forward-facing seats** can be used to transport students. Seat belts must be fitted to all seats of minibuses when used for carrying children aged under 16 in a group of three or more on an organised trip. **Seat belts** must be worn.

3.8.23 The driver is legally responsible if a passenger under the age of 14 does not use a seat belt provided. Anyone 14 or over must wear a seat belt, but is responsible for doing so. The responsibility lies with the individual student and, where appropriate, the leader of the group. Staff in charge of a group on a bus may be prosecuted if they fail to ensure seat belts are used.

3.8.24 Adequate **wheelchair passenger restraints** must be provided to enable wheelchair users to take advantage of, and travel safely on, minibuses. An occupied wheelchair must itself be held securely in position using a recognised wheelchair-securing system.

3.8.25 A driver cannot **drive and supervise** at the same time. They should not be distracted except on safety grounds. Where student needs or behaviour warrants supervision, a second adult should be present to fulfil the supervisory duty.

3.8.26 Vehicle operators and drivers must assess the likely risk of drivers suffering from **fatigue**, especially on long journeys. If a driver is going to drive for more than four hours in any one day, then they must comply with British domestic rules for driver hours if operating solely within the UK and with EU rules if operating in any other EU country.

3.8.27 **Trailers** should not be used unless unobstructed access is provided at all times to at least two doors, one on the nearside and one on the offside, in case of any incident that may cause the trailer load to slide forward and block the rear exit.

3.8.28   The yellow and black **'school bus' sign**, compulsory for home to school transport, is not a requirement for minibus use on other types of journey, but many schools choose to have it on display in the rear window as a warning notice to other traffic.

Minibus driver responsibilities

3.8.29   The driver is responsible for:

- the roadworthiness of the vehicle when it is on the road

- ensuring the minibus is not overloaded and not carrying more passengers than allowed

- doing a risk assessment for the journey

- ensuring seat belts are worn by all passengers under 14 years during journeys

- knowing how to adjust seat belts

- ensuring all passengers have their own seat – three children sharing two seats is not allowed, neither are standing passengers

- satisfying himself that passenger supervision is adequate

- ensuring luggage is securely stored with no obstructions on the floor between the seats or in front of any exit

- notifying the employer of any changes in his driving circumstances

- observing speed limits and other traffic controls – buses carrying eight passengers or more are now restricted to a maximum stabilised speed of 100kph (62mph) with lower speeds according to the type of road being travelled (further information is available from www.minibusclub.co.uk/minibus_information.php)

- knowing the locations and use of the fire extinguisher and first aid kit

- driving with the doors unlocked and good visibility through all windows.

3.8.30   **Safe embarkation** and disembarkation are important. The location should be away from the roadside where possible. It is advisable for passenger loading to be allowed only by the side doors and not the back doors where passenger safety may be compromised by passing traffic.

> **More information on minibuses can be found on the CD-ROM in *Appendix 21: Minibus Driver's Hours of Work Allowed – British Domestic Rules (Transport Act 1968).***

Cars

3.8.31   When using cars to transport students, a clean driving licence is usually expected. Definitions of a **clean licence** may vary from one employer to another. Having some penalty points may be accepted as a clean licence, and staff need to check with their employer.

3.8.32   The car must be **roadworthy** and have a valid MOT if relevant.

3.8.33   The driver needs to have appropriate **insurance**. For non-school support staff, this must be fully comprehensive, and staff insurance should cover the use of their car for school business.

3.8.34   **Charging** is not allowed for the use of the vehicle.

3.8.35   Agreed procedures should ensure **no adult is ever alone** in a car with any child other than their own. Appropriate disclosure certification should be obtained if applicable.

3.8.36   Travelling in convoy is not recommended as it can divert a driver's attention. Drivers should know the route to their destination and not rely on following others.

3.8.37   Parents should give permission for their child to travel in **another adult's car**.

3.8.38   Local requirements will apply as to whether **senior students** may use their own cars to transport their peers.

3.8.39   **Child restraints** (ie baby seats, child seats, booster seats and booster cushions) must be used where students are less than 12 years of age and under 135cm in height and seat belts are fitted. This requirement applies only to private cars and vans although it should also be applied to the use of taxis where booster seats are available. The only exceptions are:

- for a short distance in an unexpected necessity

- where two occupied child restraints prevent the fitting of a third

- where the correct child restraint is not available in a taxi (then the adult seat belt must be used).

3.8.40   Schools using staff and parents' cars to transport students to matches and events will need to apply the requirements on the use of booster seats. It is the school's responsibility, on behalf of parents, to ensure booster seats are provided and used. Seat belts must be worn.

> **More information on the issue of cars can be found on the CD-ROM in the following appendices:**
>
> - *Appendix 8: Parental Consent Form for a Student to be Transported in Another Adult's Vehicle*
> - *Appendix 22: Car Seats, Boosters and Seat Belts – Department for Transport.*

Taxis

3.8.41   Taxis are increasingly used to transport small groups as a more cost-effective means than hiring coaches.

3.8.42   Staff should check the **employer's policy** to ensure the use of taxis is allowed.

3.8.43   Staff should also check whether or not the taxi firm is **accredited** by the employer (some LAs maintain lists of approved firms who employ CRB/DBS-checked drivers). If using a firm not on an approved list, schools must make their own decisions and arrangements with the firm in relation to CRB/DBS clearance.

3.8.44   Discussion with the taxi firm to put in place a system of organisation may determine such issues as whether all taxis are to load and leave together for the journey to the venue and return to the school, and how staff supervise disembarking and check numbers.

3.8.45   The **risk assessment** should determine whether each taxi should have an adult supervisor or whether a student may be designated to carry a list of names and base contact details and what procedures are to be implemented in case of an accident or emergency during the journey.

3.8.46   **Seat belts**, where provided, must be worn.

3.8.47   Parents should be informed and their **consent obtained** prior to children being transported by taxi.

Buses and coaches

3.8.48   Where schools use buses or coaches, it is good practice to use a **reputable transport company**. Many schools and LAs maintain an approved list of companies.

3.8.49   **Coaches** are fitted with seat belts, and staff must ensure all passengers use them. However, **buses** are not required to have seat belts, and staff should therefore seriously consider whether buses should be used to transport students involved in physical education or sport activities.

3.8.50   **Supervision levels** need to be considered according to the students involved, the journey and any breaks in the journey. The adults should be positioned through the coach so they can observe all students. Evacuation procedures need to be known by all before departure. When disembarking, it is good practice for the adults to disembark first to direct students to an assembly point away from the roadside or in the car-park area.

Public transport

3.8.51   Schools should establish a **code of conduct** for students who use public transport for physical education and sports events, to ensure group interaction with the public is of an acceptable standard.

3.8.52   Some schools choose not to provide transport to off-site events and leave students' transport arrangements to parents. In such instances, schools must not be involved in any way with the parents making the transport arrangements, or the school's duty of care will continue and responsibility remain with the school, rather than the parents.

Relevant case law

3.8.53   R versus Unwin (2011):

A coach driver was late to collect a school group from an outdoor activities centre. To make up time on the return journey, he took a short cut that was wholly unsuitable. The teachers complained, and one student received whiplash injuries. The driver had 12 points on his licence already for speeding and driving while using a mobile phone but had been spared a ban. He was found guilty of dangerous driving and given a 12-month 'alternative to custody' order and banned from driving for 14 months. He was sacked from the coach company the day after the incident. There was no reported indication that the coach company was disreputable, but this case emphasises the importance of **checking the standards of coach companies**. *It would usually be sufficient to use a coach company the school is familiar with and one that has a good timekeeping record, along with evidence of good, considerate drivers and well-maintained coaches.*

More information on transport can be found in *Section 2: Safe Teaching Principles, paragraphs 2.3.118–2.3.124,* **page 40.**

Organisation-related principles

Group management

- Ratios and group sizes
- Mixed-gender activities
- Mixed-age sport
- Accidents, emergencies and critical incidents

Programme management

- Schemes of work, lessons and teaching
- Emerging activities
- Higher-risk activities
- Religious and cultural issues
- Sports fixtures, festivals and tours
- Club links
- Weather conditions

Risk management

- Risk-benefit analysis
- Risk assessment
- Reporting, recording and communicating risk
- Making risks safe – controlling risk
- Risk education – involving students in their own safety

3.9　Group Management

3.9.1 According to a school's particular circumstances, **documented procedures** may include reference to:

- the school policy on group sizes
- determining ratios
- resolving concerns
- mixed-gender activities
- mixed-age groupings
- a summary of first aid and emergency procedures in the PES context
- the use of electronic communication in the event of an incident
- information on first-aiders and/or appointed persons to manage situations
- the necessity of taking a first aid kit for all off-site events
- whether additional or specific expertise is required when taking groups to remote off-site locations
- processes and timescales for completing incident records
- relevant aspects of the school critical incident plan relating to PES off-site visits
- discussion of near misses and incident analyses.

Ratios and group sizes

3.9.2 Scotland and Northern Ireland have legal requirements that all classes in practical activities, including physical education, are restricted to a maximum of 20 students. England and Wales have no such restrictions, despite the context and organisation of PES being the same in each of the home countries. In England and Wales, the school leadership team has responsibility for making decisions that group sizes and adequate work space are safe, including the responsibility for not creating situations that would be overcrowded and thus unsafe. Where the HSE becomes involved and determines that overcrowding is sufficient to cause injury, an improvement or prohibition notice could be served on the school.

3.9.3 Some governing bodies of sport recommend or impose teacher/coach:participant ratios, particularly in potentially higher-risk activities, such as adventure activities, aquatic activities and some contact sports because of the type of environment. Subject leaders should be aware of these and take them into consideration when planning the staffing for internal school activities or where an external provider works to such ratios.

3.9.4 **Levels of supervision** should be appropriate to the nature of the activity, the students in the group and the environment in which they are participating. It is frequently difficult to define teacher:student ratios for school-organised activities because of their highly contextual nature. The same activity would merit more generous staffing levels, for instance, if it were known that the teaching groups concerned presented challenging behaviour, had very limited experience or lacked confidence.

3.9.5   Teacher:student ratios may be determined on the basis of different reasons, including:

- staff competence and specific expertise
- student age
- student behaviour
- student ability levels
- previous experience of students and staff in particular circumstances
- a higher-risk environment (such as aquatics, adventure activities, trampolining)
- the nature of the activity
- the size and layout of the work area
- the condition of the facility
- limited safety equipment
- the type, location and amount of equipment in the work area
- the way the activity is most effectively organised
- any history of accidents and/or incidents occurring.

3.9.6   A rigorous risk assessment of the **particular circumstances** in question, culminating in a professional judgement by the head teacher and teacher involved, should indicate suitable staffing arrangements in terms of competence, number and available space.

3.9.7   Where a teacher or subject leader believes group size may compromise safety in the work environment, they should consider whether the **organisation of the lesson** can be amended to establish a safe learning situation before approaching the leadership team to seek a reduction in the group size.

3.9.8   Visiting coaches working in school may question group sizes they are asked to work with because their insurance is likely to be through a governing body of sport, which may restrict the coach's insurance cover to that sport only and to a maximum group size that is not conducive to a school's organisation. Greater flexibility is obtained where the coach works under the school or LA insurance cover in the same way as a member of the school staff. Subject leaders need to clarify with their employer whether a visiting coach operates within the employer's insurance or the coach's own and, where this is so, limit the visiting coach to any restrictions imposed by that coach's individual insurance.

Relevant case law

3.9.9   Jones versus Cheshire County Council (1997):

*A teacher took a larger group to the pool than the LA ratios allowed, but used a paired system so only half the group were in the water at any time other than 'free' time at the end of the lesson, when all were in the water. A child was injured during the free time, doing an activity the group had not been taught. The teacher was held responsible for going beyond the **LA ratios** and not limiting the end of lesson activity to pre-learnt skills instead of free time.*

Mixed-gender activities

3.9.10   Mixed-gender teaching and participation in activities have increased over the years. There are many safety advantages to this practice, including the potential for improved attitudes to learning, improved behaviour, improved learning and the use of specific staffing expertise.

3.9.11   It is recommended that strength, confidence, previous experience, ability and attitude are **key considerations** in the need to match students in learning activities, whatever the gender involved. Being a girl or a boy in football activities or dance should not imply that one gender has advantages over the other in a particular sport.

3.9.12   Age alone, as a safety factor, is not relevant unless it affects attitude and behaviour. **Physical contact and strength** translated into power are fundamental considerations as students mature. In instances where bodily contact, support and power applied to actions such as tackling or hitting a ball form part of the context, separating the genders for practical experience does become a key consideration.

3.9.13   Staffing single-gender student groups with members of the **opposite gender** should be acceptable unless there are significant elements of relatively intimate contact that may affect the dignity, comfort and confidence of either students or staff. In these instances, specific gender staffing becomes a key consideration.

Mixed-age sport

3.9.14   Some governing bodies of sport stipulate team selection restrictions to **narrow age bands** for reasons of safety, particularly in contact sports, such as rugby, and combat sports. This is intended to address possible differences in size, ability and confidence. Where any competitive situation occurs within the aegis of that governing body of sport, the requirement must be met.

3.9.15   While the principle to promote safe practice through **matching student size and experience** is generally sound, it is not necessarily appropriate to make decisions solely on chronological age due to variations in rates of physical development, confidence and skill.

3.9.16   There may well be occasions of competition, outside the remit of the governing body of sport and provided the safety and welfare of all students is not adversely affected, where the principle is considered as part of a risk assessment but not applied as strictly as the governing body of sport dictate sets out. For example, where a slightly younger but experienced, skilful and well-developed player would benefit from playing in an age band slightly outside his chronological age, a risk assessment could determine that the selection is safe.

Relevant case law

3.9.17   Mountford versus Newlands School (2007):

See Section 2: Safe Teaching Principles, paragraph 2.3.150, page 44, for details.

Accidents, emergencies and critical incidents

3.9.18   The priorities that should be evident in establishing and putting into practice **emergency procedures** are:

- saving life

- avoiding personal injury

- minimising damage

- reducing loss.

3.9.19   To this end, employers have a **duty to provide** their employees with:

- detailed, written policy and procedures for dealing with accident and emergency situations (in practice, school leadership teams and governing bodies draft their own, specific to their particular situations)

- access to first aid provision at all times; because schools deal with children, this entitlement extends to the students as well.

3.9.20 Policies and procedures dealing with accidents, emergencies and critical incidents are, therefore, **whole-school issues**. Subject leaders need to ensure all teachers of physical education, including visiting staff, are familiar with the school procedures and apply them when necessary in order not to detract from the efficient delivery of the PES programme.

3.9.21 These school procedures should be checked to ensure they **adequately apply to the context of physical education and sport**, including taking account of injuries that may occur at the extremities of the school site and also during off-site activities that frequently extend beyond the normal school day. A risk assessment of the PES programme and the contexts in which it is delivered will aid consideration as to whether the whole-school procedures adequately cover PES situations.

3.9.22 Effective and efficient **communication** with the office or leadership team is essential, whatever the time of day. Electronic communication systems (mobile phones and walkie-talkies) enable immediate response to an emergency and have become common forms of emergency communication from playing fields and other facilities at the extremities of school sites, as well as for events on or off the school site extending beyond the normal school day.

3.9.23 Schools must have one or more nominated **'qualified' first-aiders or appointed persons to manage first aid situations**. First aid qualifications are not essential for all staff though many feel that a higher professional standard is set by holding a current first aid qualification. It is important that teachers have a **working knowledge** of dealing with emergency situations to the extent that they can manage an initial injury situation effectively and summon the appointed person or first-aider to take over management of the injury.

3.9.24 A **travelling first aid kit** must be taken as a minimum provision for injury situations when groups go off site.

3.9.25 At least one **fully equipped first aid kit** must be provided on each site – often, many more are strategically placed across a school site. It is the role of the appointed person who manages first aid to ensure the kits are regularly checked and items replaced as necessary. Where an effective school system does not exist, PES staff need to implement a procedure for checking and replacing items used, particularly in the travelling first aid kit.

3.9.26 Where teachers take groups to environments **remote** from immediate help, additional training in first aid, specific to the hazards likely to be encountered, is advisable.

3.9.27 It is important that accidents are **reported** on the employer's official report form or accident book as soon as is reasonably possible. This aids the reporting process and is also of benefit in the event of a complaint or claim. It is also good practice to write down the events surrounding an incident as soon as possible to ensure a clear recall at some later date.

3.9.28 An official report form invariably provides a brief report of an accident. It may not contain all the information a school may be required to submit in the event of a liability claim. Additional information, not contained in the official report, may be attached, according to school policy.

3.9.29   It is very worthwhile for someone to **analyse** the incident report forms, typically termly, to establish whether there is any pattern in the causes of injury as this forms valuable evaluative evidence to inform and influence review of practice.

3.9.30   The HSE encourages the recording and discussion of **near misses** – where an incident occurred, but injury was avoided – because there are many more of these than actual injuries, and the causes of a near miss can also inform practice.

3.9.31   Employers must **report certain injuries to the HSE** to fulfil the requirements of the Reporting of Injuries, Diseases and Dangerous Occurrences Regulations 1995 (RIDDOR). It is therefore incumbent on schools to ensure records and reports are completed quickly and submitted to the employer. In some instances, employers have devolved the task of reporting to the HSE directly to schools. The school leadership team has responsibility for ensuring the necessary reporting occurs within the designated timescales.

3.9.32   Requirements for **reporting injuries** in schools to the HSE have recently changed. It is now a requirement to report an accident involving a student only if the accident:

   • results in a student being killed or taken to hospital for treatment of an injury

   • arises out of or in connection with the work activity – ie is **attributable** to:

      – the work organisation (eg poor organisation, management or supervision of an activity)

      – any equipment or substances (eg fitness machines, gymnastic equipment, swimming pool chemicals)

      – the condition of the premises.

   Injuries arising out of normal participation in an activity (ie not related to failing in the organisation or management of an event or faults in the premises) are no longer reportable to the HSE. Neither are situations where a visit to a hospital occurs, but no injury is identified.

3.9.33   Many schools have a **critical incident plan**, crisis management plan or disaster plan – disconcerting titles for the same thing – a pre-planned response to a major incident that one member of staff cannot manage alone and where communication of the incident with parents, emergency services and possibly the media needs to be coordinated, involving the leadership team, governors and LA, where relevant.

3.9.34   Major crises occur very rarely, but when they do happen, there is very little **time** to plan what to do. Every event tends to move rapidly so staff having planned any necessary contingency prior to it occurring will be at a great advantage. This should form part of a risk assessment of activities that take place off site.

3.9.35   Some school critical incident plans take account of on-site crises only. This is inadequate to cover the PES context fully. Where only on-site consideration is given by the governors and leadership team, it is important that discussion takes place with those responsible for the content of the plan in order for it to fully support and inform teachers taking groups off site for PES activities.

3.9.36   School policy should make staff aware of the relevant aspects of such a plan, and teachers of physical education should make themselves familiar with how they would respond, to what would be a small section of the plan, should they ever become involved in a major incident while taking teams to fixtures, festivals or on sports tours.

3.9.37   In practice, this can be summarised as:

- identifying potential critical incidents that could occur on the trip

- identifying potential support agencies and personnel who could provide immediate help

- developing a contingency plan specific to the event to deal with any critical incident

- clarifying roles and responsibilities for all staff involved

- effective and immediate communication with the school leadership team

- implementing the school system for contacting parents

- minimising the potential for students involved in the incident to communicate inaccurate or misleading information to family, friends or the media.

> **More information on accidents, emergencies and critical incidents can be found in *Section 2: Safe Teaching Principles, paragraphs 2.3.103-2.3.107, pages 37-38, Section 4: Essential Learning about Safe Practice, paragraph 4.3.5,* page 169, and in the following appendices on the CD-ROM:**
>
> - *Appendix 3: First Aid Qualifications and First Aid Kits: An Explanation of the Health and Safety Executive Approved Code of Practice (HSE ACOP) on First Aid 1997*
> - *Appendix 4: School Accident Report Form*
> - *Appendix 5: Standard Accident Procedures.*

3.10   Programme Management

3.10.1	According to a school's particular circumstances, **documented procedures** may include reference to:
	• the need for all teachers of physical education to plan lessons based on the assessed needs of students in conjunction with dynamically developed and developing schemes of work
	• structured lessons
	• afPE and/or governing body of sport guidance with regard to activity-specific requirements
	• student safety education learning outcomes being included in planning
	• the creation of a safe learning environment that is influenced by teaching positions to observe the maximum space and number of students, regular scanning to check safety, matching student expertise and confidence, accurate demonstrations and the importance of a strict application of a sport's rules for reasons of safety
	• any restrictions or pre-requirements on the introduction of emerging and challenging activities or higher-risk activities
	• protocols about religious and cultural issues
	• requirements for leading teams and squads on sports fixtures, festivals or tours
	• club links
	• extended sports provision for the community
	• protocols for accommodating students' cultural and religious principles.

Schemes of work, lessons and teaching

3.10.2 Planning means order, and order contributes significantly to safe teaching. Staff should assess students' **learning needs** against well-structured schemes of work that set out staged learning targets, essential techniques and skills, stages of progression and relevant safe-practice information not contained in other documented procedures. It is necessary for all schools to have such schemes of work on which lessons may be planned, consistent with any prescribed curriculum, as well as local circumstances and needs.

3.10.3 Assessing students' learning needs against operable schemes of work provides the cohesion, continuity and progression that ensure students' experiences are at all times appropriate, with risks assessed and managed so safe practice is addressed and implemented.

3.10.4 In cases involving negligence, the issue of whether students have experienced appropriate **preparation** for a particular physical task is frequently raised. Devising suitable challenge and **matching student capability to task** is enhanced when founded on progressive and structured learning experiences, enabled through comprehensive and dynamically evolved schemes of work. Planning should take account of, and accommodate, all levels of competence and confidence to ensure effective, meaningful and relevant content.

3.10.5 Schemes of work should make reference to relevant aspects of the risk assessment for PES and should include guidance on the organisation and teaching of safety.

3.10.6 Lessons need to be orderly and well organised. Poor discipline on the part of staff and reckless behaviour from students elevate risk beyond an acceptable level and can needlessly contribute to injury and harm. Lack of concentration and application cannot be tolerated within the context of physical activity, requiring staff to intervene rapidly to secure an appropriate focus on, and attention to, the task in hand.

3.10.7 Alternative **inclement weather lessons** should be planned on the same principles as the intended learning experiences. Doubling up of classes to provide some form of activity should be planned and managed with care, with particular thought being given to whether such circumstances may make injury more likely.

> **More information on the following topics can be found in** *Section 2: Safe Teaching Principles:*
>
> - **learning outcomes and lesson structure** - *paragraphs 2.3.142-2.3.145, page 43*
> - **registers and records** - *paragraphs 2.3.113-2.3.117, page 39*
> - **progression** - *paragraphs 2.3.158-2.3.169, pages 45-46.*

Emerging activities

3.10.8 Staff may wish to introduce into a physical education programme new, emergent or hybrid activities for which **codes of safe practice** are still under development. In these circumstances, head teachers should be consulted for approval, with careful forethought as to the implications of offering such potentially high-risk activities. Examples might include parkour, street surfing, kite surfing, free diving, land boarding, slacklining and street games.

3.10.9   Teachers may need to contact their LA advisory service, a relevant consultant, expert staff in other schools, their insurer, or the relevant governing body of sport or awarding body to obtain the best advice available as to whether to proceed.

3.10.10 Because emerging activities are often **not regulated** by a governing body of sport or national association, principles relating to safe practice are inevitably in their infancy and lack an effective communication network. Some emerging activities groups would not welcome intervention and oversight in the sense of compromising and limiting independence, creativity and individual choice in seeking out extreme and potentially dangerous pastimes. This poses particular difficulties for staff charged with a duty of care in safeguarding students' health and well-being.

3.10.11 It should be noted that anyone can establish a 'governing body' for a 'new' sport. afPE recognises only those governing bodies of sport that are acknowledged by the home country national sports agencies – Sport England, **sport**scotland, Sport Wales and Sport Northern Ireland. For a governing body of sport to be acknowledged in this way, certain **quality standards** have to be met. This provides some degree of reassurance as to the integrity of the organisation and some indication of consistency across the sport or activity involved.

3.10.12 It is advisable for staff to **refrain** from actively promoting students' involvement in activities that lack a regulatory structure and identified code of practice, whether within the curriculum or as part of wider sport provision.

3.10.13 **Freestyle gymnastics** is a relatively new aspect of gymnastics that is well regulated by the appropriate governing body of sport, British Gymnastics (BG). It consists of adapted existing gymnastic skills, is an activity for indoors only, should use recognised gymnastic apparatus and only be delivered by coaches with a minimum of a Level 2 gymnastics qualification and a BG Freestyle add-on module. Further information on this new aspect of gymnastics can be obtained by contacting the governing body of sport.

3.10.14 Parkour UK is now established as the governing body of sport for **parkour**. afPE is working closely with Parkour UK in the development of a professional learning course for teachers, covering aspects for Key Stages 1–4 (5–16 years). Until this is available, schools wanting to introduce the activity into the school curriculum or school sport programme should only do so using suitably qualified parkour coaches, following the afPE guidance regarding the use of coaches in schools. afPE will regularly update its position paper on parkour as the Parkour UK resources evolve (see www.afpe.org.uk).

3.10.15 **Street surfing** – the British Street Surfing Association (BSSA) is the governing body of sport for casterboard sports in the UK. A practical workshop for teachers is available, which provides a comprehensive element of safe practice, as well as safe development in the sport.

3.10.16 afPE will continue to liaise, where requested, on similar emerging **'street games'**, which are being adapted for use in schools, and communicate developments in these areas through its website (www.afpe.org.uk).

3.10.17 Where schools are approached by organisations offering activities not previously known to the school, they would be recommended to contact afPE, their LA, a known consultant or other colleagues to discuss any issues.

Higher-risk activities

3.10.18 Activities deemed to be higher risk may form part of a school's PES programme because of staff interest and expertise, student requests, the school's location, current trends in emerging and hybrid activities or as part of a broad, balanced and relevant curriculum that seeks to meet the student population's needs and interests.

3.10.19 Higher-risk activities may be **defined** as those activities where:

- there is a requirement for a high level of specific skills by participants

- specialist equipment is needed

- physical contact at speed and with power forms a central part of the activity

- there is a potentially hostile environment

- there is evident potential danger that needs to be addressed in the organisation, teaching and participation of the activity.

3.10.20 **Typical activities** deemed to be higher risk, unless managed appropriately, include:

- adventure activities

- aquatic activities

- athletic throwing events

- some contact sports, such as rugby

- combat sports

- high rebound activities (trampolining and trampette work)

- some gymnastics activities

- street-game activities adapted for schools, such as parkour or skateboarding.

3.10.21 In such instances, there is a need for:

- head teacher and/or governor approval for the activity to be undertaken

- a thorough risk-benefit analysis

- supervision ratios to be calculated carefully and based on a thorough risk assessment of the particular circumstances, taking note of governing body of sport guidance

- students to be fully informed of the risks and management of those risks

- teaching to be highly competent

- teachers to demonstrate up-to-date knowledge

- a careful development from basic progressive practices to high-level skills based on regular and consistent involvement

- specific teaching for specific techniques and skills

- student understanding to be checked

- competition to be introduced carefully and only when the students are ready

- specialist equipment and clothing to be carefully checked

- avoiding improvisation

- venues to be vetted regularly or at a time close to an occasional event

- clear procedures to be known by all involved

- contingency planning in the event of injury occurring or environmental conditions changing

- consideration of any need for:
  - specific parental approval
  - ability grouping
  - particular levels of fitness
  - a required code of practice
  - selection criteria to be applied (based on behaviour, attitude, previous experience etc)
  - monitoring of inappropriate peer-group pressure
  - careful and staged reintroduction following any student absence or illness
  - specific or additional insurance cover.

Religious and cultural issues

3.10.22 The religious and cultural diversity of modern society has brought with it a number of health and safety issues within the context of PES. **Careful and sensitive management**, however, should enable all students to experience the full benefits of a broad and enriching programme of physical activity, whatever their faith commitment and cultural background, while allowing schools to have due regard to the relevant education, health and safety and equality legislation.

3.10.23 The requirements of the Health and Safety at Work Act 1974 establish that **safe practice must never be compromised**. Whatever solutions and strategies schools decide on to maintain meaningful participation, this principle must be upheld in order to ensure the health and well-being of students in their care.

3.10.24 The most frequent health and safety **concerns** arise from:

- the wearing of certain items of clothing and/or religious artefacts
- the impact of religious/cultural festivals (eg Ramadan – Muslim month of fasting, which changes from year to year)
- cultural expectations relating to prescribed areas of activity and procedures
- participation in single- or mixed-gender groups
- language issues, which may put newly arrived students at risk due to difficulties in understanding the requirements of the task, safety procedures, expectations relating to conduct and the simple ability to stop work immediately in the event of danger or emergency.

3.10.25 In seeking to maximise safe and meaningful participation, staff should ensure the following in relation to **clothing and religious artefacts**:

- Any clothing worn to comply with a faith commitment is appropriate to the activity being taught. It should be comfortable and allow for freedom of movement. Loose or free-flowing clothing is generally not suitable for most physical activities and may compromise both the safety of the wearer (eg in gymnastics) and others in close proximity (eg in invasion games). It should be remembered that a tracksuit is considered perfectly acceptable clothing for Muslim students and is not seen as offending the principles enshrined in *Haya* relating to modesty and decency.
- Headscarves, where worn, are tight, secured in a safe manner, particularly at the side of the face, and unlikely to obscure vision or catch on anything that may put the wearer at risk.

- Any religious artefacts are removed or made safe. Wherever removal is expressly forbidden and the article cannot be made acceptably safe by taping, padding or covering, the activity and involvement of the wearer must be suitably modified to mitigate undue risk. Case law relating to human rights legislation has established that a student does not have the right to manifest their belief at any time and place they choose at school, and this includes the wearing of jewellery. Generally, to succeed in making a claim on the grounds of human rights, there would be a commonly acknowledged religious obligation on a follower to wear the jewellery.

3.10.26 Staff need to be aware that certain religious and cultural **festivals** (eg Ramadan, which involves fasting from dawn to dusk over the period of a month) require some students to exercise specified dietary regimes. Normal energy resources may thus become temporarily depleted, and the risk of dehydration is increased. In such situations, staff expectations relating to performance (eg sustained running) may need to be reviewed and levels of challenge adjusted to accommodate individual need.

3.10.27 Younger students, particularly, may be prone to a lowering of concentration levels when opting to participate in **fasting**. This has clear implications for the supervision and management of physical activity, and care needs to be taken in maintaining a safe working environment. Thus, work on apparatus in gymnastics, for instance, may require modification, and intensity levels in games activities may need to be lowered to a point where fasting students may continue to participate safely.

3.10.28 Staff need to remain responsive to student needs in this area at all times, but, because of the potential for higher activity levels in the summer months, particular care needs to be taken when Ramadan or similar festivals fall at this time of year.

3.10.29 Religious and cultural customs and beliefs fundamental to certain faiths may initially be seen to conflict with the demands made by some activities within a prescribed curriculum. **Swimming**, for instance, presents particular issues for some communities, associated with unacceptable exposure of the body, mixed-gender settings or the wearing of adornments. From a health and safety perspective, however, the ability to swim extends far beyond simply recreational or competitive activity. It embodies a potentially lifesaving skill that all children have an entitlement to access. In securing this access, school staff should apply all practical means to sustain a meaningful swimming programme that at least meets the requirements of the given curriculum, while seeking to respect any religious or cultural sensitivities involved wherever possible. Staff should try to ensure:

- discussion with local faith leaders and parents is ongoing, and policies concerning swimming provision are effectively communicated to parents and the local community

- adjustments are made in swimming attire to accommodate religious and cultural sensitivities

- changing arrangements take into account any mixed-gender issues and provide acceptable levels of privacy

- the management of the swimming programme builds in single-sex teaching, whenever practical and wherever this preference is feasible.

3.10.30 **EAL students** who do not fully understand the requirements of, or how to set about, a particular physical activity pose a risk to themselves and the rest of the group. Students at an early stage in the acculturation process may initially have limited English language capability and consequently may struggle to interpret what is required of them in a physical education lesson. It cannot be assumed that the complexity of the language used in physical education is any less demanding than elsewhere in the curriculum, and the speed of response often required puts further pressure on the ability of such students to comprehend. The following procedures will assist in encouraging safe participation:

- Where learning support staff are available, they should be effectively briefed about the learning outcomes of the lesson and alerted to any safety features.

- Initially, time should be taken to ensure individual EAL students clearly understand the command 'Stop!' and know an immediate response to cease activity is required, should this command be necessary. Over time, other key phrases, identified through risk assessment procedures, can be introduced into EAL students' vocabulary.

- Staff should be familiar with the names of EAL students in order to quickly attract and maintain their attention.

- The use of focused demonstration can sometimes overcome linguistic difficulty, linked to an acknowledgement by the students that they have understood what is required.

- The use of a 'buddy' system, where practical, pairing an EAL student with another student known to have a responsible and mature disposition, reflects good practice.

Relevant case law

3.10.31   Begum versus the Head Teacher and Governors of Denbigh High School (2006):

The outcome of this case, having progressed all the way to the House of Lords, was that a school had the right to set and enforce a **school policy on uniform**. *The decision was based on the facts that the school had discussed the matter with the community and taken great pains to devise a policy that respected religious and cultural beliefs, and that the policy was in place when the student joined the school, therefore choosing to accept the rules in place at that time. It is important that* **clothing for PES seeks to respect religious and cultural beliefs without compromising health and safety standards**.

3.10.32   Watkins-Singh versus the Governing Body of Aberdare High School and Rhondda Cynon Taff Unitary Authority (2008):

A claim for indirect racial discrimination was brought against a school because the governors' interpretation of the school's restrictive policy on wearing jewellery prevented a Sikh student attending school wearing the kara (a plain steel band about 5mm in width). The judgement for the student was based on the school's interpretation of the policy being 'procedurally unfair' and allowing no exemption at all. Consideration of the issue was totally about wearing the kara in school generally and not about the implications relating to a specific context of health and safety within PES.

The student was prepared to remove or cover the kara with a sweatband during PES where health and safety was an issue. The judge made particular reference to her willingness to do this in recognition of health and safety concerns in his summary of the judgement and thus acknowledged the need for exceptions to be made in specific health and safety situations.

Another important consideration by the judge was that the restrictive school jewellery policy was formally recognised by the governors after the dispute had arisen. Prior to that, it was described as being in place but unsigned by the governors, incomplete in content and in a generic form from a neighbouring authority. Schools need to ensure that all policies are specific to the school, fairly detailed and approved by the governors before implementation.

More information on personal effects, including cultural or religious adornments, can be found in *Section 2: Safe Teaching Principles, paragraphs 2.3.49-2.3.55*, pages 30-31, and in this section, *paragraphs 3.5.58-3.5.65*, pages 90-91.

Sports fixtures, festivals and tours

Sports fixtures

3.10.33   Sports fixtures at home and away from the school site are a standard aspect of school sport. Procedures should be routine, and all staff and students who participate in the programme should be familiar with them. The school leadership team must be aware of and **approve**, specifically where appropriate, all activities the students undertake within school sport.

3.10.34   Safety issues relating to home fixtures should be addressed within an on-site risk assessment for PES as normal procedures should apply.

3.10.35   **Away fixtures** often fall within a school's procedures for regular off-site visits. As school fixtures generally follow the same organisational procedures, it is acceptable for a single risk assessment to cover the whole off-site school-sport fixture list for a full year, or it may be reviewed on a seasonal basis. It is not necessary for individual sports fixtures to have a written risk assessment.

3.10.36   Normal school procedures for informing parents and requirements for consent forms should be followed.

3.10.37   General **pre-planning** for away fixtures should ensure the following, as appropriate, have been addressed:

- Is the head teacher aware a fixtures programme is taking place?

- Have the relevant school policies and procedures been considered and applied as necessary?

- Are consent forms required? Have they been obtained? What happens if a consent form is not returned to school?

- Have parents been made aware of the itinerary, programme, particular needs and conditions, insurance provision, emergency contact system, venue address – typically through a fixture list or the school bulletin?

- Do equality in size, experience and confidence need to be part of the pre-event discussion?

- Have staffing roles and responsibilities, required ratios, necessary expertise, group-management competence and knowledge of the group been communicated to the staff involved?

- Is a group register available?

- Are medical backgrounds known?

- Have the school's risk assessment requirements been followed?

- Are any reciprocal arrangements with the host school clear and confirmed?

- Have weather issues – sun protection, rehydration needs, storms and any other seasonal considerations – been addressed?

- Has other contingency planning been thought through?

3.10.38   **Team assembly** for the event should consider whether:

- duty of care from the school day continues or whether it is broken and parents assume total responsibility for their child reaching the venue

- a register is taken and a list left at school

- a kit check is necessary

- students have personal responsibility for taking any necessary medications

- emergency contact information is to hand

- students know and apply the code of conduct

- a staff or school mobile phone is to hand in case of emergency.

3.10.39   Consideration of any **journey** issues should include:

- school requirements about the mode of transport being met for coach, minibus, taxis or staff and volunteers' cars

- the availability of a first aid kit and an appointed person to manage any injury situation

- whether the embarkation and disembarkation points are safe

- a head count before leaving

- action in the event of illness on the journey

- knowledge of the emergency action plan should a critical incident occur

- student dispersal point(s) after the event

- a supervision strategy if parents who will collect their child from the dispersal point(s) are delayed

- arrangements in the event of delays in the journey.

3.10.40   Forethought about the **venue** to be visited should include:

- whether information has been received about the venue risk assessment from the host staff and, if not, the need for a visual check to be carried out on arrival

- whether first aid cover and any other reciprocal arrangements with the host have been confirmed

- any group- or activity-management issues, such as there being only one member of staff with two teams or that the staff are required to officiate and supervise

- consideration of staff roles and responsibilities; for example, at a festival or competition for primary schools organised by junior sports leaders on a high-school site, the secondary staff may be responsible for the direct supervision of junior sports leaders, but the primary-school staff may be responsible for ensuring any activities are suitable for the age and experience of the children

- how acceptable behaviour will be assured

- whether periodic 'head counts' are necessary at the venue

- whether kit and footwear are appropriate to the weather and playing surface

- who is responsible for students' personal effects

- whether any necessary PPE – such as pads, helmets and mouth guards – is provided by school or students have responsibility for their own provision

- whether the officials are competent and qualified, where necessary.

3.10.41   All events should be **evaluated** to inform future planning. In the case of away sports fixtures, this should include:

- whether there are near misses or incidents to review

- the recording of any injuries and follow-up of any related outcomes

- whether any improvements can be made for the next event

- whether any feedback is necessary to the head teacher, fellow staff, students or parents

- any adjustments that may be needed to the risk assessment.

> *Appendix 11: Risk Assessment Form for School Games Level 2 Inter-school Sport, Level 3 Centrally Organised Events and Other Off-site Fixtures* on the CD-ROM provides a format for completing a risk assessment for an away fixture programme.

Sports festivals

3.10.42   Festivals are simply one example of a centrally organised event in which individual schools are invited to participate. Such events need three separate planning and risk assessment responsibilities.

> Further detail is set out in *Appendix 23: Managing a Sports Event – Some Planning Issues Identified* on the CD-ROM.

3.10.43   The venue manager/owner/host needs to have a risk assessment that identifies the hazards, evaluates the risks and establishes appropriate controls to make the **venue** safe for the purpose for which it is being offered to the user group. This may be known as a risk assessment or normal operating procedures and emergency action plan.

3.10.44   The event organiser needs to know the content, issues and required procedures and standards arising from the venue risk assessment that are relevant to the planned event and group involved. These need to form part of the **pre-event guidance and information** provided to the staff managing groups from the schools involved.

3.10.45   Swimming pools, leisure centres and independent arenas are usually thorough in doing risk assessments though school venues vary widely. Where the venue risk assessment is **lacking or not available**, the event organiser needs to complete a venue assessment prior to the event.

3.10.46   The event organiser then needs to take account of the venue issues and the organisation of the planned event to complete an **event risk assessment**. The relevant issues from this assessment need to be clearly communicated to the staff managing groups attending the event, usually in the form of event programming, procedures, essential information or guidance for the staff.

3.10.47   The school staff need to take account of the information received from the event organiser about the venue and organisation of the event and carry out a **risk assessment for their group**: preparing for the event; getting there; managing and supervising the group while at the event; and getting them back to school/into the parents' care safely.

3.10.48   Attendance at sports festivals should **include consideration of the issues for fixtures and also address**:

- **pre-event planning:**

  - whether additional staffing is needed to cover supervision, officiating or other roles

  - the clarification of group issues, such as the relevant age, ability, behaviour and selection criteria

  - whether some form of cascading communication system is required to convey messages back to parents

  - the need, where possible, for a pre-visit to the venue if the staff involved are not familiar with it

  - whether additional or specific risk assessment is required

  - whether first aid is provided by the host or is a school responsibility

- **assembly and the journey:**

  - whether students and parents know the time to meet and what to do if they miss the coach

  - whether additional drivers are needed

  - the management of breaks in the journey (eg motorway service areas)

  - the need for head counts after any break in the journey

- **the venue and event:**

  - whether the programme allows sufficient rest and recovery periods

  - whether the total playing time the students will be involved in is within their capability

  - who provides refreshments and rehydration

  - a contingency plan in case of early completion or abandonment of the programme

  - whether consent is necessary, and has been granted, for any photography that may be involved

  - what sunshade or rain cover is available

  - whether a change of clothes is needed

  - what supervision requirements will be appropriate.

Sports tours

3.10.49   Sports tours in the UK and abroad have increased in regularity. Whether the tour will be arranged through a commercial agency or less formally by the school staff, the planning and management of tours is complex.

3.10.50   The **employer's requirements** for events that are at considerable distance from the school base and residential in nature need to be known and applied.

3.10.51   Planning and managing a sports tour should **follow the advice for regular fixtures plus the additional requirements for single-day festivals** set out above and additionally consider issues such as:

- **pre-event planning:**

  - whether LA and/or governors' approval is needed, all set requirements are met, and the relevant paperwork or online forms submitted

  - all paperwork is checked, including passports and additional insurance if needed, and passports have the required period of time left before expiry as set by the country to be visited

- whether any injections or specific medications will be required prior to and during the tour

- whether the student code of conduct needs to be developed from the basic school visit requirements, such as the inclusion of requirements about communication, the mountain code or country code or safety on water

- parents have a copy of the itinerary, contact details and other relevant information

- the necessary leadership skills are evident

- what additional staffing requirements need to be identified, such as for residential adventure activities, city tours or the inclusion of swimming in the itinerary, and implications for students with SEND

- consideration of any implications of taking non-school staff and adjustments made

- all relevant safeguarding issues checked about the host location and host families

- how students need to be adequately prepared for the tour, physically, emotionally and behaviourally

- **assembly and journey:**

  - whether the Package Travel, Package Holidays and Package Tours Regulations 1992 will apply (www.legislation.gov.uk/uksi/1992/3288/contents/made)

  - any implications of foreign law, standards, health and language

  - whether international driving requirements need to be considered

  - supervision at airport, ferry or train terminals

  - the information to be carried by students in case of separation from the main group

- **the event and venues:**

  - the itinerary

  - the security of any accommodation

  - home care abroad, including safeguarding requirements and standards

  - how the student code of conduct will be applied

  - whether any additional insurance is needed

  - what 'down time' issues need to be considered

  - the policy on student use of mobile phones

  - the importance of students having an accessible point of contact for staff in the host country if not boarding together

  - any reciprocal arrangements are clarified if hosted by another school or group.

> **Guidance on safeguarding the security and welfare of students on residential sports tours in the UK and abroad can be found earlier in this section, paragraphs 3.5.130–3.5.137, pages 105-106.**
>
> **Risk assessment formats for centrally organised events such as festivals and school games can be found on the CD-ROM in *Appendix 11: Risk Assessment Form for School Games Level 2 Inter-school Sport, Level 3 Centrally Organised Events and Other Off-site Fixtures.***

Club links

3.10.52   It is essential that schools ensure safeguarding is addressed in all school-club/community sport links to provide the best possible protection in fulfilling their duty of care towards children and young people and specifically to 'have in place arrangements for ensuring that their functions are exercised with a view to safeguarding and promoting the welfare of children' (section 175 of the Education Act 2002).

3.10.53   The **link club** should:

- have adopted the appropriate LA (or governing body of sport where no LA guidance is provided) safeguarding policy and set of procedures

- promote the policy and procedures to all club members and parents to show the club's commitment to a safe, friendly and supportive environment

- have guidance in place covering a range of activities and practices relevant to the sport or activity

- provide appropriately qualified, trained and CRB/DBS-checked coaches to work with children and young people

- ensure appropriate training is available for coaches and others working with children and young people

- have a designated person to deal with safeguarding and welfare issues.

3.10.54   In addition, where a club link is established, the **school** should ensure safeguarding protocols are in place that clarify the shared roles and responsibilities in the event of a concern arising.

3.10.55   All of the above, where relevant, apply to individual coaches and volunteers who are working with children and young people. In addition, the adults who are responsible for **managing activities should be alert** for any of the following signs:

- activities where other adults are discouraged from staying to watch

- any individual who appears to ignore organisational guidelines

- staff who appear to show favouritism or personally reward specific children or young people

- any engagement in inappropriate physical contact, such as taking part in physical activities, other than demonstrations, or physically supporting where little or no support is necessary

- poor communication from the adults and negative responses to the children and young people

- a 'win at all costs' attitude towards the sport or activity

- children and young people who drop out of an activity for no apparent reason (registers are important for curriculum, school sport and off-site activities)

- invitations offered to specific children or young people to spend time alone with the adult, such as on the pretext of individual coaching.

3.10.56   In addition, coaches who are providing high quality delivery and have been monitored, checked and are aware of all school procedures, including evacuation and end of season procedures, may work at a distance from supervising staff.

3.10.57   Many sports have adopted a **club accreditation scheme**, and included within this are minimum standards for safeguarding that provide assurance for schools and others commissioning links. Clubmark is the Sport England cross-sport quality accreditation for clubs with junior sections, and governing bodies of sport accredit clubs that comply with minimum operating standards in four areas:

- the playing or participation programme
- duty of care and child protection
- sports equity and ethics
- club management.

3.10.58   Clubmark, or a sport-specific version (eg FA Charter Standard, Swim21, GolfMark), is an **indication of quality**, and schools should seek to build links with clubs that have achieved or are working towards achievement of club accreditation.

> **General information on safeguarding can be found earlier in this section, paragraphs 3.5.121-3.5.145, pages 99-106.**

Weather conditions

3.10.59   Weather conditions require careful consideration for all outdoor activities, whether on or off site. The physical demands of athletics, games and adventure activities are such that the body is often moving quickly so it is essential that the weather conditions do not impede safety. On damp or frosty mornings, the risk of slipping on a **grass or court surface** is increased and needs to be carefully assessed.

3.10.60   The position and brightness of the **sun** in relation to the students and types of activities they undertake can impact on safe performance. Similarly, in the indoor environment, the effectiveness of **artificial lighting** needs to be taken into account. It would be hazardous to ask students to undertake any activity where their safety was compromised due to inadequate or overly bright lighting.

> **Information on protection from the sun can be found earlier in this section, paragraph 3.5.91, page 95, and in *Section 2: Safe Teaching Principles*, paragraphs 2.3.177-2.3.179, page 47.**

3.11 Risk Management

3.11.1	According to a school's particular circumstances, **documented procedures** may include reference to:

- the need to constantly apply risk-benefit principles
- the importance of constant dynamic risk assessment and making appropriate adjustments as necessary
- the five-step risk assessment process
- the format, frequency and location of written risk assessments for on- and off-site activities
- the requirement for all staff to read current risk assessments
- fire safety precautions
- staff participation in periodic written risk assessments
- student participation in ongoing risk assessment
- reporting concerns
- procedures for informing staff, students and the community, as appropriate, of changes to practice resulting from risk assessments
- strategies to make situations safer.

Risk-benefit analysis

3.11.2 Risk-benefit analysis is the **comparison** of the risk of a situation to its related benefits – a systematic consideration of the relative importance of risks and benefits to identify a net benefit of offering the activity or experience – ensuring situations are as safe as necessary, not as safe as possible.

3.11.3 Where the calculation is **negative**, the event should not be undertaken. A positive outcome needs to be evident in order to pursue participation.

3.11.4 Analysing the risk of a situation is very dependent on the individual doing the analysis.

3.11.5 In practice, risk-benefit analysis is the completion of a suitable and sufficient risk assessment that brings together the risks and benefits in a **descriptive form**. It highlights the considerations and decisions made, from which it can be determined whether to provide, modify or remove some activity, event, facility or feature.

3.11.6 It is an essential aspect of the **teacher's role** to make an analysis of the perceived risks balanced against the learning benefits of an event and identify a positive benefit before commencing the event. This is part of the teacher's duty of care – part of the **forethought** necessary in sound planning. Everyone has the right to be educated in a safe and healthy environment. However, risk (the possibility of injury) is inherent in all physical activity and needs to be assessed and managed effectively. It is neither possible nor desirable to remove all risks from physical activity, but it is important that the different hazards and risks involved in different activities are recognised. Some activities are clearly more hazardous than others and involve a higher possibility of injury or harm. Sports involving a high degree of physical contact, for instance, record a greater number of injuries than activities in which contact is expressly forbidden or simply not part of the context. Whatever the activity, the generic safety principles listed here should be considered and, where appropriate, applied to, and integrated into, the risk-management process.

Risk assessment

3.11.7   Risk assessment is central to safe practice. It involves **managing the risk** (or possibility) of injury by:

- deciding what to risk assess – the PES programme as a whole or each activity, facility or special event

- identifying the hazards that could cause harm (injury)

- judging whether or not existing safety precautions are sufficient to provide a safe learning environment

- deciding whether there is any significant risk of harm remaining

- identifying who could be harmed by the significant risks

- reducing, or controlling, any remaining significant risk of harm to an acceptable and reasonable level by some additional form of corrective action or control measure

- recording the findings of the risk assessment and implementing them

- informing participants, staff and any other relevant people about any changes (additional controls and procedures) that have been implemented to make any situation safer

- reviewing and updating the risk assessment regularly.

3.11.8   There are three main types of risk assessment:

- **Ongoing risk assessment** (sometimes referred to as dynamic risk assessment) – continuously carried out before and while an activity or event is taking place, taking into account and responding to unforeseen issues, such as an unsafe response to a task, sudden illness, changes in climatic conditions or ineffective officiating. This expertise evolves over time and is applied during the activity, in forward planning and also to inform future risk assessments. Ongoing risk assessment is unwritten and represents a dynamic process where staff remain vigilant, constantly reassessing the precautions they have put in place. Students should also be taught to be vigilant for risk during activity, and to report any concerns.

- **Generic risk assessment** – general principles that might apply to an activity wherever it may take place. This will usually be the starting point and is usually provided in written form by the employer, governing body of sport or similar organisation. Generic guidance needs to be amended to be applicable to a school's particular circumstances and will inform both ongoing risk assessment and the periodic written risk assessment for the site or activity.

- **Site- or activity-specific risk assessment** – usually carried out for each location, facility or activity with specific consideration of the people involved, the context and the organisation of the situation. This is usually in a written form and reviewed periodically.

3.11.9   The HSE has the power to **confirm** that risk assessments have been carried out and instigate action against those organisations that fail to do so.

3.11.10   Under the terms of the Management of Health and Safety at Work Regulations 1999, **employers have a duty** to ensure periodic formal, activity- or site-specific risk assessments are carried out in the establishments for which they are responsible. In the context of community and voluntary controlled schools, the employer is the LA. In the case of free, foundation, trust, voluntary aided and academy schools, governors are the employer. The employer in independent schools may be the proprietor, governors or a board of trustees.

3.11.11   In practice, the majority of voluntary aided schools and some academies and foundation schools 'buy in' to LA insurance provision and consequently comply with LA health and safety regulation, but this does **not abnegate their responsibility** for maintaining up-to-date policies. Responsibility for health and safety is usually delegated to head teachers and governors on a day-to-day basis. Under these arrangements, a careful examination must be carried out of what might cause harm to students, staff and visitors during all activities organised by the school. Systems need to be put in place to mitigate and manage the potential for such harm.

3.11.12   Under the terms of the Regulatory Reform (Fire Safety) Order 2005, schools are obliged to include a specific, written **fire risk assessment** within their overall risk-management provision. The fundamental purpose is to establish measures to minimise the risk of fire and ensure safe evacuation in the event of fire. In the **context of physical education**, this should involve:

- the identification of escape routes from designated working areas
- safety procedures relating to enclosed areas from which there is no escape (eg storerooms)
- the safe storage of flammable items (eg mats)
- the clear display of, and easy access to, fire extinguishers
- contingency planning for any emergency evacuation in cold or inclement weather.

3.11.13   Opportunities should be provided for **students** to become involved in the assessment and management of risk associated with the activities in which they participate. The definitive, formal risk assessment will always be undertaken by staff, but students should be expected to contribute at their own level wherever possible.

3.11.14   Risk assessments are most effectively carried out:

- as a team exercise using collective expertise
- in or around the facility/location in which the activity is planned to take place
- using the people, context, organisation model
- based on existing documentation, procedures and practice, establishing whether any additional precautions are necessary over and above those currently in place.

3.11.15   Where concerns are identified in the risk assessment, the record should be annotated to indicate progress made in reducing the risk to a safe level.

The risk assessment process

3.11.16   The table on the pages that follow illustrates a typical range of **generic issues** that might be helpful in compiling on-site or activity-specific risk assessments.

Table 9: Typical generic risk assessment issues to consider

People: Staff

- Do staff feel confident/competent/have adequate qualifications and experience to fulfil their teaching commitments safely?
- Has the teaching and discipline capability of all staff been checked?
- Does anyone require some form of professional development or support for reasons of safe teaching?
- Is staff supervision of students appropriate to their behaviour, age and development stage, and the facility layout?
- Are there any times when additional supervision is required but not provided?
- Are there any times when students are not supervised that give cause for concern?
- Do staff have sufficient knowledge of individuals and groups they teach to maintain a safe situation?
- Are there any control/discipline/behaviour problems with any student/group and any adult teaching them that cause safety concerns?
- Are student medical conditions known by any adult teaching an individual?
- Is relevant medical information always passed on to visiting staff before they teach a group?
- Are staff observation and analysis skills adequate?
- Is staff clothing or personal effects appropriate for teaching PES?
- Do all staff occupy appropriate teaching positions in relation to participants?
- Do all staff know their role and responsibilities?
- Is effective communication between the teacher and support staff evident?
- Do all adults teaching groups have appropriate insurance cover where needed?
- Have disclosure certificates been seen for all support staff?

People: Students

- Are group sizes and teacher:student ratios always safe?
- Is clothing and footwear appropriate for each activity?
- Is the policy on jewellery and other personal effects applied consistently?
- Is safety equipment/PPE available and used where needed (eg shin pads)?
- Are the school policies on physical contact (supporting) and substantial access (1:1) known and applied effectively?
- Are there any concerns about Equality Act requirements for access and involvement in PES for those with cognitive, visual, hearing or motor impairment?
- Do the students know and safely apply PES routines and procedures appropriate to their age/ability?
- Are any individual care issues met?
- Are there any safety issues about participation in any specific activity?

Context: Procedures/routines

- Has the head teacher been made aware of/approved all activities offered?
- Have off-site visit requirements been met – lists, first aid etc?
- Have parents been informed and any necessary permission obtained?
- Is movement to the work areas safe and orderly?
- Is access to each facility safely managed?

- Is first aid equipment provided, and are procedures and responsibilities known by staff and (where appropriate) students?
- Are safety information notices evident, clearly positioned, effective, shared and applied?
- Are emergency evacuation procedures known?
- Are safeguarding procedures and training in place?
- Is the policy on digital imagery known and applied, and have the required permissions been obtained?
- Are all procedures monitored adequately?

Context: Equipment

- Is equipment used for the purpose for which it was designed?
- Is all equipment in good condition and used safely, including electrical items?
- Is equipment suitable in size, type, weight, quality for the age, build and strength of students?
- Have students been taught to carry, move, place and retrieve equipment safely?
- Is supervision of the carrying/placing of equipment managed, where appropriate?
- Do staff check equipment before use by participants?
- Do staff regularly check equipment before use and report any faults found?
- Is equipment easily accessed and safely stored?
- Are routines for the collection, retrieval and changing of equipment known and applied by staff and students?
- Are there any other equipment handling, carrying or siting concerns in any activity?
- Is there an annual gymnastics, play and fitness equipment inspection check by a specialist company?
- Is any improvised use of equipment allowed?
- Is all required safety and rescue equipment present?

Context: Facilities

Changing:
- Is the changing area safe (space, pegs, floor surface, supervision)?
- Is the route from the classroom/changing room to activity area safe, especially for young/disabled students?

Work area:
- Is access to the facility safe (steps, doors, disability issues)?
- Are fire exits clear, with emergency egress possible?
- Are fire extinguishers/notices etc present?
- Are safety signs present, in correct locations and illuminated?
- In case of emergency evacuation, are doors unlocked?
- Is the first aid provision/system suitable for the facility/students etc?
- Does the playing/work surface provide secure footing?
- Is the work area an optimum size for the group/activity/organisation?
- Are there any obstructions (heating, columns, piano etc)?
- Is the lighting safe and adequate for activities?
- Does the location of windows cause sunlight on to work area?
- Are there any display and other furniture issues?
- Are the storage space/system/routines safe?
- Are there any obvious entrapments?

- Are goalposts/nets etc safe, secure and in good condition?
- Are there plastic/glass/stone problems on pitches?
- Are there any activity-specific safety concerns?

Context: Transport (where used for PES)

- Is a clear policy applied where any form of transport is used?
- Are school vehicles checked for roadworthiness before use?
- Is a reputable coach/taxi company used?
- Are there clear procedures about the use of parents' cars?
- Are embarkation points safe?
- Are seat belts always used?
- Are booster seats available where required?
- Is there always a check on numbers leaving and returning to the transport?
- Are driver requirements and responsibilities known and applied?
- Is there an emergency contact system in place?
- Are there any concerns about supervision while driving?
- Is there a procedure for dismissing students after an event away from school that is understood, accepted and applied by all staff, students and parents?
- Are procedures in place in the event of a transport problem arising?

Organisation: Class organisation/management

- Are group numbers always known/checked?
- Is a register check taken for every session/lesson (secondary)?
- Do staff regularly scan or do head counts at the beginning/during/end of lessons?
- Are group organisation/management procedures safe and consistently applied?
- Are demonstrations accurate and safely performed?
- Are students with visual, hearing, motor or cognitive impairment catered for appropriately to enable them to participate safely?
- Are there any activity-specific safety concerns?

Organisation: Teaching

- Does the demand/challenge in sessions match students' abilities, needs and confidence?
- Are appropriate teaching styles used to ensure safety?
- Is regular and approved practice used at all times?
- Are physical support and manual handling techniques known and applied, where appropriate?
- Is intervention appropriate to individual student needs?
- Are tasks differentiated to meet individual abilities and confidence?
- Are rules consistently applied in games?
- Do staff know the limits of their involvement in games, practices and demonstrations involving students?
- Does the play schedule allow appropriate activity/recovery periods?
- Are there any activity-specific safety concerns?

- Do written schemes of work/other guidance set out safety issues to be followed?
- Do lessons provide appropriate and effective warm-up/cool-down?
- Is student-led warm-up monitored by staff?
- Is progression based on ability? Are progressive practices known and applied?
- Are rehydration/sun protection planned for?
- Are overplay/overtraining implications checked/known?

Organisation: Emergency action

- Are accident and emergency procedures to address potential incidents during lessons and visits set out, known and applied by all?
- Can first aid support be summoned and provided quickly?
- Are contingency plans to address potential incidents during lessons and visits set out, known and applied by all staff?

The questions in Table 9 are provided in an editable format that can be adapted for schools' specific needs in *Appendix 10: Risk Assessment for On-site Physical Education, Including Level 1 School Games Intra-school Sport* on the **CD-ROM**. A Welsh version is provided in *Appendix 12*.

3.11.17 All risks should be evaluated during the risk assessment. This involves making an **informed judgement** about whether an identified hazard is capable of causing injury or harm in some way. Risks can be categorised simply as **safe or unsafe**, based on using one's professional judgement. Some may prefer the slightly expanded form of high, medium or low risk. It is not necessary to rate risks in any more complex manner than these, which are wholly acceptable.

3.11.18 The **level of risk** in a particular environment or setting is determined by a number of contextual and organisational features, including the:

- extent of unpredictability in the task, event or activity
- speed of decision making required to stay safe
- complexity of the task or activity
- severity of any potential injury, should things go wrong.

Relevant case law

3.11.19 R versus Porter (2008):

See Section 1: Basic Principles, paragraph 1.2.1, page 18, for details.

3.11.20 R versus Chargot and Ruttle Contracting (2008):

See Section 1: Basic Principles, paragraph 1.2.2, page 18, for details.

3.11.21 R versus HTM (2008):

*This case determined that **foreseeability** relates to the likelihood of the risk being realised (ie the injury occurring) and not simply the test for the existence of risk (ie the potential to cause harm – a hazard). Foreseeability (the likelihood of harm) only becomes relevant when it is established that a risk exists.*

3.11.22   Liverpool City Council versus The Adelphi Hotel (2010):

*A hotel guest went swimming in the hotel pool and drowned. There was no lifeguard present. The hotel had carried out a risk assessment seven years before that identified the risk of drowning but had not determined that lifeguard supervision was necessary. A breach of section 3(1) of the Health and Safety Act was found – **failing to ensure a customer's safety**. The hotel was fined £65,000 plus costs.*

The following risk assessment materials can be found in the appendices on the CD-ROM:

- *Appendix 10: Risk Assessment for On-site Physical Education, Including Level 1 School Games Intra-school Sport*
- *Appendix 11: Risk Assessment Form for School Games Level 2 Inter-school Sport, Level 3 Centrally Organised Events and Other Off-site Fixtures*
- *Appendix 12: Welsh Language Risk Assessment Form*
- *Appendix 13: Welsh Language Version of Risk Assessment Form for Off-site Inter-school Away Fixtures.*

Reporting, recording and communicating risk

3.11.23   All staff **must** report any concerns about hazards they become aware of to the appropriate person in school. Schools have different arrangements for such reporting requirements. It is advised that an individual teacher makes a note of any concern reported and dates the note in case there should be a need to provide evidence that statutory action was carried out.

3.11.24   Findings should be **recorded** as the risk assessment is carried out. There is no set format for a formal written risk assessment. The statutory requirements are that it should:

- demonstrate that the assessment has been carried out
- identify any significant risks
- identify who is affected by them
- identify what action is to be taken to reduce risk to an acceptable level.

3.11.25   **Local requirements** must always be complied with, and staff should always check with their employers whether a particular format for recording risk is required.

3.11.26   Whenever health and safety procedures or practices are amended, the school has a duty to **inform all those affected**. This may be done verbally, in writing or diagrammatically.

3.11.27   Written risk assessments should be **reviewed** on a regular basis, typically annually or when circumstances change. The date of review should be indicated and the report signed off by the person(s) responsible.

3.11.28   All staff should **know the location of and read** the written risk assessments. It is increasingly common for schools to require all staff to **sign** to confirm they have read the risk assessments and all other safety-related documentation.

Appendix 10: Risk Assessment for On-site Physical Education, Including Level 1 School Games Intra-school Sport on the CD-ROM sets out the **recommended format** for completing a risk assessment for on-site physical education.

Appendix 11: Risk Assessment Form for School Games Level 2 Inter-school Sport, Level 3 Centrally Organised Events and Other Off-site Fixtures on the CD-ROM provides a format for an away fixture programme and attendance at centrally organised sports events, such as festivals.

Relevant case law

3.11.29   R versus Ellis (2003):

*A teacher was convicted of manslaughter and a failure to provide adequate care for the rest of the group when a student died during a pool plunging activity where the prevailing conditions required the activity to be cancelled and **adequate contingency planning** to be in place.*

3.11.30   Poppleton versus Portsmouth Youth Activities Committee (2008):

*An adult's claim for compensation was dismissed when he was seriously injured following an attempt to jump from one part of an indoor climbing wall to another. He **ignored warnings and warning notices** not to climb high. The judge stated that no amount of matting would avoid totally the risk of serious injury, the risk of an awkward fall is an obvious inherent risk in climbing, and the adult should have realised this without a need for warning.*

3.11.31   Edwards versus NCB (1949):

*This case set the ruling on **'reasonably practicable'** as being a term narrower than 'physically possible'. The interpretation is a calculation of the degree of risk against the 'sacrifice' (in terms of time, trouble and financial cost) involved in averting the risk. Where this is clearly disproportionate, with the **risk being insignificant in relation to the 'sacrifice' (cost)**, there is no requirement to address the risk.*

Making risks safe – controlling risk

3.11.32   Once a significant risk has been identified, an action plan or control measure is required to manage the risk(s) involved.

3.11.33   **Control measures** may be provided through improving:

- supervision
- protection
- education.

3.11.34   These three strategies will often involve the use of everyday measures to control risks, such as:

- **supervision:**
  - staff being present when a group is working – with any remote supervision of older students being introduced progressively
  - staff being competent, qualified and experienced to organise and lead the session safely
  - improving the ratio of staff to students
  - increasing the training and qualifications of staff

- explaining any inherent risks
- emphasising playing within the rules
- stopping the activity if unsafe
- avoiding the area if unsafe
- using a safer alternative
- amending the pace, progress and challenge of the tasks

- **protection:**
  - providing or advising the use of PPE or protective clothing
  - devising appropriate procedures
  - inspecting the facility periodically
  - placing warning notices/protective devices (such as barriers) where unacceptable risks exist
  - using good quality equipment
  - inspecting the equipment regularly
  - repairing and servicing the equipment regularly
  - using different equipment if necessary
  - amending how the equipment is used
  - using equipment more compatible with the students' stage of development
  - changing the way the activity is carried out
  - limiting/conditioning the activity
  - matching the students in terms of strength, experience, ability and confidence where physical contact and competition are involved

- **education:**
  - providing any necessary training to establish safe practice
  - applying regular and approved practice
  - setting appropriate discipline and control standards
  - developing students' observation skills
  - teaching how to use the equipment and or facility correctly
  - teaching progressive practices thoroughly.

Risk education – involving students in their own safety

3.11.35   This issue is addressed in *Section 4* of this handbook, where guidance is given about what students should learn in relation to:

- safeguarding (feeling safe)
- assessing and managing risk
- first aid and accident procedures
- exercise safety
- space
- tasks
- equipment
- people.

> For more information on risk education, see *Section 4: Essential Learning about Safe Practice*, pages 165-173.

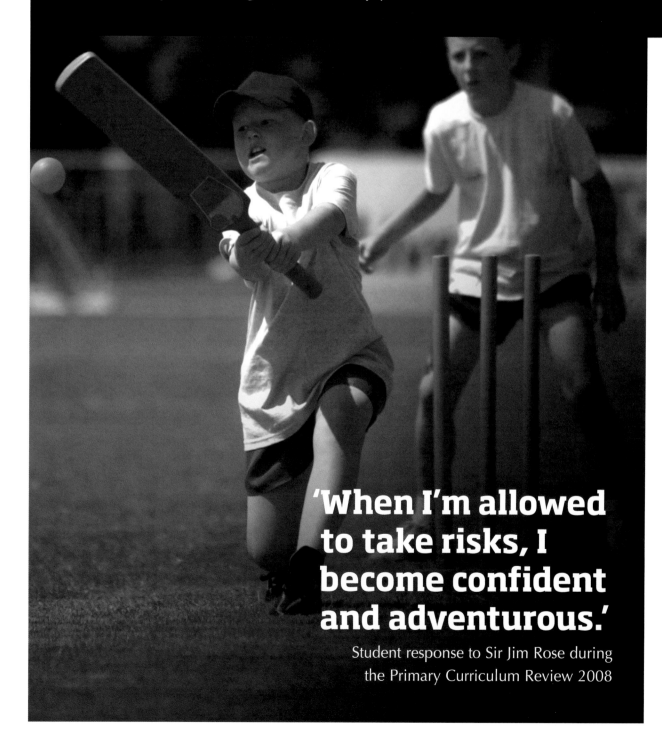

Section 4:
Essential Learning about Safe Practice

This section is important reading for all who teach physical education.

'When I'm allowed to take risks, I become confident and adventurous.'

Student response to Sir Jim Rose during the Primary Curriculum Review 2008

4.1 Safety Education

<table>
<tr><td>4.1.1</td><td>According to a school's particular circumstances, documented procedures may include reference to:</td></tr>
<tr><td></td><td>
<ul>
<li>applying the whole-school policy for safety education in the physical education and sport (PES) context</li>
<li>building into schemes and units of work general principles on educating about what is safe, what is unsafe, how unsafe situations can be made safe, and the importance of abandoning any activity that cannot be made safe</li>
<li>learning outcomes related to students being able to understand, assess and respond to risks</li>
<li>educating students about safe-practice principles in particular contexts then developing the application of these into other activities</li>
<li>the importance of positive, interactive, experiential and relevant contexts for learning about safe practice</li>
<li>which safe-practice principles should be learnt</li>
<li>how evidence of learning can be seen.</li>
</ul>
</td></tr>
</table>

4.2 Overview

4.2.1   Safety education is about developing students' knowledge, skills and understanding to:

- identify relevant hazards
- identify the potential risk associated with the hazard
- assess the appropriate actions required
- take steps to manage the risk to themselves and others.

4.2.2   It is neither possible nor desirable to eliminate the risks related to participating and leading in PES. Risk needs to be managed and a **clear awareness developed** in students of the following:

- what is safe
- what is unsafe
- whether unsafe situations can be made safe
- if something cannot be made safe, it should not commence or continue.

4.2.3   Safety education is often ad hoc and lacking coherence even within schools where health and safety requirements are fully met. A **whole-school approach** to learning about safe practice is advisable. Learning needs to be context-specific (eg in PES) and based on educating about principles that can be applied across the range of activities within that context. **Learning outcomes** should focus on students being able to understand, assess and respond to risks. From this, the students can then learn to apply generic safety principles to wider contexts and other curriculum areas.

4.2.4   Effective teaching, leadership and management (organisation) are the major contributors to effective learning about safe practice. Enabling students to learn about safety is as important as the teacher creating and managing safe environments.

4.2.5   Learning will be **most effective** where it is interactive, experiential, relevant to the student and delivered in a practical and positive manner; where the student seeks information, develops skills, is engaged in problem solving and applies safe practice through a range of roles as participant, official and coach.

4.2.6   This section outlines the **'what'** and **'how'** of safety education, ie what students need to learn, and how they can learn effectively, to become safely independent in lifelong physical activity.

4.3   What Safe-practice Principles Should Students Learn?

4.3.1   It can be helpful to teachers and students alike to have an easily remembered acronym as a reminder of important principles. As an example, STEP (Space, Task, Equipment, People) has become an accepted acronym when considering factors that can be adapted to enable learning experiences to more readily suit the needs of learners.

4.3.2   A similar approach can be helpful in relation to safety education by using the acronym **SAFE STEP**:

> - **S**afeguarding (feeling safe)
> - **A**ssessing and managing risk
> - **F**irst aid and accident procedures
> - **E**xercise safety
> - **S**pace
> - **T**ask
> - **E**quipment
> - **P**eople.

Safeguarding

4.3.3   Students should learn:

- that it is their right to be safe from abuse
- to tell staff if they feel at risk from an adult or other student
- to avoid being alone or going alone to unknown places
- to keep an adult informed of their whereabouts, using agreed procedures to keep in contact with others
- to determine what contact from adults is acceptable and what is not
- to go for help and advice about abuse and bullying.

> **More information on safeguarding can be found in** *Section 2: Safe Teaching Principles, paragraphs 2.3.61-2.3.64,* **page 32,** *Section 3: Safe Management Principles, paragraphs 3.5.121-3.5.145,* **pages 99-106, and** *Appendix 9: Aspects Relevant to Safeguarding Within a Physical Education and Sport Context* **on the CD-ROM.**

Assessing and managing risk

4.3.4   Students should learn:

- the concept of risk

- that PES involve risk (the possibility of injury) and require a responsible attitude

- that safe practice (managing risk) applies in some form to all areas of physical activity and sport

- safe methods of learning

- that it is acceptable to express anxiety about a particular activity

- that advice, rules and procedures relating to safe practice, whether verbal or written, should always be followed

- to recognise hazards and make decisions about how to make situations safe for themselves and others

- to apply the risk assessment process at their particular level, taking into account their age, ability and experience

- that safe-practice principles can be applied in various contexts

- that safe practice involves thinking ahead, wherever possible, about potential hazards and having a plan to keep everybody safe

- to apply the risk-benefit analysis principle before commencing an activity

- to understand the safety procedures, at their level of development and ability, for any activity or event they take part in whether as participant, official, coach or spectator

- to take responsibility for ensuring behaviour, personal effects, kit, footwear and any necessary items of equipment appropriate to the activity meet safety expectations

- before and during activity to check:

  - kit

  - equipment

  - work area

  - weather and environmental conditions

  and be able to offer solutions to minimise risk

- how useful it is to reflect on performance and analyse whether it was safely performed and how it might be improved

- that active involvement in assessing and managing risk, and reflecting on the subsequent effects, are key to learning how to become safely independent in lifelong physical activity.

> **More information on risk assessment can be found in *Section 2: Safe Teaching Principles*, paragraphs *2.3.151-2.3.157*, pages 44-45, *Section 3: Safe Management Principles*, paragraphs *3.11.7-3.11.22*, pages 155-161, and *Appendices 10 and 11 (Welsh versions in Appendices 12 and 13)* on the CD-ROM.**

Safe Practice in Physical Education and Sport 2012 Edition

First aid and accident procedures

4.3.5   Students should learn:

- the causes and types of injury

- to report, should anyone be injured

- the type of information to provide about accidents

- to keep themselves and others safe at the site of an accident

- that it is vital to only move anyone who is injured if they are in greater danger

- how important it is to obtain permission from an adult before administering first aid to someone who is injured or, if working independently without staff close by to take responsibility, to be qualified to administer first aid.

> **More information on first aid and accident procedures can be found in *Section 2: Safe Teaching Principles, paragraphs 2.3.103–2.3.107,* pages 37–38, *Section 3: Safe Management Principles, paragraphs 3.9.18–3.9.37,* pages 137–140, and in the following appendices on the CD-ROM:**
>
> - *Appendix 3: First Aid Qualifications and First Aid Kits: An Explanation of the Health and Safety Executive Approved Code of Practice (HSE ACOP) on First Aid 1997*
> - *Appendix 4: School Accident Report Form*
> - *Appendix 5: Standard Accident Procedures.*

Exercise safety

4.3.6   Students should learn:

- to recognise which exercises are safe and which may induce strain and injury

- to adopt safe exercise principles

- how warming up and cooling down feel when done effectively

- to adopt recommended principles for warming up and cooling down and, to ensure lessons make the most effective use of learning time, incorporate these principles into appropriate introductory and concluding activities

- to make introductory and concluding activities relevant to the content of lessons and/or specific to the activity in which they are to be engaging

- to recognise when tiredness can affect performance and put individuals at risk

- to hydrate appropriately during activity

- how important it is to consider any safety implications if they have a medical condition

- to understand the risks and hazards associated with participation in PES

- what personal clothing is suitable and safe for participation in particular activities and manage it so it presents no danger to others

- when and what type of personal protective equipment (PPE) is appropriate for a particular activity or sport

- that PPE can reduce, though never eliminate, the possibility of injury

- how important it is to replace PPE after damage or normal wear and tear

- to judge whether an item of PPE offers protection and fits appropriately

- to consider the hygiene implications of sharing PPE and when sharing is not advisable

- to manage effectively the potentially harmful effects of the sun and other extreme weather conditions

- that sports footwear should be checked regularly and maintained well, with laces tied

- that jewellery and other adornments should always be removed before active participation and how any exception to this rule must always be sanctioned by a member of staff.

Space

4.3.7   Students should learn:

- to check their personal space is safe for activity

- to check it is safe to move into an activity space before doing so

- to recognise and respond appropriately to potential hazards within and around their activity spaces

- to assess whether personal skill level renders the amount of designated activity space large enough to ensure safe participation

- to utilise appropriate markers for the demarcation of activity spaces

- how to modify activities and/or use alternative equipment to enable safe use of restricted space

- to be vigilant and alert to what is going on around them when in an activity area

- to avoid moving into the activity space of other groups (eg to retrieve a ball) without first of all checking safety implications

- to look before throwing, kicking or hitting any type of implement or equipment in a work area, and judge that it is safe to do so.

Tasks

4.3.8   Students should learn:

- to always ask for guidance when tasks are confusing or uncertain

- to learn and apply techniques, skills and tactical or choreographic principles accurately in their work in order to minimise the likelihood of injury

- to apply principles of movement to a range of activities, such as establishing a firm base to maintain balance in gymnastics, combat sports or tackling in games

- to recognise that rules in sports have evolved to make competition safe as well as fair and play within the rules and spirit of a sport, as participant, official or leader

- that repetition and consolidation are a necessary part of the skill-learning process

- to make progress according to their individual ability, experience and confidence, selecting alternatives where necessary

- to cope with and avoid impatience and frustration when progress is slow

- that concentration is the key to improvement in performance and safe participation

- to ensure understanding of any technical language that may be used and seek explanation where it is not understood.

Equipment and facilities

4.3.9   Students should learn:

- to lift, carry, place and use apparatus in a safe and responsible manner

- to work as a team when setting out and putting away larger items of equipment

- to check the condition of equipment before and during use, and the importance of reporting defective equipment to the appropriate person

- to recognise the scope and limitations of apparatus (eg mats and landing modules) in protecting personal safety

- to use equipment only for the purpose for which it was designed

- to use a facility only with permission

- to check the facility before use – that it provides secure and safe footing, protected lighting and a clear work area

- to check the safety procedures for any facility made available to them

- to understand notices and signs

- to summon staff in an emergency where supervision is remote

- that faults should be reported

- to be vigilant when being transported and to pay particular attention to the following:

  - seat belts, where provided, must be worn

  - anyone over the age of 14 has the responsibility to ensure they wear the seat belt provided

  - they should only attract the driver's attention in an emergency (eg if someone has fainted, been sick or dropped something out of the window)

  - they should remain seated throughout a journey

  - aisles should be kept clear of any luggage to allow emergency evacuation safely

  - they should not be alone in a car with an adult other than their parent

  - care should be taken when embarking and disembarking, particularly in public locations where traffic may be passing.

People

4.3.10   Students should learn:

- that behaviour should help learning and safe practice

- to resist inappropriate peer pressure to attempt a task they genuinely feel to be beyond their own capability

- that they need to consider their peers who may not be as confident, adventurous or skilful as they are

- when it is appropriate to place their trust in other people.

4.4 How Can Students Learn and Effectively Apply the Principles of Safe Practice?

4.4.1 There is an old adage that teachers should 'teach safely and teach safety'. Often, the focus has been on controlling safe standards in teaching situations – **teaching safely** – sometimes with little thought about students learning about safety in order to become independent in their activity – **teaching safety**. Both aspects are important, but if students are to be able ultimately to organise their own games, performances, competitions, training programmes and expeditions, it is important that the 'teaching safety' aspect is addressed.

4.4.2 In many ways, helping students learn and effectively apply the principles of safe practice is no different to helping them learn and effectively apply the principles underpinning performance, problem solving, communication and teamwork. In essence, approaches to safety education should seek to:

- motivate students to appreciate the relevance of and need for safety education

- provide students with a clear set of guiding principles that enable them to make well-informed and increasingly complex decisions regarding the safety of their learning and performing environment

- engage students actively, at a level appropriate to their age and ability, in risk assessment and risk-management activities

- allow increasing degrees of responsibility to be taken by students for their own and others' safety

- ensure safety education is truly experiential.

4.4.3 In order to be safe, feel safe and learn how to ensure their safety, students need to learn how to take **responsibility** for their own safety at an appropriate level. The teacher will always be the responsible 'safety manager', but this is a role that does not require the teacher to always be the one making the assessments, devising appropriate management procedures and evaluating their effect. Learning to assess and manage risk are **vital life skills** for students to develop, which will enable them to explore their immediate and ultimately wider environments with a greater sense of security, confidence and adventure.

4.4.4 Students learn effectively where **high expectations** are set that are appropriate to age, ability and previous experience, and where the learning process enables them to acquire and develop an awareness of safe-practice principles, to use and apply that awareness, and evaluate and review what is safe and what may be unsafe.

4.4.5 Achievement results from progressively developing responsibility, providing experiences that **appropriately challenge** students without placing them in foreseeable harm and providing learning contexts where they learn new principles by **building on** what they have previously learnt. Teachers utilising these principles will more readily empower students to achieve independence at whatever level of personal best each individual works.

4.4.6 **Evidence** of successful learning could be:

- Foundation stage students arriving in the hall and, on being asked by their teacher, identifying anything that may harm them

- Key Stage 3 students leading a safe and effective warm-up

- older students planning and participating in work that is supervised remotely.

4.4.7   An appropriate response to instructions does not demonstrate that learning has occurred at a deep level. However, students who are questioning, observing, evaluating responses to tasks, taking responsibility for organisation and development and creating situations where safe-practice principles need to be applied in new contexts are more than likely demonstrating that it has. For example, the concept of **safe use of space** may be demonstrated at:

- Foundation and Key Stage 1 through the students' ability to move around the work area without touching others

- Key Stage 2 by students talking about possible problems they might encounter when running from one location to another

- Key Stage 3 by students identifying hazards and solutions as to how they can use space safely

- Key Stage 4 by students managing a group in a limited space.

4.4.8   Students will learn more effectively when they are motivated, involved, engaged, empowered and trusted.

Section 5:
Applying the Principles to Specific Areas of Activity

This section lists relevant teaching and organisation principles in areas of activity:

- Adventure Activities
- Aquatic Activities
- Athletics Activities
- Combat Activities
- Dance Activities
- Games Activities
- Gymnastics and Trampolining Activities
- Health-related Physical Activities
- Physically Active Play in the School Environment.

The information contained in this section reiterates, reinforces and also builds on the information set out in Section 2 on safe teaching and Section 3 on safe management and leadership.

5.1 Adventure Activities

5.1.1 The inclusion of both outdoor and adventurous activities in the curriculum recognises the value of these activities in contributing to students' educational development. A progressive programme of activities, which emphasise the benefits of environmental education and adventure, offer real-life experiences and encourage students to take responsibility for their own actions in appropriately challenging situations, lies at the heart of this approach to education.

Typical school outdoor activities provision

5.1.2 Many schools limit the scope of their outdoor activities programme to the school site and immediate locality where the level of demand in the activities and level of risk are relatively low and easily managed by teachers with limited experience in this aspect of the physical education and sport (PES) curriculum.

5.1.3 In such circumstances, the technical demand on teachers is such that experience is often sufficient qualification, along with knowledge of the locality and the school's system for managing groups off site. However, where the activities become more challenging and more remote from the school site, evidence of appropriate qualification is advised.

More challenging adventure activities

5.1.4 Competent leadership and appropriate safety-management systems (which anticipate the many variables inherent in working with people in the natural environment) are essential in delivering safe, high quality adventurous activities. The spirit of adventure needs to be balanced against a concern for the well-being and safety of those participating in these activities.

5.1.5 Many governing bodies of sport relating to adventure are constantly updating and developing their awards, resources and current best practice relating to safe organisation, leadership and risk assessment of specific adventure activities. As such, afPE advice is to refer to the relevant websites for the latest information and standards relating to adventure activities. Relevant website details are provided at the beginning of the information about each individual adventure activity later in this section.

Basic outdoor activities

General safe-practice issues

5.1.6 **The general principles set out in *Section 2: Safe Teaching Principles, Section 3: Safe Management Principles* and below apply to all outdoor activities and should be read and applied to each of the areas described later in the section.** In addition, **activity-specific guidance** is given within each part of this section. The overall guidance thus builds through common principles to activity-specific guidance. Staff should familiarise themselves with this information and apply it to their unique set of circumstances.

Useful websites

Outdoor Education Advisers' Panel (OEAP)	www.oeapeg.info
Handsam	www.handsam.co.uk support@handsam.co.uk
eduFOCUS	www.edufocus.co.uk

People

5.1.7   Good judgement is most likely to be made when the teacher with a group has:

- the relevant qualifications and/or skills depending on, and related to, particular environments

- experience or knowledge of the intended location, taking into account weather conditions/forecasts and other variables

- clear educational objectives in mind

- a good knowledge of the students for whom they will be responsible

- taken reasonable steps to ascertain the fitness and experience of students and matched the proposed activity to them

- proven qualities of leadership and responsibility that are evident from other aspects of their work

- a flexible approach to altering the plan appropriately if conditions dictate

- the necessary mental and physical fitness to undertake the proposed activity

- established safe adult:student ratios, taking into account all relevant variables

- recognised, and remains within, the extent of their competence.

5.1.8   Where the activity makes **basic demands** on the students and staff, such as using the school and its immediate local environment (eg problem solving, orienteering using the school grounds or walking in local lowland countryside), self-regulation of competence is acceptable based on thorough application of general safe practice and appropriate risk assessment.

5.1.9   Employers should ensure periodic monitoring of teachers leading activities to ensure they work within their levels of competence and in line with current good practice.

5.1.10   **Mixed groups** benefit from having staff of each gender, particularly for overnight stays. Where this is not possible, parents should be informed of the situation so they can decide whether to consent to their child participating.

Context

5.1.11   If students are to use their own clothing and equipment, this should be checked prior to the activity to ensure it is appropriate.

Organisation

5.1.12   It is good practice to introduce students to basic outdoor activities through a **progressive series of activities** in which they gradually develop appropriate levels of skill.

5.1.13   A suitable **risk assessment** must be carried out for the group/venue/activity. This responsibility is normally delegated to the visit/activity leader, who should ensure the risk assessment meets employer requirements.

5.1.14   Where groups are working on site or in the immediate vicinity of the school site, the risk assessment may simply form part of the teacher's normal planning and indicate no risks identified. More challenging activities or locations would require further detail as to the safe organisation and management of the event.

5.1.15   Any employer requirements for ratios when taking groups off site must be observed at all times. Otherwise, adult:student **ratios** should be determined through an informed risk assessment taking account of:

- relevant factors within the three key dimensions of people, context and organisation
- any employer guidance
- the students' age, ability, aptitude and needs
- staff expertise and confidence
- the demands of the activity and designated area
- potential variables, such as the weather, that may be encountered.

5.1.16   In anticipating the possibility of **changed circumstances**, staff should make sure adult:student ratios are always sufficient to ensure safety by having workable and realistic contingency plans.

5.1.17   The leader, and other staff where appropriate, should have **recent knowledge and experience** of any off-site venue or location or make a **pre-visit** before the group activity commences. Where a pre-visit is not possible, a thorough risk assessment must be made on arrival to determine whether a planned activity can proceed.

5.1.18   It is preferable that two responsible adults accompany a group off site to allow for dealing with unanticipated events. An **assistant leader,** capable of fulfilling the leader's role, should be identified where there is more than one member of staff with the group.

5.1.19   Where a leader operates alone, effective communication with the school is essential, and the group should be trained to take appropriate action in the event of the leader being incapacitated.

5.1.20   When operating off site, relevant **information** should be left at the school or base to enable effective emergency action if required. This should include:

- contact information (eg school and parent emergency communication)
- activity location
- expected time of arrival and return
- equipment carried
- names and number of students and staff
- any agreed procedures to be followed in the event of an accident or emergency.

5.1.21   Even with basic outdoor activities, discipline must be maintained at all times, and school staff must be prepared to intervene if students take potentially unsafe action.

5.1.22   It is accepted practice, and an integral part of high quality provision, for students participating in activities such as the Duke of Edinburgh's Award scheme to undertake carefully planned expeditions under progressively more **remote supervision,** providing they have been properly trained to do so. Before taking part in more independent activities, students should first demonstrate sufficient skill, experience and maturity under supervision. Adequate safeguards should be put in place by relevantly qualified and experienced staff before proceeding with these activities.

5.1.23   Staff should not unduly pressure group members; individual apprehensions and levels of ability should always determine progress.

5.1.24   If external providers contribute to the activity programme with school staff, then clear identification and understanding of roles and responsibilities is important.

5.1.25   When external agents or **tour operators** are used, schools should follow their employer's requirements for engaging their services. Systems should be in place to ensure tour operators:

- are reputable

- meet relevant statutory requirements, including financial bonding arrangements

- are able to fully satisfy the school's duty of care expectations.

5.1.26   When dealing with commercial agencies, some knowledge of the Package Travel, Package Holidays and Package Tours Regulations 1992 will enhance safe planning.

5.1.27   **Long-term planning** for off-site outdoor activities should:

- ensure employer (school or local authority [LA]) requirements with regard to outdoor activities are met

- allow sufficient time for necessary planning and coordination and, where appropriate, visit approval

- clarify necessary staff competence, availability (eg enforced staff-substitution arrangements) and staff ratios

- identify timescales covering important aspects of the itinerary; depending on the duration and nature of the activity, this might include:
  - a preliminary visit to the intended location
  - educational visit coordinator (EVC) clearance and submission of any necessary paperwork (eg risk assessment), as required by the employer
  - a detailed plan for the proposed trip, with timescales
  - written information to parents if it is an optional activity, including outline plan, consent forms, educational aims and a proposed programme of activities
  - expectations and codes of behaviour
  - times of meetings and information evenings if this requirement is relevant to the event
  - any finance details and student costs
  - travel arrangements, including the management of breaks in the journey
  - any accommodation details with arrangements for mixed-gender groups
  - information concerning personal insurance and the limit of the school's liability
  - appropriate equipment lists
  - disclosure and vetting – Criminal Records Bureau/Disclosure and Barring Service (CRB/DBS) – checks
  - designation of approved-adult status where relevant
  - responsibilities and supervision arrangements for the duration of the trip
  - meal arrangements
  - individual needs, such as diet, educational and medical information
  - an accurate register of participants and appropriate adult:student ratios
  - contingency arrangements for use when adverse circumstances prevent the planned programme from taking place

- anticipation of staff changes and their effects on continuity

- agreed and workable emergency procedures

- the appointment of a named school contact

- allowing sufficient time for the submission of plans to the leadership team, and, where appropriate, school governing body for approval

- ensuring an appropriate level of challenge for participants with a progressive approach to skill acquisition.

5.1.28 **Medium-term planning** for off-site outdoor activities should:

- establish a schedule for the supervision of students

- provide for contingency arrangements in the event of accident, illness or inability to participate in the proposed programme

- establish the necessary equipment requirements and ensure it is:

  - in good condition

  - fit for purpose

  - correctly sized to fit the students involved

- ensure students are emotionally prepared and physically fit for the proposed activity

- include the leader obtaining a weather forecast and the interpolation of general information about the proposed venue, and take account of this corrected forecast

- identify workable accident-reporting procedures.

5.1.29 **Short-term planning** for off-site outdoor activities should:

- provide for flexibility on the day, taking into account variables such as weather, the presence of other groups and the disposition of the group in question

- include ongoing consideration of:

  - the educational aims of the event

  - staff ratios and appropriate supervision arrangements for the group

  - the capabilities, individual needs and physical state of students and staff

  - the development of weather systems as the day progresses

  - site-specific issues relating to the proposed venue

  - transport logistics and travelling times

- enable the adult in charge to:

  - follow accepted current good practice in the conduct of the activity

  - provide an appropriate level of challenge for the range of individuals involved

  - ensure the group is adequately clothed and equipped

  - ensure the group is adequately briefed on the plan for the day

  - take into account the medical background of students and staff and ensure prescribed medication, such as asthma inhalers, is accessible

  - ensure accessories such as watches and jewellery are removed if they pose a danger or are liable to be damaged; long hair is tied back and spectacles secured if necessary

  - check any equipment used is fit for purpose

180

- monitor and take account of changes in the physical and mental state of students during activities

- carry out the plan, unless unforeseen circumstances dictate otherwise, so the group can be located in the event of an emergency

- ensure emergency equipment is adequate and readily accessible

- consider the experience and abilities of other members of staff, clearly define roles and responsibilities and delegate only appropriate levels of supervision

- consider communications systems and emergency procedures in the event of an accident

- modify the activity as necessary to ensure safe participation.

Handsam offers an online 'School trip (LOtC) organisation and management system' that aids the planning, administration and coordination of off-site visits. More information is available at www.handsam.co.uk/products/45--school-trip-lotc-organisation-and-management-system

eduFOCUS offers a somewhat different online educational visits notification, approval and database system called EVOLVE. This is a managed online service specifically designed to enable the efficient processing of educational visit proposals. More information is available at www.edufocus.co.uk/evolve.asp

Further information on specific outdoor activities typical of school programmes

Angling

5.1.30   Angling is popular with many young people. It can provide opportunities to develop an awareness of environmental issues, address conservation matters and promote respect for other water users.

Useful website

Environment Agency fishing information	www.environment-agency.gov.uk/subjects/fish

People

5.1.31   Group leaders should be proficient anglers who have practical experience of the waters in which angling will take place.

5.1.32   Group leaders are strongly recommended to ensure at least one member of the angling party is trained in lifesaving and first aid.

Context

5.1.33   Angling can take place in many environments:

- fast-flowing rivers

- meandering streams

- ponds, lakes and reservoirs

- from the seashore

- on the open sea.

5.1.34 An accurate weather forecast and knowledge of local water conditions (eg susceptibility of the venue to flooding, tide times and the effects of wind on tide and sea states) should inform the risk assessment.

Organisation

5.1.35 When fishing from a **boat**:

- it should be fit for purpose and appropriately licensed

- it should not be overloaded, and there should be sufficient space

- there should be a method to retrieve anyone who falls in

- that is hired, the boat should conform to the requirements laid down by the Maritime and Coastguard Agency (MCA) and other relevant agencies

- staff members should be vigilant at all times.

5.1.36 Students need to be adequately equipped for the prevailing weather conditions.

5.1.37 Appropriate footwear (usually wellingtons) should be worn.

Camping

5.1.38 There are various forms of camping, ranging from standing camps, with some permanent on-site facilities, to lightweight camping and backpacking expeditions, which demand greater levels of skill and knowledge. It is essential that potential hazards relating to sites and associated activities are identified at the planning stage.

Useful websites

| OEAP | www.oeapeg.info |
| Mountain Leadership Training (MLT) | www.mltuk.org |

People

5.1.39 For camping in the school locality or the hills, staff should be appropriately experienced, trained and, if relevant, qualified for the terrain, in accordance with MLT guidelines.

5.1.40 If the party is to camp **near water**, group leaders should be familiar with the issues relating to water safety.

Context

5.1.41 All sites should be thoroughly **risk assessed** by an appropriately experienced person and appropriate control measures put in place.

5.1.42 Sites close to mines and quarries, busy main roads and steep ground should be avoided wherever possible.

5.1.43 A first camp should be held under controlled conditions, located near permanent shelter and close to vehicle access.

Organisation

5.1.44　Group leaders should ensure students receive **adequate training** in key aspects of camp craft, including effective pitching of tents for anticipated weather, the importance of hygiene, the safe packing and carrying of loads and a minimum-impact approach to the environment.

5.1.45　**Contingency plans** for alternative routes, venues or activities, in the event of bad weather, should be agreed at the planning stage.

5.1.46　Careful thought needs to be given to the training and supervision required for safe use of stoves, including:

- the type(s) of **stove** used
- fuel storage
- careful refuelling:
  - after the stove has cooled
  - in a ventilated area
  - when other nearby sources of ignition have been extinguished.

5.1.47　Menu planning should reflect the need for:

- healthy nutrition
- cooking convenience and hygiene
- fuel efficiency
- palatability.

5.1.48　Students should be taught how to safely prepare and store food and clean utensils with environmental and hygiene considerations in mind.

5.1.49　Sufficient space should be left between tents to allow free movement and prevent the spread of fire.

5.1.50　All rubbish should be taken away and disposed of thoughtfully.

Cycling and mountain biking

5.1.51　There are many forms of cycling, ranging from recreational activities in the rural environment to competitive events in mountainous terrain, from cycling as a way of getting to school or work to competing at the highest levels in the velodrome. In all its guises, cycling, as an aerobic activity, provides the type of exercise that is particularly effective at promoting good health. There are, of course, many other benefits of cycling, not least its potential to encourage young people to explore the wider world in a local context.

5.1.52　There is the potential for serious accidents in all forms of cycling, and great care should be exercised when planning and organising activities.

Useful websites

British Cycling	www.britishcycling.org.uk
CTC mountain-biking and cycling courses	www.promtb.net
Scottish Cycling	www.britishcycling.org.uk/scotland

Context

5.1.53 **Weather** variables will have effects on the riding surface, as well as on the physical capabilities of the group. Wind strength and direction, wind chill and the possibility of frozen ground will have significant effects on progress and safety margins.

5.1.54 **Bikes** should:

- be roadworthy, with all parts in good condition

- have tyres that are appropriately inflated for the nature of the riding

- have wheels that are locked in place and not buckled, with hubs running smoothly

- have correctly adjusted brakes that are capable of stopping the cyclist effectively

- be correctly sized with securely adjusted handlebars, brake levers and saddle

- have correctly adjusted and smooth-running gears

- be fitted with suitable lights (if appropriate)

- have safe stowage and pannier systems (if appropriate).

5.1.55 Cyclists should wear **clothing**, and carry equipment, suitable for the activity, venue and conditions. This will normally include:

- gloves

- helmet

- appropriate footwear; trainers are normally acceptable, but it should be remembered that riders can be susceptible to cold feet when wet

- long sleeves and full-length, close-fitting trousers

- waterproof/windproof top (in warm weather, it is usual to carry this in a rucksack; otherwise, riders may suffer from overheating).

5.1.56 Each **group** should carry equipment to deal with foreseeable emergencies. Depending on the route and other variables, this will normally include:

- first aid kit

- group shelter

- puncture repair/maintenance kit

- map and compass

- emergency procedures aide-memoire

- mobile phone

- water.

Organisation

5.1.57 Cycling frequently involves transporting bikes and students by minibuses and trailers; the legal requirements must be observed.

> General information on minibuses can be found in *Section 3: Safe Management Principles, paragraphs 3.8.7-3.8.30,* pages 128-131, and *Appendix 21: Minibus Driver's Hours of Work Allowed - British Domestic Rules (Transport Act 1968)* on the CD-ROM.

5.1.58   The competence of the group should be assessed before taking to the road or trail, and this assessment should take place in controlled conditions in a safe area.

5.1.59   In deciding on appropriate rides for young people, risk assessments should take into account the levels of technical difficulty, objective dangers, overall distance (including height gain and loss), escape routes and whether a leader with a mountain-biking qualification will be required (and available) to ensure acceptable margins of safety.

5.1.60   Cyclists should be briefed on key safety measures relevant to the planned route. These will normally include:

- bike controls
- body positions when ascending and descending
- braking
- skid control
- riding as part of a group at different speeds
- specific venue hazards, including traffic or weather variables.

5.1.61   Students need to maintain safe braking distances between their bike and the one in front.

5.1.62   **Venues** should be chosen that take account of the fitness, ability and experience of the group.

5.1.63   Consideration needs to be given to the position of staff in the group when riding; this 'position of most usefulness' may involve the leader dismounting to check individuals at certain points.

5.1.64   Students should be forewarned of **hazards** such as very steep descents, difficult bends, unusually rough terrain or other unusual riding surfaces, and other track users. Such situations should be managed according to the ability of the group, whether on or off-road. Safe progressions with appropriate levels of challenge and development should characterise the session.

Forest School activities

5.1.65   The philosophy of Forest Schools is to encourage and inspire individuals of any age through positive outdoor experiences. By participating in engaging, motivating and achievable tasks and activities in a woodland environment, each student has an opportunity to develop intrinsic motivation, and sound emotional and social skills. Activities should be adapted to students' ability levels, educational needs, weather and terrain. Activities linked to the prescribed curriculum and personal and social development include hide and seek, shelter building, tool skills, lighting fires, building dens and environmental art.

5.1.66   Forest School activities are commonly offered to early-years groups, some primary school groups and in secondary schools seeking to engage or re-engage disaffected students.

Useful website

| Forest Schools | www.forestschool.com |

People

5.1.67   A Forest Schools Level 3 practitioner award (or equivalent) is advised as the standard for leading Forest School sessions. However, competent adults with some experience of Forest School may be able to deliver basic activities in the school grounds, local parks or small areas of woodland with clear boundaries and observable paths.

Context

5.1.68   Where Forest Schools take place outside school grounds, prior **permission** needs to be sought from the landowner; and Forest School sites must be risk assessed and prepared before use.

5.1.69   Wherever possible, the Forest School area should not be close to busy roads or major geographical hazards (eg crags or deep water). Where there is access to the public, appropriate procedures should be in place to ensure child safety.

5.1.70   Appropriate boundary setting is an essential part of the risk-management process.

5.1.71   Appropriate **clothing** should be worn to suit the prevailing conditions and type of activity. Complete coverage of the arms and legs is strongly advised for events in thick vegetation and woodland.

5.1.72   **Footwear** should be suitable for the terrain, activities and prevailing weather conditions.

5.1.73   Secure storage of tools and equipment is important.

Organisation

5.1.74   Where Forest School activities take place over a number of sessions, a progressive plan of activities should be developed.

5.1.75   Students should be briefed with clear and unambiguous ground rules. All foreseeable hazards they may come across should be identified and brought to their attention. A briefing area (often with a **circle area and fire pit**) is recommended as a focal point for starting and finishing activities.

5.1.76   Fire making and tool use are practised in Forest Schools in a traditional woodland manner and should be carefully introduced by demonstration and supervised throughout. Supervision and monitoring of tools and fires is essential. However, students should be encouraged to think about and assess their actions and become aware of safety issues in order to manage risk.

5.1.77   For all activities, consideration should be given to:

- educational aims
- the potential hazards associated with the environment and activities
- the potential threat from other people
- emergency procedures in the event of injury or getting lost.

5.1.78   If appropriate, **escape instructions** may be issued to enable students to retreat safely to a prearranged point.

5.1.79   Procedures for locating students who get lost should be handled by the leader.

5.1.80   First aid kits should be available.

> General information on first aid kits can be found in *Section 3: Safe Management Principles, paragraphs 3.9.24-3.9.25*, page 138, and *Appendix 3: First Aid Qualifications and First Aid Kits: An Explanation of the Health and Safety Executive Approved Code of Practice (HSE ACOP) on First Aid 1997.*

Horse riding and pony trekking

5.1.81   Horse riding and pony trekking are popular activities with many young people. Schools should use only approved riding schools, trained horses and qualified staff when offering equestrian activities.

Useful websites

| Association of British Riding Schools (ABRS) | www.abrs-info.org |
| British Horse Society (BHS) | www.bhs.org.uk |

Context

5.1.82   Only BHS or ABRS approved centres should be used.

5.1.83   School staff should discuss the needs of their students with the riding school to ensure the standards of rides chosen are appropriate for the needs of the group.

5.1.84   Horses and riders should be relevantly equipped in line with BHS standards and guidelines.

Organisation

5.1.85   Staff **ratios** should reflect the:

- demands of the terrain

- needs of the group

- risk assessment requirements of the riding centre.

5.1.86   Clear, comprehensive and concise guidance from the centre's staff should be given to all responsible adults if they are to lead particular horses.

Journeys and low-level walking

5.1.87   Walking can take place in a variety of locations, from local walks in urban areas to high-level mountain and fell walking in remote areas. There are hazards associated with low-level walking, particularly on or near beaches, rivers, cliffs and quarries.

Useful websites

MLT England	www.mlte.org
MLT Northern Ireland	www.tollymore.com
MLT Scotland	www.mltuk.org/MLTS/about.php
MLT UK	www.mltuk.org
MLT Wales	www.mltw.org

Context

5.1.88   **Staff competent** in the activity should carefully choose appropriate venues and plan routes, taking into account all variables. Where more remote and challenging journeys are proposed, it is advised that the group leader holds the MLT Walking Group Leader Award for lowland country.

5.1.89   The **weather** can change quickly and significantly, even at low levels, causing increases in wind speed and rainfall intensity, and reductions in temperature.

5.1.90   Wind chill and topographical funnelling effects should also be anticipated by the staff in choosing appropriate venues.

5.1.91   Venues should offer levels of educational, environmental and/or activity challenge appropriate to the abilities, confidence and experience of the group.

5.1.92   If the route to be taken involves planned scrambling or gorge walking, the use of helmets may be required. Gorges may also require the use of wetsuits and buoyancy aids.

> **General information on personal protective equipment can be found in** *Section 2: Safe Teaching Principles, paragraphs 2.3.56–2.3.60, pages 31–32,* **and** *Section 3: Safe Management Principles, paragraphs 3.5.66–3.5.92,* **pages 91–95.**

Organisation

5.1.93   **Planning** should include:

- suitable stops for rests

- an estimated time for completing the journey

- consideration of equipment needs

- a level of demand appropriate to the abilities and experience of the group

- possible hazards and how they might be managed

- emergency procedures that may need to be implemented.

5.1.94   Each **group member** should carry or wear suitable clothing and equipment to ensure their comfort. This will typically include:

- waterproof and windproof clothing

- food and drink

- appropriate spare clothing

- appropriate footwear.

5.1.95   In addition, the **group** should carry equipment to allow them to deal with emergencies. This will typically include:

- first aid kit

- map and compass, where appropriate

- emergency procedures aide-memoire

- mobile phone.

5.1.96   Low-level walking may be an appropriate context for groups to be **remotely supervised**. In these situations they need to:

- be clearly briefed

- be informed of potential hazards

- be left in no doubt as to action to take in the event of emergencies

- carry suitable emergency equipment to deal with foreseeable incidents

- be able to contact the leader if required.

5.1.97   The group leader should be satisfied that the students have acquired the necessary skills and have the necessary confidence, physical ability and judgement to be left without direct supervision. The withdrawal of direct supervision should be a gradual **four-stage process**, evolving through:

- accompanying the group

- shadowing the group

- checking regularly at agreed locations

- checking occasionally at agreed locations.

Orienteering

5.1.98   The challenge, excitement and achievement of orienteering is in finding the fastest route between a series of controls on an orienteering course, using physical and mental abilities in combination. Many schools establish adequate activities and short courses on the school site. Some are able to develop this into the immediate locality and provide exciting orienteering sessions during lesson times.

Useful website

| British Orienteering | www.britishorienteering.org.uk |

People

5.1.99   Competent adults with some experience of orienteering are perfectly able to deliver a basic introduction in the school grounds, local parks or small areas of woodland with clear boundaries and observable paths.

Context

5.1.100   On-site orienteering routes should take account of the hazards relating to car-park areas, boundaries and particular aspects of the school site.

5.1.101   Prior **permission** should be sought from any landowner; the existence of orienteering maps does not necessarily indicate a right of access.

5.1.102   Wherever possible, the orienteering course should not require students to cross busy roads or negotiate major geographical hazards (eg crags or areas very close to deep water).

5.1.103   Appropriate route setting is an essential part of the risk-management process.

5.1.104   Appropriate **clothing** should be worn to suit the prevailing conditions and type of orienteering course. Complete coverage of the arms and legs is strongly advised for events in thick vegetation and woodland.

5.1.105   **Footwear** should be suitable for the course terrain and prevailing weather conditions.

5.1.106   All students should carry a whistle or other means of calling for help if orienteering in areas where they will be out of sight of the leaders.

Organisation

5.1.107   Students should be briefed with clear and unambiguous ground rules. All foreseeable hazards they may come across should be identified and brought to their attention.

5.1.108   A **call-back signal** and prearranged cut-off time should be agreed. Escape instructions may be issued to enable students to retreat safely to a prearranged point.

5.1.109   Inexperienced students should compete in pairs or small groups and remain together, though it is recognised that orienteering skill development in pairs is less effective than solo orienteering.

5.1.110   If groups are to be left **unaccompanied**, consideration should be given to:

- educational aims

- the potential hazards associated with proposed routes

- the potential threat from other people

- emergency procedures in the event of injury or getting lost

- a realistic cut-off time

- the boundaries of the course.

5.1.111   Only experienced and relevantly trained students should take part in **night-time orienteering**, except on the most straightforward sites (eg school grounds or fully enclosed areas of limited size).

5.1.112   Procedures for locating students who get lost should be handled by the leader.

5.1.113   First aid kits should be available.

> General information on first aid kits can be found in *Section 3: Safe Management Principles, paragraphs 3.9.24-3.9.25, page 138*, and *Appendix 3: First Aid Qualifications and First Aid Kits: An Explanation of the Health and Safety Executive Approved Code of Practice (HSE ACOP) on First Aid 1997* on the CD-ROM.

Problem-solving activities

5.1.114   Problem-solving and team-building activities can develop trust, communication and leadership skills using simple equipment in safe, controlled environments. Activities that are easy to set up, using resources that are obtainable locally, can address the central challenges of education by:

- helping individuals find solutions by discovering the right balance of creativity and subjectivity on the one hand, and logic and objectivity on the other

- encouraging individuals, through adopting the techniques of critical thinking, to realise they can make a difference to the outcomes of their own lives

- fostering and developing teamwork.

Useful website

OEAP	www.oeapeg.info

People

5.1.115 Students often think creatively when problem solving, and experienced staff's active approach to risk management is crucial. Sensible precautions can reduce risk without stifling initiative, enterprise and excitement.

5.1.116 These activities can appear contrived and innocuous on occasions. There is a danger that students may not fully appreciate the real risks involved. All participants should act in a safe manner and take responsibility for their own and others' well-being.

Context

5.1.117 Special consideration should be given to the height from which students could fall.

5.1.118 Some common activities involve working in awkward positions some distance from the ground, and there may be a need for protective equipment, such as helmets, for some activities. In these cases, it is vital staff have the specialist knowledge and competence to lead the activity safely.

5.1.119 The required levels of skill and expertise for particular activities should be stipulated in the risk assessment.

5.1.120 Students should be adequately clothed and equipped to afford acceptable levels of protection.

5.1.121 Consideration should be given in the risk assessment process to the appropriateness of all equipment to be used in problem-solving activities. This is particularly important when using equipment that has not been designed specifically for the task. Due consideration should also be given to the nature and size of the equipment relative to the capabilities of the group and individuals concerned.

Organisation

5.1.122 Students should be adequately **briefed** on the potential hazards of the activity, and the parameters within which they may act independently should be carefully defined.

5.1.123 The hazards and consequences of overtly competitive activities should be considered.

5.1.124 If the activity involves **independent** work, staff should be positioned at specified locations if hazards, such as busy roads, entrances and exits and deep water, are to be managed.

5.1.125 Activities that involve students physically supporting each other should be carefully managed, with time given for familiarisation and practice.

Improvised rafting

5.1.126 Improvised rafting using barrels and planks as building materials is an outdoor activity that is often used for team building and management-development programmes.

Useful website

| OEAP | www.oeapeg.info |

People

5.1.127 For improvised rafts, group leaders should be experienced in construction techniques. Rafts may distort when placed on the water, and care will be needed, during design and construction, to anticipate the effect of this.

5.1.128 An appropriately staffed **safety boat** may be required for rafting activities that take place on stretches of open water where individuals may have difficulty reaching the shore in the event of capsize.

Context

5.1.129 For improvised rafts, all students should be made aware of the hazards involved in lifting and handling the construction materials, which should be fit for purpose. Clear construction and safety guidelines should form part of the initial briefing.

5.1.130 At the construction stage, helmets may be useful.

5.1.131 Students should be adequately **dressed for immersion**, and helmets and buoyancy aids should be worn, even in shallow water. The risk of entrapment needs to be anticipated and managed appropriately.

Organisation

5.1.132 Clear **communication** will be necessary to ensure safe lifting and handling techniques are used.

5.1.133 A **capsize or break-up** of the improvised raft should be considered a real possibility and an appropriate action plan established to rescue anyone in the water.

5.1.134 If safety boats are to be used, appropriate procedures should be followed in the event of capsize or break-up. Safety boat 'kill cords' should be used, and the instructor should carry a knife.

Skating

5.1.135 The advice in this section applies to ice, roller and in-line skating.

Useful websites

British Artistic Roller Skating	www.british-roller-skating.org.uk
Federation of Artistic Roller Skating	www.fars.co.uk
National Ice Skating Association (NISA)	www.iceskating.org.uk

People

5.1.136   Students should be taught how to skate safely. To assist with this process, many leaders introduce the acronym **SLAP**, which means skaters should be:

- **S**mart:
  - always wear protective gear
  - master the basics, including stopping and turning
  - skate at a speed that is safe and appropriate for the level of competence
- **L**egal:
  - observe the venue's protocol for overtaking
- **A**lert:
  - skate in control at all times
  - watch out for hazards
  - be vigilant for changes to the skating surface
- **P**olite:
  - announce an intention to pass
  - always yield to novices and pedestrians
  - accept the need to skate thoughtfully and with care.

5.1.137   Leaders should have previous experience of skating at rinks and leading groups in similar environments.

Context

5.1.138   The **skating surface** should be:

- on an even surface
- free from obstructions
- regularly checked
- maintained and inspected before use.

5.1.139   Though in-line skating is increasing in popularity, guidance should be sought from the relevant LA or employing organisation for its policies on skating in public areas and/or on highways.

5.1.140   A pre-visit inspection of the **location** by the leader is highly recommended prior to its use by the school.

5.1.141   Students should wear suitable **clothing** that provides adequate protection. Beginners should wear gloves. Helmets may be required in certain circumstances. Elbow and knee protection is advisable. Ice/roller boots should provide firm ankle support.

> **General information on personal protective equipment can be found in** *Section 2: Safe Teaching Principles, paragraphs 2.3.56-2.3.60,* **pages 31-32, and** *Section 3: Safe Management Principles, paragraphs 3.5.66-3.5.92,* **pages 91-95.**

Organisation

5.1.142   For recreational skating, the terms and conditions of the particular commercial venue must be observed, and duty of care arrangements should be explicit.

5.1.143   For taught sessions, skating should be supervised by school staff, and a competent instructor should always be present.

5.1.144   It is sensible, in pre-visit information to parents, to explain the nature of the risks inherent in visits to skating rinks.

5.1.145   The group should observe any local requirements for direction of skating. This is usually an anticlockwise direction, skating on the right and passing on the left.

5.1.146   Where possible, it is advisable for beginners and advanced skaters to skate in separate groups.

Traversing

5.1.147   Low-level traversing, sometimes referred to as bouldering, is becoming a common provision, particularly in primary schools. Adjustable holds are attached to a wall and provide for students to manoeuvre along the wall at very low heights. It does not involve the use of ropes and requires a minimum level of expertise to manage while offering challenging situations to the students involved.

Useful website

MLT	www.mltuk.org

Context

5.1.148   Traversing walls for beginners should incorporate holds along the floor level in order to enable those lacking in confidence to complete the traverse at their level.

5.1.149   Adjustments to the holds should involve expert advice in order to provide a range of routes along the wall to accommodate different levels of ability and confidence.

5.1.150   **Matting** under traversing walls is designed to provide a more comfortable landing for anyone who may fall or jump. Students should be made aware that it should not be assumed that matting makes the climbing any safer.

Organisation

5.1.151   Traversing is safer when done initially in pairs with a partner behind the traverser to 'spot' in case of a fall.

5.1.152   Sufficient space should be provided so individuals have the opportunity to look at the location of holds and devise their own route along the wall without the pressure of others crowding them.

5.1.153   Clear safety rules should be established before traversing begins. It is good practice to involve the students in devising the safety rules.

5.1.154   Careful consideration needs to be given to the control and supervision of all members of the group.

Activities at outdoor and residential centres

5.1.155 Many schools use outdoor and residential centres to provide students with experience of the outdoors, and specialist staff can do much to further schools' educational aims. Centres may be run by LAs, charitable bodies or commercial/private agencies.

Useful websites

Adventure Activities Licensing Authority (AALA)	www.aals.org.uk
OEAP	www.oeapeg.info
Council for Learning Outside the Classroom (CLoTC)	www.lotc.org.uk
Adventuremark	www.adventuremark.co.uk
British Adventure Holidays Association (BAHA)	www.baha.org.uk/safety.aspx
Institute for Outdoor Learning (IOL)	www.outdoor-learning.org

5.1.156 At the time of publication, centres offering activities that are subject to licensing under the **Adventure Activities Licensing Regulations 2004** must demonstrate to the licensing authority that they meet acceptable standards of safe practice in those activities; accredited centres are then issued with a unique licence number. This gives assurance that good safety-management practice is being followed by the provider. Centres that hold a current AALA licence can be searched for on its website: www.aals.org.uk/aals/provider_search.php

5.1.157 However, at the time of printing, the government has announced its intention to amend the above legislation and replace the AALA with a **voluntary code of conduct**. Currently, there are a number of accrediting schemes for outdoor providers, including:

- the CLoTC Quality Badge (www.lotc.org.uk/lotc-quality-badge)
- the Adventuremark scheme (www.adventuremark.co.uk)
- the BAHA accreditation scheme (www.baha.org.uk/safety.aspx)
- the IOL approved provider scheme (www.outdoor-learning.org).

5.1.158 The AALA scheme does not cover activities offered by voluntary associations to their members, schools to their students or provision for young people accompanied by their parents. However, its guidance on safety in the outdoors is clearly appropriate to schools' provision. Alternatively, the CLoTC Quality Badge, Adventuremark or accreditation by IOL or BAHA provides some assurance that recognised safety-management practices are being followed by the provider.

People

5.1.159 Where centre specialist staff are used, they are responsible for technical aspects. School staff maintain overall duty of care for the students (subject to new case law being relevant – see *Section 3: Safe Management Principles, paragraphs 3.4.24–3.4.26*, pages 60–61). Clarity of role and responsibility is essential.

Organisation

5.1.160   Prior to booking at a centre, checks should be made to ensure:

- the centre is appropriate for the students and planned learning outcomes

- the education credentials and reputation of the centre are sound

- whether an AALA licence is held and, if so, what it covers

- fire and emergency procedures are satisfactory

- which facilities and services are offered

- whether sole use is possible or shared use with other groups will occur

- insurance arrangements are appropriate and acceptable

- who is responsible for what and when

- regular meetings with centre staff are scheduled to resolve issues and evaluate progress.

5.1.161   Any unsatisfactory issues should be resolved before booking.

5.1.162   Wherever possible, there should be sufficient school staff to accompany each activity group under instruction. Where the school staff are concerned about any unreasonable or unnecessary risk, they should approach the specialist staff, and measures should be taken to ensure the continued safety and well-being of the students.

Adventure activities

5.1.163   The websites of governing bodies of sport for specific activities will provide up-to-date guidance and information on relevant coaching, leading and personal performance awards, recommended leader:participant ratios, current best practice and risk assessment considerations.

5.1.164   afPE recommends that teachers planning to provide challenging adventure activities for students should regularly check the latest guidance provided by the relevant governing bodies of sport and ensure that staff leading students are appropriately qualified to the appropriate level of challenge and/or specialist experts are used.

5.1.165   Proven **competence to lead** groups in challenging adventure activities is essential. Teachers should ensure anyone leading groups in adventure activities holds the relevant qualification or endorsement.

5.1.166   Technical competence to lead an activity can be demonstrated by holding one of the following:

- a relevant and current governing body of sport award for the appropriate activity/terrain plus logged evidence of recent and relevant experience

- an assessment of competence by an appropriate technical adviser that confirms the leader has the required experience, leadership and technical skills for the specified activity.

5.1.167   Teachers leading **higher-risk activities** need to follow the employer's requirements for qualification, experience and management.

5.1.168   Where activities are led by an external provider, the **provider** assumes responsibility for risk assessing its **services and provision**. School staff should note that they retain responsibility for risk assessing those elements of the visit/activity falling directly under their supervision. This allocation of duty needs to be understood and agreed by both parties, but see *paragraph 3.4.25*, pages 60–61.

5.1.169   Teachers should check **external providers** deploy competent and qualified staff before engaging with the provider. Details of current activity-specific qualifications can be obtained from governing body of sport websites.

Information relating to specific adventure activities

Canoeing, kayaking and paddle sports

5.1.170   Canoeing and kayaking take place in a wide variety of contexts and environments; from open boating to flat-water marathon racing and offshore sea kayaking. They epitomise, in every way, the notion of sport as a route to adventure.

5.1.171   The governing body of sport awards, administered and regularly updated by the home-nation boards, are divided into two areas: coaching and personal skills/leadership. They are specific to a variety of craft and a wide range of environments. Specialist knowledge (for kayaks and canoes) is available in the following areas:

- racing
- slalom
- wild-water racing
- surfing
- open canoeing
- polo
- freestyle
- sea kayaking
- white-water kayaking
- flat water.

Useful websites

British Canoe Union (BCU)	www.bcu.org.uk
Canoe Association of Northern Ireland (CANI)	www.cani.org.uk
Canoe Wales	www.canoewales.com
Scottish Canoe Association (SCA)	www.canoescotland.org

Caving and mine exploration

5.1.172   Underground systems, other than show caves and tourist mines, present many of the challenges and adventure opportunities associated with mountains and water, and these, associated with darkness and confined spaces, make the underground experience uniquely challenging and exciting. Well-organised underground activities can provide numerous educational opportunities for personal and group development.

Useful website

British Caving Association (BCA)	www.british-caving.org.uk

Climbing and abseiling

5.1.173   Climbing and abseiling require degrees of balance, agility, strength, endurance and mental control that are dependent on the standard of routes selected at the chosen venue. The activities also require that individuals take responsibility for their own and others' safety in what can be potentially hazardous environments.

Useful websites

British Mountaineering Council (BMC)	www.thebmc.co.uk
MLT England	www.mlte.org
MLT Northern Ireland	www.tollymore.com
MLT Scotland	www.mltuk.org/MLTS/about.php
MLT UK	www.mltuk.org
MLT Wales	www.mltw.org
National Indoor Climbing Award Scheme (NICAS)	www.nicas.co.uk

Coasteering

5.1.174   Coasteering is a mixture of swimming, climbing, scrambling and traversing the coastline. When it is safe to do so, coasteering also allows participants to jump into the sea from height and explore areas of the coast that are not normally seen.

Useful website

British Coasteering Federation	www.britishcoasteeringfederation.co.uk

Combined water/rock activities

5.1.175   Combined water/rock activities are adventure activities where those hazards associated with the rock environment may, at times, combine with those of the water environment. These include:

- gorge walking
- sea-level traversing
- canyoning
- adventure swimming
- river running.

Useful websites

BCA	www.british-caving.org.uk
BMC	www.thebmc.co.uk

Dinghy sailing

5.1.176   Sailing is a long-established adventure activity that has become a core component of outdoor education. It offers opportunities for developing physical skills, self-confidence and self-esteem and is used frequently for team building, leadership and management-development programmes.

Useful websites

National School Sailing Association (NSSA)	www.nssa.org.uk
Royal Yachting Association (RYA)	www.rya.org.uk
Royal Yachting Association Northern Ireland (RYANI)	www.ryani.org.uk
Royal Yachting Association Scotland	www.ryascotland.org.uk
Welsh Yachting Association (WYA)	www.welshsailing.org

Overseas expeditions

5.1.177   Challenging overseas expeditions are an area of growth in adventure activities, with significant issues involving insurance, quality assurance of activities and providers, and communication with school.

Useful websites

MLT	www.mltuk.org
BMC	www.thebmc.co.uk
OEAP	www.oeapeg.info
Royal Geographic Expedition Advisory Service	www.rgs.org
Foreign and Commonwealth Office (FCO)	www.fco.gov.uk
Young Explorers' Trust	www.theyet.org

Rafting

5.1.178   White-water rafting involves paddling purpose-made inflatable rafts on white-water rivers. School staff should ensure that raft guides are appropriately qualified for the level of river and that coaches with Level 1 raft guide qualifications have been passed as competent for the specific site.

Useful website

BCU	www.bcu.org.uk

Rowing

5.1.179 Rowing, as a leisure sport, provides high quality aerobic exercise that benefits the heart and lungs and strengthens all the major muscle groups in a smooth, impact-free, rhythmic motion. Competitive rowing, in which anaerobic and strength conditioning form an integral part of the training regime, has a long tradition as an Olympic sport in Britain. Whether for leisure or competition, rowing offers diverse opportunities for training and enjoyment, both on and off the water. Perhaps more importantly, with increasing obesity rates in children now posing major challenges for the future of the nation's health provision, it should be noted that rowing burns calories faster than cycling at the same perceived level of exertion.

Useful website

British Rowing	www.britishrowing.org

Skiing and snowboarding

5.1.180 Skiing and snowboarding can encourage students to develop a wide range of physical skills and qualities, including general fitness, coordination, balance and strength. Foreign residential visits, as cultural experiences, also offer wide-ranging opportunities for personal and social development in challenging new environments.

5.1.181 The wearing of **ski helmets** has become compulsory in several countries. LAs and schools are currently formulating their own guidance on this issue. afPE endorses the principle of wearing safety helmets when skiing.

More information on ski helmets can be found in *Section 3: Safe Management Principles, paragraph 3.5.80*, page 93.

Useful websites

British Association of Snowsport Instructors (BASI)	www.basi.org.uk
Snowsport England	www.snowsportengland.org.uk
Snowsport Scotland	www.snowsportscotland.org
Snowsport Wales	www.snowsportwales.net

Sub-aqua activities

5.1.182 Underwater exploration often begins with snorkelling, but the proficient use of scuba equipment significantly enhances the levels of enjoyment, challenge and opportunities for sub-aqua activities farther afield. Due to the specialist nature of sub-aqua activities, only recognised and fully **accredited teaching centres** should be used to deliver diving programmes.

Useful websites

British Sub-Aqua Club (BSAC)	www.bsac.org
Professional Association of Diving Instructors (PADI)	www.padi.com

Surfing

5.1.183   Surfing provides cardiovascular exercise by using upper-body muscles to paddle through the surf and leg muscles to guide the board once up and riding. It develops balance, strength and coordination while demanding high levels of personal commitment to learning about, and staying safe in, surf.

Useful websites

Surfing GB	www.surfgb.com
Royal Life Saving Society (RLSS) UK	www.lifesavers.org.uk or http://rlssonline.com
Surf Life Saving Association of Great Britain (SLSGB)	www.slsgb.org.uk

Windsurfing

5.1.184   Taught on lakes and the sea, windsurfing is a fun activity that requires mental and physical skills to convert wind power into controlled motion. It develops balance, strength and coordination, as well as an understanding of the wind and waves in a dynamic environment.

Useful website

RYA	www.rya.org.uk/startboating/Pages/Windsurf.aspx

5.2   Aquatic Activities

Useful websites

5.2.1   The following websites provide detailed guidance on the safe organisation and risk assessment of aquatic activities:

Amateur Swimming Association (ASA)	www.swimming.org/asa
Swimming Teachers' Association (STA)	www.sta.co.uk
Scottish Swimming	www.scottishswimming.com
Royal Life Saving Society (RLSS) UK	www.lifesavers.org.uk or http://rlssonline.com
Chartered Institute for the Management of Sport and Physical Activity (CIMSPA)	www.imspa.co.uk
Marine and Coastguard Agency (MCA)	www.dft.gov.uk/mca
Government safety advice on water sports and coastal activities	www.direct.gov.uk/en/TravelAndTransport/Boatingandtravellingbywater/Keepingsafeatthecoast/DG_185550

5.2.2   Swimming and its related activities are health-promoting and provide great satisfaction to all practitioners. Learning to swim and being confident in water provide the essential foundation for many water-based recreational choices.

5.2.3   Due to the evident hazard of drowning, the teaching and learning of swimming and related water skills require the utmost care on the part of all concerned. The aim should be to teach the basic skills to as many young people as possible. Competence in aquatic activities is a genuine life skill.

5.2.4   School swimming lessons are **programmed activities** with structure, supervision and continuous monitoring from the poolside where the risk is limited due to the nature of the activity and degree of control exercised. The Health and Safety Executive (HSE) has clearly identified a reduced level of risk to the safety of swimmers when undertaking programmed activities, compared to swimming in an **unprogrammed** public session, in 'free' swimming when allowed as a contrasting activity at the end of a structured session or in 'fun' activity sessions.

5.2.5   Diving, by its very nature, can be dangerous, and there have been a number of serious diving accidents in recent years.

General safe-practice issues

People

5.2.6   Whatever the aquatic activity, whenever there are students in the water, a **suitably qualified adult** should be present at the poolside who is able to effect a rescue from the water and carry out cardiopulmonary resuscitation (CPR).

5.2.7   A minimum of **two** people on the poolside is common and good practice to cover eventualities in the teaching and safety aspects of aquatics. Where only one adult is present, the risk assessment needs to indicate clearly why this ratio is acceptable and should highlight alternative emergency arrangements.

5.2.8   Where specialist aquatics teachers are employed to lead the lesson, it is essential the **school staff remain on poolside** to provide an assisting role.

5.2.9   Specialist aquatics staff may also provide essential **lifesaving cover**. Another responsible adult should be available to supervise the students in any situation where the specialist aquatics teacher has to enter the water to effect a rescue.

5.2.10 Aquatics teachers and school staff who have responsibility for the water safety of the class in **programmed activities** should hold, as a minimum, either of the following awards:

- the National Rescue Award for Swimming Teachers and Coaches (NRASTC)

- the STA Level 1 Award in Pool Emergency Procedures.

5.2.11 Aquatics teachers and school staff who have responsibility for the water safety of the class in **unprogrammed activities** or shared space where programmed and unprogrammed activities take place should hold a current **swimming pool lifeguard** award such as:

- the RLSS National Pool Lifeguard qualification

- the STA Level 2 Award for Pool Lifeguard.

5.2.12 All lifeguards, lifesavers and supporting staff need to:

- update their skills in lifesaving and water safety regularly, where relevant to their role

- practise their previously learned lifesaving skills and, where appropriate, lifeguarding skills regularly

- remain diligent and effectively organised throughout a swimming lesson

- be aware of the standard pool operating procedures for the venue they use

- be appropriately dressed so they can fulfil the requirements of their role without restriction.

5.2.13 Pool lifeguard staff should be trained in the use of **spinal boards/special recovery stretchers**, which more easily meet the need of recovering patients, especially where such patients may have suffered head and neck injury. School staff and those on poolside duty should know how to assemble and use such equipment, where it is available and where their role may include responsibility for water rescues.

5.2.14 All **adults accompanying students** to aquatics lessons should:

- be given a clear role

- understand the limits of the role

- be confident on the poolside

- communicate with the other adults on safety issues

- have the necessary discipline and control standards

- regularly carry out head counts during, as well as at the beginning and end of, sessions

- know, understand and be able to apply the pool normal operating procedures (NOPs) and emergency action plan (EAP)

- be suitably dressed for the role they are to play in the lesson.

5.2.15   Teachers should not be deployed to aquatic responsibilities who:

- **lack confidence** in the role

- cannot swim

- are reticent about being on the poolside.

5.2.16   Teachers should have the opportunity to express such a lack of confidence or ability before being deployed in a poolside role.

5.2.17   The supervision of activities such as canoeing or scuba diving in pools requires **specialist knowledge** in both teaching and lifesaving, which needs to be identified in the appropriate risk assessment.

5.2.18   All students should be made aware of the necessary procedures and **safety routines**, including:

- removing, or making safe, all jewellery

- not to chew sweets or gum

- carrying out the usual hygiene procedures

- reporting any illness

- not to run on the pool surround

- to remain away from the pool edge until told to approach the water

- the emergency procedures for stopping activity and evacuating the pool

- reporting unseemly or unacceptable behaviour that may compromise safety

- responding immediately to all instructions.

5.2.19   Students with **medical problems** may need clearance provided through the written permission of parents before they are allowed to participate in school aquatics programmes. Additional advice may also be necessary from relevant organisations with regard to specific risk factors relating to aquatic activity.

5.2.20   The needs of students with **epilepsy** may vary according to whether a medication regime applies. According to need, they should:

- be observed from the poolside

- work alongside a responsible person in the water when out of their depth

- according to their particular needs, work within a 'buddy' system of a co-student or helper in the water to provide an **unobtrusive** system of paired supervision that avoids embarrassment.

Context

5.2.21   **Swimwear** should be suitable for the purpose. For reasons of safety, swimwear should be sufficiently tight-fitting to allow freedom of body and limb movement without causing unsafe water resistance. Cultural or religious sensitivity needs to be demonstrated, but staff should ensure the correct balance between safety, cultural requirements and the need to be able to see the limb movements of students to ensure appropriate learning and safe practice.

> **More information on religious and cultural issues associated with swimming can be found in** *Section 3: Safe Management Principles, paragraph 3.10.29,* **page 145.**

5.2.22 Students with long hair should wear caps to prevent vision being affected (this will also reduce the amount of hair that becomes trapped in the grilles and filters).

Guidance on the wearing of goggles in swimming lessons can be found in *Section 3: Safe Management Principles, paragraphs 3.5.82–3.5.90,* page 94.

5.2.23 **Safety equipment**, such as poles, throwing ropes or throw bags, first aid provision and emergency alarms, needs to be:

- fit for purpose

- sufficient in quantity

- regularly checked

- positioned so as to be readily available when needed without creating additional hazards to pool users.

5.2.24 Any **electrical equipment** on the poolside needs to be:

- designed to be used in an aquatic environment

- of low voltage or battery operated

- located so as not to create an additional hazard

- have current circuit breakers attached

- be checked regularly.

5.2.25 No one in the water should handle any electrical equipment.

5.2.26 Leisure or **play equipment** is often large and may adversely affect supervision, requiring observation from both sides of any large inflatables. Careful thought should be given to the wisdom of introducing such equipment into the water where additional lifeguarding provision is not available.

5.2.27 A variety of teaching and **floatation aids** should be available. Equipment should:

- conform to any BS EN standard, where available

- be checked before the session to ensure it is safe to use

- be close at hand for easy access and use during the lesson

- be placed tidily on the poolside to minimise tripping or other safety hazards

- be used appropriately to avoid over-reliance on it

- be appropriate and safe for the needs of the students

- be correctly fitted or held according to the design and purpose of the aid.

5.2.28 Safe supervision of lessons will need to take account of whether the group has **sole or shared use** of the pool. Shared use with the general public would have further implications for the supervision and designated responsibility for safety, which would need to be satisfactorily addressed.

5.2.29 Schools will often use pools on **premises other than their own**. By law, the responsible manager must ensure the facilities are safe and present no risk to health for visiting groups. This applies equally when schools use swimming pools belonging to other schools. It is regarded in law as a place of work under the responsibility of the host school. However, staff with the duty of care for the lesson should always ensure they make whatever checks they can on each visit before allowing students to use the facility.

5.2.30   School staff and/or specialist aquatics staff should be able to see all the students throughout the lesson. The bottom of the pool should be **clearly visible**, and any problems of **glare** or light reflected from the water surface should be satisfactorily overcome.

Organisation

5.2.31   The **management and monitoring** of the school aquatics programme should be delegated to nominated teachers, particularly in relation to:

- student progress

- accompanying staff confidence and competence

- the application of policies and procedures

- informing other staff of procedures and standards

- ensuring risk assessments are carried out.

5.2.32   Unprogrammed sessions, such as leisure and play sessions, or where the pool space is shared between unprogrammed and programmed activities, may require **higher levels of supervision** and lifeguard expertise because of the less-controlled nature of the session.

5.2.33   Whoever is responsible for the water safety of the group should be told the **number in the group** by the school staff so regular scanning and accurate head counts can be carried out during the lesson.

5.2.34   Where an adult has responsibility for teaching more than two students, the recommended **teaching position** is from the side of the pool as this provides the best position to oversee the whole group and respond quickly to any teaching or emergency situation.

5.2.35   **Additional adults** may be in the water to assist individual students or small groups according to the age, ability and confidence of the students. Where manual support is provided, care needs to be taken to:

- avoid embarrassment to student or adult

- ensure support is provided in an appropriate form.

5.2.36   Adult:student **ratios** should meet the particular safety requirements and be determined by a thorough risk assessment based on considerations of the staff, students, facility, equipment, activity and organisation of the session as set out in the risk assessment format in *Appendix 10* on the CD-ROM. However, where **local requirements** are set, such as by a local authority (LA) or pool management, these must be followed. Numbers should be low enough for all students to be managed safely.

5.2.37   Some governing bodies of sport and other professional bodies set maximum generic adult:participant ratios. These should be considered within the risk assessment as useful guidance, but they do not take into account the variable circumstances each teacher may encounter. Decisions on ratios may vary according to the specific circumstances. For example, the number of adults per student is likely to be increased where the students are very young, have special needs or exhibit challenging behaviour.

5.2.38   **Pool safety operating procedures (PSOPs)** consisting of NOPs and an EAP should be known, applied and practised, as relevant, by all staff working in the lesson.

5.2.39 NOPs are simply the day-to-day organisational systems based on risk assessment and would typically include information relating to:

- pool design and depth
- potential areas of risk
- arrangements for lessons
- responsibility for safety
- staffing levels and qualifications
- supervision and student conduct
- arrangements for students with particular needs (eg very young children, those with special educational needs and disabilities [SEND] or medical conditions)
- pool safety and equipment
- clothing and equipment
- maximum numbers
- first aid provision
- water quality.

5.2.40 EAPs should establish who assumes leadership in managing emergencies and the action to be taken in relation to such issues as:

- serious injury to a bather
- dealing with casualties in the water
- sudden overcrowding in a public pool
- sudden lack of water clarity
- disorderly behaviour
- emergency evacuation due to:
  - fire alarm
  - bomb threats
  - power failure
  - structural failure
  - toxic-gas emission.

5.2.41 Safety notices should be clear and understandable to users who may have difficulties with reading and brought to the attention of the students.

5.2.42 Separate school **changing areas** should be made available where possible. Where this is not possible, changing times different to the public should be attempted. Whatever the circumstances, changing rooms should be **adequately supervised**. Ideally, a male and female member of staff should accompany each class in order to fully supervise the changing areas. Staffing pressures may mean a known adult volunteer of the opposite gender is used. They would need disclosure and vetting clearance due to the situation of supervising children while undressing. Where this level of staffing is not available, it may be possible to enlist the cooperation of pool staff to supervise the other changing room. This arrangement, through the pool management, needs to be assured and consistent. If only one suitable adult is available, they would need to establish procedures to deal with any emergency in the other changing room. If these arrangements are not to the school's satisfaction, it may be necessary to combine classes and take single-gender groups, where appropriate staffing allows this. Adults supervising students need to be familiar with, and adhere to, the relevant safeguarding policies.

General information on changing provision can be found in *Section 2: Safe Teaching Principles, paragraphs 2.3.74-2.3.81, pages 34-35,* and *Section 3: Safe Management Principles, paragraph 3.7.2, page 120.*

5.2.43 Consideration needs to be given to the fact that, during an **emergency evacuation**, students will have bare feet, little clothing and may be outside for an extended period of time. Pool operators should make provisions for these factors in their EAPs. Some pool management systems provide, for example, space blankets and, in some instances, rubberoid surfaces near the emergency exits.

5.2.44 Access to a **telephone** giving direct contact from the pool to the emergency services is essential. The system for providing this access should be guaranteed during all hours when the pool is in use.

5.2.45 Teachers should **count** the students off the poolside and **walk around the pool** at the end of each aquatics lesson to ensure it is clear of all students.

General information on the use of swimming pools can be found in *Section 3: Safe Management Principles, paragraphs 3.7.19-3.7.34, pages 123-124.*

Diving

People

5.2.46 **Prior** to any dives being taught, students should have developed watermanship, confidence and competence in aquatic practices, followed by safe feet-first and head-first entries from the poolside.

5.2.47 Students should check the diving area is clear before commencing any dive.

Context

5.2.48 Where diving is to form part or all of a lesson, the pool **freeboard** (the distance from the poolside to the water surface) should be less than 0.3m with a sufficient **forward clearance** (the horizontal distance at which the minimum depth of water is maintained) typically in excess of 7.5m.

5.2.49 Where diving provision is made in a main pool rather than a diving pit, the designated diving area should be **clearly defined** and other swimmers discouraged or prohibited from entering that area.

5.2.50 The water **depth for diving**, other than racing starts, should ideally be standing height plus arms and fingers fully extended. However, this advice is exemplary as some pools do not provide sufficient depth to meet this requirement for tall students. Where this is not practicable, the deepest water available, with a minimum depth of 1.8m, should be used with the exercise of additional caution. Staff should ensure dives are executed into the deeper end of the swimming pool as a matter of routine safety.

5.2.51 Prolonged underwater swimming after a dive should be discouraged.

5.2.52 Generally, entry into water less than 1.5m in depth may best be effected from a sitting position on the side of the pool.

5.2.53 Care should be taken with feet-first entry jumping, which may cause damage to the ankles, arches of the feet or lower spine from striking the pool bottom with force in shallow water. Variables affecting safe entry in such a way include:

- the extent of knee bend
- water depth
- freeboard height
- size and weight of the student.

5.2.54 Progression in diving, following feet-first and head-first entries, is normally via the plunge dive. As well as students being taught the technique, they should also appreciate when to use the dive.

5.2.55 Anyone commencing a swimming race with a plunge-dive entry should be checked for their competence to do so safely, especially when the entry is from a starting block.

5.2.56 Diving blocks should always be fitted at the deepest end of the swimming pool.

5.2.57 Where vertical plain header dives are taught, the water should be a minimum of 3m in depth.

Organisation

5.2.58 The depth of a dive is affected by:

- the height from which the dive is made – higher will be deeper
- the angle of entry – a steeper entry leads to a deeper dive
- flight distance – a short flight leads to a deeper dive
- the strength and drive from the diver's legs.

5.2.59 Students should be thoroughly familiar with the water space and environment in which they learn to dive. Diving should never take place in unknown waters.

5.2.60 To avoid the risk of collisions during simultaneous dives, there should be:

- sufficient pool space
- sufficient forward clearance
- no underwater obstructions
- clearly understood exit routes from the entry area on resurfacing from a dive.

5.2.61 Good class organisation and discipline are paramount in diving activities. Staff and students need to be fully aware of the additional safety implications for diving, over and above those for general aquatic activities, to ensure safe practice. These include the following:

- Divers should not wear goggles.
- Toes should be curled over the pool edge for each dive.
- Dives should be performed from a stationary position.
- Arms should be extended beyond the head with the hands clasped for a safe entry.

5.2.62 Competitive shallow-entry dives should be taught into water no less than 1.8m in depth. When students have achieved the standard of the ASA Competitive Start Award and can execute a competitive shallow dive consistently, they may execute such a dive in water of no less than 0.9m in depth.

5.2.63   Raised starting blocks for racing dives should only be used by capable swimmers who have received instruction on the techniques required and with the approval of school staff. It is not recommended that raised blocks are used for school swimming instruction.

5.2.64   Vertical poolside dives and diving from a board should not form part of mainstream school swimming unless only delivered in a specialist environment by a qualified diving teacher.

5.2.65   Where students participate in board diving, additional safety factors should be applied, including the following:

- Diving boards should be checked before use to ensure security of footing will not be affected by damage or slipperiness.

- Only one student should be allowed on any part of the board at any time.

- Both the student and staff should check the water is clear of other swimmers or obstruction.

- Progression should be from low level to greater heights.

- Dives of 3m or more require the water surface to be disturbed, by a specialist facility or hosepipe with a spray nozzle played across the surface to identify the water level and avoid mistiming of entry, possibly causing injury.

Lifesaving

Organisation

5.2.66   When teaching lifesaving, only reaching with a pole or similar item and throwing rescues should be taught to children below eight years of age. **Contact rescues** should not be taught to children under 13 years of age.

5.2.67   Advice on teaching packs and awards for lifesaving at the appropriate key stages in primary and secondary education is available from the RLSS, STA and ASA.

Personal survival skills

Organisation

5.2.68   It is important that personal survival skills are taught. Students should understand the **effects and dangers of cold water**, their ability to assess a survival situation and the application of the principles of personal survival.

5.2.69   **Swimming in clothes** differs considerably from styles and techniques used in normal swimming lessons. Students should be taught how to conserve energy and body heat through the use of gentle swimming movements and holding particular body positions. Wearing everyday clothing helps simulate real situations.

Swimming in open water

People

5.2.70   Swimming in open water needs to be closely supervised by **competent staff**, able to affect rescue and resuscitation procedures.

5.2.71   Staff must be able to rescue any swimmer in difficulty. Depending on the nature of the event, this may involve the need for lifeguards with an **open-water endorsement**.

Context

5.2.72 **Adequate clothing** needs to be available for swimmers to change into when they leave the water.

5.2.73 Appropriate **footwear** is advisable when swimming in open water in order to avoid the likelihood of foot injuries.

5.2.74 Before allowing anyone to enter the water, precautions should be taken to check:

- for easy entry and exit points
- for underwater obstructions
- the depth of the water
- the extent of weed
- the composition of the bottom
- the likelihood of hazardous rubbish
- for any possible effects of current, tidal flow, wave height or wind-chill factor
- water traffic is not impinging on safety.

5.2.75 While the extent of pollution is difficult to establish, a professional judgement may need to be made on the quality of water and its suitability for recreational or competitive swimming.

Organisation

5.2.76 **Inform parents** and obtain their consent before offering open-water swimming to students.

5.2.77 Carry out a thorough **risk assessment** prior to allowing open-water swimming to take place. Consultation with agencies that have local knowledge of the venue needs to be part of the risk assessment wherever possible. A local weather forecast is an important part of the risk assessment.

5.2.78 **Brief groups** thoroughly and make them aware:

- that the temperature of open water is often less than what they would be familiar with in a swimming pool
- they should proceed with caution when first entering the water
- of set boundaries that should be clearly visible and over a manageably contained area
- they should not venture outside the boundaries
- weaker swimmers should keep to areas where it is easier to stand.

5.2.79 Supervising staff should be positioned around the boundaries to **monitor** swimmers in relation to:

- ability
- cold
- fatigue
- discomfort
- fear
- preventing any excursions outside the boundaries
- the effects of sun, wind, tide, sea state, current or weather forecast.

5.2.80	Regular **head counts** should be standard practice.
5.2.81	A review of whether to continue the event or occasion should be made according to the particular circumstances at any given time.
5.2.82	As well as the possible need for additional lifeguards, consideration should be given to the benefit of safety boats, rescue equipment, provision of facilities to treat hypothermia, the presence of emergency services and changing accommodation.
5.2.83	Additional information may be obtained from the ASA, STA and MCA.

Hydrotherapy pools

5.2.84	Hydrotherapy pools in special schools provide the opportunity for students to exercise in warm water. This is of particular benefit to students with complex physical difficulties.

People

5.2.85	Hydrotherapy-pool activity programmes usually involve **team teaching** by the class teacher, learning support/care assistants and a physiotherapist.
5.2.86	Whether a specialist swimming teacher is present is an issue to be determined by the particular circumstances.
5.2.87	As hydrotherapy pools tend to be shallow in depth and small in size, it is not usual to require a lifeguard to be present. However, the staff involved need to be confident and have the competence to complete any water-based rescue that may become necessary.
5.2.88	A **pool watcher** should be present on the poolside, whose sole duty is to observe all pool activities and draw attention to any problems developing in the water.

Context

5.2.89	Due to the temperature, it is recommended that **regular maintenance** of the plant, and filtration and sterilisation systems, and a comprehensive programme of water testing are carried out to ensure the safe use of hydrotherapy pools.

Organisation

5.2.90	The adult:student ratio should not be determined in accordance with any swimming-specific written guidelines that may exist. A safe ratio can only be determined by carefully examining individual students' medical profiles and healthcare plans in conjunction with relevant medical staff.
5.2.91	As the pool will be used by students with complex physical difficulties, particular attention should be given to the development of risk-management schemes for:

- lifting and carrying students
- transporting students between the changing rooms and the pool
- dressing/undressing areas and support staff
- emergency equipment and procedures.

5.3 Athletics Activities

Useful website

5.3.1 See the UK Athletics (UKA) website for detailed guidance on the safe organisation and risk assessment of age-related athletics activities:

UKA	www.uka.org.uk

General guidance relevant to throwing, jumping and running events

Context

5.3.2 Damaged equipment should never be used.

5.3.3 Equipment should be clean.

5.3.4 Equipment should be safely stored when not being used.

5.3.5 Any equipment that is considered to be unsafe should be labelled and removed from the area.

5.3.6 Great care must be taken if equipment is to be used for a purpose for which it was not primarily designed.

> General information on athletics equipment can be found in *Section 2: Safe Teaching Principles, paragraph 2.3.94*, page 36.

5.3.7 Allow sufficient **space** between participants to avoid collisions.

5.3.8 Condition, limit or abandon activities if the **grass surface** of the work area is wet.

5.3.9 Check that the work areas for approach and release in throwing events, take-off in jumping events and all running areas are stable, level, smooth and non-slip.

Organisation

5.3.10 Teach basic **techniques** thoroughly and through progressive practices (eg standing throws before adding turns and run-up).

5.3.11 Ensure distances and types of event are suitable for the student **age groups** involved (eg for Key Stage 2, short sprinting distances, low hurdles, light throwing implements, feet-to-feet jumping styles).

5.3.12 Students need to be sufficiently mature before progressing from soft, light, low equipment to competition-style implements.

5.3.13 Regularly remind students of required safety procedures as well as correct technical points.

5.3.14 Students should be encouraged to get involved with safety checks to promote good health and safety practice.

5.3.15 Students should be advised not to chew sweets and chewing gum during sessions.

5.3.16 Restrict **multi-event lessons** to a maximum of four activities with only one to be a directly supervised throwing event.

5.3.17	Direct any spectators to specific safety zones.
5.3.18	Any officials need to be appropriately positioned before and during an activity.
5.3.19	Staff and officials in competitive situations need to be competent to supervise the event or activity safely. This is particularly, but not exclusively, important for throwing events, pole vault and any 'Fosbury flop' type of high-jump style.
5.3.20	Auditory and visual **ready and response signals** help heighten student awareness as to what is expected of them at particular times, such as the retrieval of throwing implements, clearance to begin a run-up in a jumping activity or for the start of a running event.

Throwing activities and events

Context

5.3.21	Provide the appropriate **age-related** type, weight and dimensions of throwing implement (eg soft for primary students).
5.3.22	Use only purpose-made hammers with a free spindle and wire in good condition. Do not improvise.
5.3.23	Remind students that a dry grip on the throwing implement is essential.
5.3.24	All throwing implements need to be carried and retrieved at **walking pace**.
5.3.25	Throwing implements should be carried and retrieved singly using two hands (preventing mock throwing actions) with javelins upright and ends protected if possible. (Multiple discuses may be carried in baskets provided the overall weight is not excessive.)
5.3.26	All throwing implements need to be carried back to the throwing line and **never** thrown back.
5.3.27	Implements need to be placed on the ground, not dropped.
5.3.28	Javelins, when not in use, should be placed on a rack or, when a rack is not available, laid flat on the ground.
5.3.29	Ensure **throwing lines** and zones for lessons and competition are clearly identified and demarcated.

Organisation

5.3.30	Ensure procedures for entering throwing zones, in lessons and competition, are known and reinforced.
5.3.31	**Left-handed** discus throwers should be positioned at the left side of a throwing group to minimise the likelihood of injury in the event of an early release.
5.3.32	Those waiting to perform need to stand well behind the throwing line or circle and focus on the thrower until told to move forward.
5.3.33	Throwers in group situations should throw **sequentially** and in a predetermined order.
5.3.34	Wide margins of error should be allowed for the release and direction of throws.

5.3.35 Staff and students need to check possible lines of flight are clear before staff allow throws to commence.

5.3.36 Throwers need to remain **behind** the throwing line until told to retrieve their implement.

5.3.37 In higher-level competition and when students employ a turn technique in training or competition, safety nets and cages that meet UKA standards should be used.

Jumping activities and events

People

5.3.38 Students need to understand and be competent in basic **feet-to-feet** jumping before progressing to more advanced techniques.

Context

5.3.39 Brightly coloured boards placed on the runway help indicate when jumping is not allowed.

5.3.40 Round bars are recommended for feet-to-body high-jump styles.

5.3.41 The uprights for flexi-bars need to be secured so as not to collapse on jumpers.

5.3.42 Multi-unit high-jump landing beds should:

- be large enough to extend beyond the uprights
- conform to UKA standards when used for competition
- be deep and dense enough to prevent bottoming out
- be fitted with a coverall to prevent athletes falling between the modules
- be inspected regularly.

5.3.43 Take-off markers or zones should be used to indicate take-off positions in the early stages of learning high jump to ensure the bar is negotiated at the midpoint and landing occurs in the centre of the sand pit or landing module.

5.3.44 Fibre-glass vaulting poles need to be checked regularly for damage and:

- discarded if cracked or spiked
- stored suitably to prevent bending
- be used only in planting boxes with a sloping back plate (not vertical).

5.3.45 Only suitably qualified staff should teach students how to bend a vaulting pole.

5.3.46 Regularly dig and rake sand landing areas to avoid compacted sections.

5.3.47 Maintain sand levels to the top of the pit and level with the runway.

5.3.48 Sharp sand – non-caking – should be used and be at least 30cm deep to prevent jarring on landing.

5.3.49 **Check** sand areas for fouling and dangerous objects.

5.3.50 Ensure take-off boards are flush with the runway.

5.3.51	Sand areas are only suitable for horizontal and low-level jumping for height involving feet-to-feet landings and with no danger from wooden or concrete surrounds.
5.3.52	Landing areas need to be sufficiently large to accommodate all levels of ability.
5.3.53	Digging and raking implements should be left stored at least 3m from the landing pit and with prongs and sharp edges into the ground.
5.3.54	Students should be taught how and when to dig and rake the pits.
5.3.55	Multiple take-off boards are helpful to ensure jumpers of different abilities land safely in the sand area.

Running activities and events

Context

5.3.56	Hurdles for competition need to conform to UKA standards and be positioned properly so as to **topple over** if struck. Hurdling should never be allowed in the wrong direction, with the struts on the far side of the hurdle.
5.3.57	Finishing tapes, historically used to indicate winners, should be avoided wherever possible.
5.3.58	Spiked shoes need to be stored and placed with the spikes facing down.
5.3.59	**Firearms** are not acceptable as starting devices in schools, with the exception of very small-calibre cap-firing pistols. Clapperboards or similar implements are preferred.
5.3.60	The Olympic 380 BBM imitation handgun, the most commonly used model of imitation handgun used by lower graded starters, clubs and schools, has been reclassified as a prohibited weapon, which now requires the individual to hold a Firearms Certificate with authority to possess the particular weapon on it. It is illegal to possess one of these handguns. Where starting pistols are used in competition, UKA risk assessment guidelines should be fully complied with.
5.3.61	**Cross-country** courses should be based on:

- ease of supervision
- maximum visibility of participants by staff
- suitability for the age and capability of the runners
- allowance for tracking the slowest runner
- a wide start and long clear approach before any constriction of the course
- ease of counting runners out and in.

Indoor athletics

Context

5.3.62	Throwing implements should be made from plastic, foam or rubber to prevent damage or injury.
5.3.63	Clearly designated training and competition areas should be identified, where relevant.

5.3.64	Work areas need to be clear of obstructions.

5.3.65   Ideally, walls should have no indentations or projections, but where these exist, they should either be protected or care should be taken that activities with likely collisions or tripping hazards are conducted at a safe distance.

Organisation

5.3.66   Participants should be taught how to use rebound boards safely.

5.3.67   Horizontal jumping activities should have a restricted run-up (typically four strides) with mats (but not weight-absorbing mattresses – 'crash/safety mats') to cushion landings. Thin 'crash/safety mats' are not suitable, and thicker gymnastics mats should only be used for standing jumps or jumps from very short approaches. Care should be taken that the mats do not move on the floor and that tripping over the edge of a mat at take-off is avoided.

5.3.68   The programme of activities should be appropriate to the available working space.

Sports days

People

5.3.69   All officials should receive appropriate **induction** in safe procedures with rules and safety reminders appended to the recording sheet or clipboard.

Context

5.3.70   Activity areas need to be clearly laid out.

5.3.71   Throwing areas should be roped off at some distance from the throwing sector lines.

Organisation

5.3.72   Spectators and athletes need to be marshalled effectively.

5.3.73   Strict rules should be enforced for the safe movement to and from events.

5.3.74   A suitable balanced programme of events should be based on the students' experience and abilities.

5.3.75   Throwing implements need to be stored safely and supervised at all times.

5.3.76   First aid arrangements should be known by all.

5.3.77   Water stations should be easily available.

5.3.78   Appropriate precautions need to be taken to protect spectators and athletes from the harmful effects of the sun.

5.4 Combat Activities

5.4.1   Schools are increasingly offering a range of combat activities to enrich and expand both curricular and school-sport provision.

5.4.2   Combat activities involve outmanoeuvring an opponent, often utilising physical means, using a series of techniques and skills having their origins in martial combat.

5.4.3   Although many combat activities are regulated by a **recognised governing body** under the auspices of the national sports agency, others are not, although this does not necessarily imply unsafe practice.

5.4.4   Some local authorities (LAs) have introduced 'in-house' training programmes to accredit specified combat and self-defence instructors.

5.4.5   Combat activities taught in schools include:

- boxing
- fencing
- judo
- martial arts
- self-defence
- wrestling.

5.4.6   They take place in a range of locations, including:

- gymnasia
- sports halls
- dojos
- specialist rings for boxing and wrestling
- specialist pistes for fencing.

General issues

People

5.4.7   As the potential for injury is high, coaches appointed to teach combat sports in schools should have appropriate **accreditation** that reflects:

- technical and subject knowledge through the relevant governing body of sport qualifications
- coaching expertise
- familiarity with working with young people
- officiating skills in accordance with the rules of the activity
- attendance at a sports coach UK 'Safeguarding and Protecting Children' workshop or reference to the relevant governing body of sport list of instructors to ensure approval to work with young people.

5.4.8   Where appropriate, schools are advised to contact the relevant national, regional and/or county agencies to check the coach's **suitability** to deliver contact sports in schools.

5.4.9 Schools should check the coach has a **valid licence** to coach the combat activity and that this provides appropriate indemnity insurance to complement the public liability cover provided by schools.

5.4.10 **Mixed combat** sports lessons are becoming common, providing a 'taster' of several different sports. Where schools offer more than one combat sport in any one lesson, the coach should be appropriately qualified in each of the activities involved. This form of providing experience of different combat sports within a single lesson is not to be confused with **'mixed martial arts'** (more commonly known as 'cage fighting'), which **afPE does not condone** in any way.

5.4.11 Students should be made aware of their **personal responsibilities** for safety in combat sports, including:

- adequate preparation

- participation according to the rules

- accepting the official's decisions

- respecting their peers, coach and working environment

- avoiding being excessively competitive

- not losing their temper during activity

- contributing to the risk assessment and safe learning environment according to their age, ability and awareness

- wearing appropriate clothing, footwear and personal protective equipment (PPE) for the specific activity

- tying long hair back

- cutting nails short

- removing potentially hazardous personal effects

- not chewing food, sweets or gum as this may have fatal consequences.

5.4.12 Self-discipline and showing respect for other students and staff are essential in all combat sports.

Context

5.4.13 Combat arenas should:

- be sited in a clear area away from walls and other obstacles

- be large enough to allow safe activity

- be level, even and clean, with a non-slip surface

- provide secure footing.

5.4.14 Mats should:

- be inspected regularly

- comply with BS EN requirements for the specific activity; gymnastics mats are inappropriate.

5.4.15 Faulty equipment should be clearly marked and removed from use until repaired or replaced.

5.4.16 Potentially hazardous equipment (eg fencing foils) should be made secure and stored in a safe place that prevents unauthorised access.

Organisation

5.4.17   It is advisable to **inform parents** before introducing combat activities into the programme.

5.4.18   All combat activities should be appropriate to the age, ability, strength, stamina and experience of the students involved.

5.4.19   A progressive scheme of work is essential.

5.4.20   Basic **skills and rules** should be taught before competitive combat is introduced.

5.4.21   The number in the group should be appropriate to the space available.

5.4.22   **Mixed-gender** practice is allowed in some combat sports, but mixed-gender competition is not allowed.

5.4.23   An adequate warm-up is important.

5.4.24   Rules need to be applied fully and consistently.

5.4.25   Staff should not compete with students.

5.4.26   Great care and forethought should be given to demonstrations on students such that technical guidance is provided without placing the student in an unsafe situation. Static demonstrations are acceptable, with careful consideration given to dynamic demonstrations involving students.

5.4.27   It is recommended that weapons are **not used** in martial arts in the school context and are preferably introduced in the club situation.

5.4.28   Correct instruction is important where strike pads are used to practise punching and kicking, both on the way the pads should be held and the impact allowed. Gloves should be worn, to avoid potential soft-tissue damage, where relevant to the activity.

5.4.29   Where take-downs and throws are practised, students first need to be taught to land safely (break falls), and mats need to be used.

Specific activity guidance

5.4.30   **Where schools select to offer specific combat sports, the general guidance set out above will apply, as well as the more activity-specific guidance that follows**.

Boxing

Useful websites

Amateur Boxing Association of England (ABAE)	www.abae.co.uk
Amateur Boxing Scotland	www.amateurboxingscotland.co.uk
British Medical Association (BMA)	www.bma.org.uk/ap.nsf/Content/boxing
Irish Amateur Boxing Association (IABA)	www.iaba.ie
Welsh Amateur Boxing Association (WABA)	http://welshboxingassociation.org

5.4.31 Boxing involves two participants of similar weight fighting each other with gloved fists in a series of 1–3-minute rounds. Technical points are scored according to the accuracy, frequency and direction of blows landed on the opponent. If there is no stoppage before an agreed number of rounds, a winner is determined through a points accumulation. If the opponent is knocked down and unable to get up before the referee counts to 10, or if the opponent is deemed too injured to continue, a knockout is the result.

5.4.32 The BMA, as a body of medical experts, does not support the teaching or coaching of, or any participation in, boxing due to evidence indicating detrimental effects upon health.

5.4.33 Schools may wish to consider only **non-contact** versions of boxing, and accreditation is now available to coach this through the appropriate home country governing body of sport. Parents can then make the decision as to whether their child progresses to contact boxing within a club situation.

5.4.34 Schools should ensure all parents and students involved are aware of, and accept, the inherent and obvious risks.

5.4.35 Students should wear particular items of equipment **at all times**, including a mouth guard, protective hand bandages, gloves, cup protectors, force-absorbent headgear and a shirt to absorb sweat. Women boxers are also required to wear breast protectors. All equipment should meet national requirements.

> **General information on personal protective equipment can be found in**
> *Section 2: Safe Teaching Principles, paragraphs 2.3.56–2.3.60, pages 31–32,*
> **and** *Section 3: Safe Management Principles, paragraphs 3.5.66–3.5.92,*
> **pages 91–95.**

5.4.36 The ABAE provides guidance on the safe delivery of boxing in schools, including non-contact versions of the sport (www.abae.co.uk/aba/index.cfm/coaches/coaching-resources).

Fencing

Useful websites

British Fencing	www.britishfencing.com
England Fencing	www.englandfencing.org.uk
Welsh Fencing	www.welshfencing.org

5.4.37 The three common forms of fencing are epee, foil and sabre. Safety measures need to be thoroughly addressed in order to minimise the risks involved in these potentially dangerous activities.

Fencing with metal weapons

5.4.38 The rules and safety requirements of British Fencing, the relevant governing body of sport, need to be strictly observed.

5.4.39 Pistes (the area of play), for both competition and practice, need to be well **spaced out** at least 1.5m apart.

5.4.40   There should be a clear **run-off** at each end of a piste for the safety of participants and spectators.

5.4.41   Almost all fencing injuries are caused by broken blades. All swords should be checked regularly by knowledgeable staff. It is essential that only swords in **good condition** are used. Others should be condemned or taken out of use until repaired.

5.4.42   Students under the age of 10 should fence with weapon blades of size 0, and those under 14 should normally fence with weapon blades of size 3 or smaller, corresponding to the competition requirements for their age. Adult-sized blades (size 5) are to be used by all fencers of 13 years and older.

5.4.43   The points of swords need to be covered with purpose-made protective tips.

5.4.44   Any electrical equipment used for scoring should be stored safely and observed carefully while in use.

5.4.45   Adequate **body protection** is essential and should be worn at all times, both for practice and competition. Students should only participate in fencing activities if they are wearing:

- a plastron

- a mask, complete with bib and effective back spring or 'contour-fit' secured at three points (top and sides of mask), that fits correctly; sub-standard masks are unacceptable; all masks with a back spring need to be fitted with safety back straps

- a jacket long enough to cover the waistband of the trousers by at least 10cm when in the en garde position

- gloves with a gauntlet to cover the cuff of the jacket sleeve and protect the wrist and arm by extending halfway up the sword forearm to ensure a safe overlap

- breeches, mandatory during competition but optional during practice; if trousers are worn, any opening pocket needs to be taped, sewn or zipped closed

- knee-length socks, if wearing breeches, that are always covered by the bottom of the breeches so no bare skin is shown

- shoes with a sole that grips the floor adequately.

In addition, it is compulsory for women to wear breast protectors and strongly recommended that girls wear breast protectors from the age of 10 or from the onset of puberty if earlier.

5.4.46   Right-handed fencers need to wear right-handed garments, which have openings on the left side, and vice versa for left-handed fencers, or they can wear jackets that zip at the back.

5.4.47   Protective clothing should be labelled denoting a safety rating in *newtons (N)* with a minimum for non-electric fencing of 350N for jacket, plastron and breeches. Where electronic scoring apparatus is used, the plastron should be rated 800N for over-13s.

General information on personal protective equipment can be found in *Section 2: Safe Teaching Principles, paragraphs 2.3.56–2.3.60*, pages 31–32, and *Section 3: Safe Management Principles, paragraphs 3.5.66–3.5.92*, pages 91–95.

5.4.48   Students should be taught the basic safety requirements that they **never**:

- run in the salle (unless under the direction of a teacher or coach and then never with a weapon)

- point a weapon at anyone not wearing a mask and correct clothing

- mishandle equipment

- use a blade that shows signs of 'softness' or is badly bent or kinked

- fence against anyone whose blade shows signs of 'softness'

- carry a weapon other than by the pommel with the point towards the floor or by gripping the point with the weapon hanging down vertically, other than when practising or fencing

- remove masks until told to do so by the coach.

GO/FENCE

5.4.49   GO/FENCE is the soft form of the sport using foam or plastic swords and a simple plastic face mask.

5.4.50   Ideally, participants in GO/FENCE activities should wear a long-sleeved top and tracksuit or jogging bottoms. A cloth-covered foam protective tabard for the chest is also recommended, especially for girls.

5.4.51   The simple safety guidelines for GO/FENCE are as follows:

- Check plastic foils have a large rubber button firmly affixed at the tip, that the plastic guard and blade have no cracks and the guard is fitted securely.

- Check there is no excessive bend in the blade and that any slight curvature is in the correct direction, ie downwards (see inside guard for the word 'Thumb' and an arrow indicating where to place the thumb – the blade should be straight, but if not, a slight downward curve is allowable).

- Check the integrity of the plastic mask by ensuring all rivets are in place, especially around the visor, and that the elasticated back strap is properly fixed to the plastic and that the Velcro fastenings are intact and secure.

Judo

Useful website

British Judo Association (BJA)	www.britishjudo.org.uk

5.4.52   Judo involves two participants in a contest where the object is to throw the opponent largely on to their back with considerable force and speed. This scores 'ippon' and ends the contest. It is also possible to score ippon by pinning the opponent to the mat for a period of 25 seconds. In addition to the sought-after ippon, smaller scores are given for less successful throws and hold-downs broken before the 25-second limit.

5.4.53   A minimum ceiling height of 3.5m is needed, with no objects hanging below this level.

5.4.54   The recommended **mat area** is $2m^2$ per student, with more space depending on the type of activity and intensity of practice or 'randori'.

5.4.55   The edge of the mat area should be at least 2m away from any walls, projections or open doors.

More information on the use of mats in judo and martial arts can be found in *Section 3: Safe Management Principles, paragraphs 3.6.58-3.6.59,* pages 119-120.

5.4.56   Whenever possible, judogi (judo suits) should be worn in practice. These are mandatory in competition.

5.4.57   Only bare feet are permitted on the tatami (judo mat).

5.4.58   GCSE syllabuses provide useful guidance for the organisation of judo activities.

5.4.59   **Mixed-gender** practice is permitted but not mixed-gender competition.

5.4.60   Students should not practise throwing techniques while others are practising groundwork skills.

5.4.61   It is essential that students are taught the various ways to submit and that all understand how important it is to accept submission and stop applying technique immediately.

5.4.62   Strangle and armlocks should **not** form part of a school's programme of tuition.

Martial arts

5.4.63   Martial arts involve a diverse number of styles. The activities include:

- aikido
- karate
- kendo
- ju-jitsu
- kung fu
- taekwondo.

Aikido

Useful website

British Aikido Board (BAB)	www.bab.org.uk

5.4.64   Aikido is a martial art that has been described as being as active as tumbling and as elegant and dramatic as fencing. It involves neutralising an attack by using holds and locks that are usually taught by modern/practical or classical/ceremonial methods.

5.4.65   Students should wear a loose tunic and, preferably, the recommended trousers.

5.4.66   Mats should meet the same requirements as for judo. Only bare feet are permitted on the mat area.

5.4.67   The required ceiling height is also the same as for judo (3.5m), with additional clearance if weapons are used.

5.4.68   The recommended mat space is also as for judo – 2m² per student, increasing to 5m² per participant where weapons are used.

5.4.69   Dangerous locks, holds or movements must **not** be taught or practised.

Karate

Useful websites

| British Karate Association (BKA) | www.thebka.co.uk |
| English Karate Federation (EKF) | www.englishkaratefederation.com |

5.4.70   Karate is a Japanese weaponless martial art based on scientific principles that encompass physical culture, character development, self-defence and sport.

5.4.71   There are many different karate organisations in the UK. It is essential that only coaches from **approved organisations** be appointed to lead karate sessions in schools. Details of approved organisations can be obtained from national sports councils. It is recommended that schools contact the approved organisation to ensure the coach is registered with a recognised organisation.

5.4.72   Three square metres per student are required when practising fundamental techniques (kihon) and 4m^2 per student when practising formal exercises (kata).

5.4.73   GCSE and A Level syllabuses can provide useful guidance for the organisation of karate activities.

5.4.74   One hour is the recommended **maximum time** for curriculum time karate sessions, one and a half hours maximum for out-of-hours sessions, and both would usually emphasise technical competence and consist of:

- a warm-up
- fundamental techniques (kihon)
- formal exercise (kata)
- sparring (kumite).

5.4.75   **Non-contact sparring** should be introduced initially with careful progression to touch contact with no reckless fighting ever allowed.

Kendo, kung fu and ju-jitsu

5.4.76   As the potential for harm in these activities is high, school staff are recommended to seek guidance from appropriate organisations (eg LA advisory support services, governing bodies of sport, activity associations) before appointing coaches to deliver these activities in school.

WTF taekwondo

Useful website

| British Taekwondo Control Board (BTCB) | www.btcb.org |

5.4.77   The Korean martial art of taekwondo appeals to young people as it is characterised by fast, high, spinning kicks and energetic movements, often in sequence. In addition, participants learn to apply powerful hand and joint-locking techniques. The risk of injury may be high; to minimise this to an acceptable level, great care should be taken to ensure sound discipline and respect among students.

5.4.78   If mats are used, they need to be joined together securely so they do not move apart.

> More information on the use of mats in martial arts can be found in *Section 3: Safe Management Principles, paragraphs 3.6.58-3.6.59*, pages 119-120.

5.4.79 Headgear and knee pads of the correct size that meet recommended standards should be worn.

> General information on personal protective equipment can be found in *Section 2: Safe Teaching Principles, paragraphs 2.3.56-2.3.60*, pages 31-32, and *Section 3: Safe Management Principles, paragraphs 3.5.66-3.5.92*, pages 91-95

5.4.80 Students need to be matched according to gender, size, weight, age, experience and ability when sparring.

> General information on matching students can be found in *Section 3: Safe Management Principles, paragraphs 3.9.15-3.9.16*, page 137.

5.4.81 Holds and locks should be taught safely, with students made aware of the potential for injury.

Self-defence

5.4.82 Self-defence is a countermeasure that involves defending oneself from physical harm.

5.4.83 Self-defence involves control and restraint, self-protection, and elements of judo and some martial arts. Classes are becoming increasingly popular and, in schools, are mainly targeted at teenage girls in Key Stage 4.

Wrestling

Useful website

British Wrestling Association	www.britishwrestling.org

5.4.84 The rules and philosophy of the internationally agreed freestyle form of wrestling (ie Olympic-style wrestling) are formulated so two wrestlers can engage in hard physical combat without pain and/or injury. This should be the philosophy of all taking part in wrestling activities in schools (ie staff and students).

5.4.85 The minimum ceiling height should be as for judo, at 3.5m high, with no objects hanging below this height.

5.4.86 Any potentially hazardous walls should be padded.

5.4.87 The wrestling area should measure at least 3m², with smooth mats, in good condition, firmly secured together and meeting the Fédération Internationale des Luttes Associées (FILA) standards.

5.4.88 Mats should be **disinfected** before every session to prevent the spread of germs and disease.

5.4.89 No outside footwear should be worn on the mats.

5.4.90 Clothing should be close-fitting without being too restrictive. Swimming costumes are ideal for training, but shorts are unsuitable and should not be worn.

5.4.91   Specifically designed wrestling singlets are recommended for competition.

5.4.92   **Footwear** for beginners should be free of metal lace tags or eyelets and have smooth soles.

5.4.93   Protective arm and knee pads may be worn, and the use of ear guards should be encouraged.

5.4.94   Suitable support protection, in line with wrestling rules, should always be worn by male and female students.

5.4.95   A trained and experienced mat chairperson should be positioned at the edge of the mat during competitions. They should intervene immediately if any move or hold performed is likely to cause pain.

5.4.96   School staff/coaches should adopt the role of mat chairperson during practice sessions.

5.4.97   Moves that put pressure on, or twist, the neck are **extremely hazardous**.

5.4.98   Wrestlers aged under 17 are not allowed to execute any form of full nelson. A scissor lock with the feet crossed on the head, neck or body is forbidden. The nelson is not allowed to be used in female wrestling.

5.4.99   Students under the age of 11 are not allowed to use any form of nelson or bridging.

5.5 Dance Activities, Movement and Creative Development

Useful websites

5.5.1 The following websites provide detailed guidance on the safe organisation and risk assessment of dance activities:

Dance UK	www.danceuk.org
National Dance Teachers Association (NDTA)	www.ndta.org.uk

5.5.2 Dance is a distinct area of experience that offers unique learning opportunities within the school curriculum and is part of physical education and arts education. It contributes to students' physical, aesthetic, artistic, creative, cultural and social development, playing an important role in promoting physical fitness, well-being and maintaining a healthy lifestyle.

5.5.3 There are many forms of dance, which involve a range of styles, movements and techniques. From the Foundation Stage through to the final stages of formal education, children and young adults should be provided with opportunities to acquire and develop technical skills in order to achieve high quality performance and approaches to working creatively that are safely executed. These will range from simple actions to very complex movements, all of which should be introduced progressively.

5.5.4 Although it might be assumed that dance activities are relatively hazard-free in comparison to other areas of the physical education curriculum, comprehensive and informed risk management remains essential.

People

5.5.5 **Staff** teaching dance need to:

- be appropriately qualified or experienced
- be knowledgeable about the structure and function of the human body
- know how to prevent injury
- be aware of emergency procedures and how to implement them.

5.5.6 **Students** should:

- understand the safety procedures related to dance activities
- share in the assessment and management of risks associated with dance activities
- work in bare feet where safe to do so, with any footwear being appropriate for the activity, in good repair and with appropriate support to prevent injury during high-impact activities
- wear clothing that is safe and comfortable while allowing staff to identify any incorrect body alignment
- remove or make safe any personal effects.

Context

5.5.7   **Facilities** should:

- be hazard-free and maintained in good order
- have floors that are non-slip and, preferably, sprung
- have doorways and fire exits kept clear at all times
- have heating and lighting suited to the dance activity.

> **Information on the recommended floor area for dance activities can be found in *Section 3: Safe Management Principles, paragraph 3.7.8*, page 121.**

5.5.8   **Equipment** should be maintained in good order, with any related risks properly assessed and managed.

Organisation

5.5.9   **Teaching** should address:

- the importance of adequate preparation before strenuous exercise and appropriate cooling down afterwards
- the teaching and constant monitoring of correct technique
- group sizes in relation to the available space
- age, ability and experience
- good alignment of the head, spine, hips, knees and feet with no overarching of the back
- the neck not being cramped when rotating the head or taking the head backwards
- avoiding bumping or banging when landing or taking weight on to different body parts
- knees being positioned over toes when bending, with ankles not turning outwards when standing on the toes
- developing lifting or supporting techniques based on the use of progressive practices and ensuring students are sufficiently strong and spatially aware and mature enough to cope with the demands of the activity.

5.5.10   Good practice frequently shows partnerships between schools and external agencies, such as professional dance companies, enhance students' learning and experience. Staff need to be satisfied that any adults involved are suitable and there is an effective system of monitoring and support in place.

5.6 Games Activities

5.6.1 One of the most significant features of games activities, in terms of assessing and managing risk, is that they challenge participants to work in situations that are constantly changing, where the body may be still or moving. Participants are required to demonstrate a range of technical skills with features such as:

- physical contact

- accuracy

- maximal effort

- application of force

- timing.

5.6.2 The degree of challenge faced will vary significantly, depending on the demands of each particular game and the level at which it is played.

5.6.3 The use of a range of equipment in games activities, including projectiles – some of which are very hard – and a range of implements, such as bats and rackets, further complicates the situation. Careful planning, organisation, supervision and the direct involvement of the students in risk assessment and management will assist in significantly reducing risk.

5.6.4 Governing bodies of sport play a central role in developing games activities. They are responsible for establishing the rules, regulations and conventions of their respective activities, as well as providing guidance that supports teachers in ensuring safe practice. Teachers should be familiar with the guidance provided by the specific governing body of sport for each games activity.

General safe-practice issues

People

5.6.5 **Staff** should:

- have a current working knowledge and understanding of the rules, techniques and tactics of the activity they are supervising, teaching or officiating on

- use clear and consistent instructions and appropriate vocabulary

- know and apply the **rules** stringently and consistently

- be aware that collisions between players can occur during competitive practices and matches and ensure the correct teaching progressions have been followed.

5.6.6 **Students** should:

- be taught the risks inherent in the different types of games activity

- be fully involved in the risk assessment and risk-management processes

- be strongly advised to wear the appropriate **personal protective equipment** (PPE) according to the likelihood of contact with other players, whether hard projectiles are used or there is unpredictability in terms of speed and force; helmets should comply with official standards, where relevant

- wear kit and additional clothing appropriate to the activity and weather conditions with footwear that is in good repair, appropriate for the activity, close-fitting and provides secure footing

- be taught to carry equipment safely

- communicate with each other to ensure others are ready before activity begins

- always play within the **spirit and rules** of the game, to reduce levels of risk to themselves and others.

Context

5.6.7   **Equipment** should be:

- **stored** in a safe manner and secured appropriately when not in use

- fit for purpose and meet students' needs, abilities and developmental stages

- maintained in **good condition** through repair or replacement and not used if damaged

- appropriate to the playing surface (eg using a softer ball on a hard play area) and the capability of the players

- of the correct size and weight for the age, ability and category of player.

5.6.8   Inflatable balls should be inflated to the correct pressure and free from splits and tears.

5.6.9   **Goalposts and nets** need to be secured so as not to topple over, in good condition with all necessary bolts in place, and have protective padding applied where relevant, taking note of governing body of sport guidelines.

5.6.10   **Facilities** should:

- be suitable for the activity and the needs of all students, such as those with reduced mobility

- be **checked regularly** for items that may create risk to the students' safety, including:
  - holes, significantly uneven surfaces, stones, glass, sharp plastic shards, animal excrement and unsecured goalposts on outdoor grass or artificial pitches
  - significantly uneven surfaces, excessive grit or silt, missing post socket covers and sharp fencing projections on hard play areas
  - excessive dust, wet patches, slippery surfaces, uneven surfaces, hazardous projections, unprotected windows, low-level mirrors or fixed equipment that encroaches on to the playing area on indoor courts

- be regularly maintained to provide a safe working environment

- be kept free of all equipment not in use during the activity

- provide a suitable **run-off** distance between the playing area and the perimeter of the working space, typically 1–2m depending on the sport, but reference should be made to 'Comparative Sizes of Sports Pitches and Courts' (Sport England); where such a run-off space is not possible, the activity rules and organisation need to be adjusted accordingly or the activity abandoned.

5.6.11   **Organisation** should ensure:

- weather conditions do not affect safety (eg on a damp or frosty morning, the risk of slipping on a grass or hard play area is increased, or the position and brightness of the sun affecting the students' vision)

- rules are applied consistently to provide a safe context

- progression is provided through conditioned practices and mini games that match the age, experience, ability and confidence of the students involved

- particular care and well-structured development are applied where contact in the sport is involved and competition is introduced.

Additional safety advice for invasion games

5.6.12   'Invasion games' is a collective term applied to team games in which the objective is to attack and defend parts of the playing area with the aim of scoring more goals or points than the opposition. They include fast-moving activity, frequently involve physical contact and, in some games, hard implements. Consequently, the most common causes of accidents include:

- unintended collision with other players

- being struck by a hard implement or ball

- poor application of technique, such as when tackling.

Association football/soccer

Useful websites

The Football Association (FA)	www.TheFA.com
Football Association of Wales (FAW)	www.faw.org.uk
Irish Football Association	www.irishfa.com
Scottish Football Association	www.scottishfa.co.uk

Context

5.6.13   Care needs to be taken in maintaining studded and bladed **boots** to an appropriate safety standard.

5.6.14   **Shin pads** offer protection to the lower leg and should be worn for competitive matches and whenever there is a risk of injury.

5.6.15   Halls with hazardous projections, unprotected windows, low-level mirrors or fixed equipment that encroaches on to the playing area should not be used for indoor football.

Basketball

Useful websites

basketballscotland	www.basketball-scotland.com
Basketball Wales	www.basketballwales.com
England Basketball	www.englandbasketball.com

People

5.6.16   Players should keep fingernails well trimmed.

Context

5.6.17   The court perimeter should be free from hazard with a safe zone of at least 1m around the edge.

5.6.18   Protruding **obstacles** should be removed or made safe behind and in line with the backboards. Where this is impracticable, careful officiating and management of the situation is essential.

5.6.19   Backboards should have an overhang of 1.25m on match courts and 0.75m on practice courts.

Gaelic games

Useful website

| Gaelic Athletic Association (GAA) | www.gaa.ie |

Context

5.6.20   In all hurling games and practice sessions, it is mandatory for all players up to and including under-21 grade to wear a **helmet** with a facial guard.

5.6.21   GAA policy with regard to the use of hurling helmets is that they should comply with IS 355 (ie the official hurling helmet specification that was set out by the National Standards Authority of Ireland [NSAI] in 2006).

Handball

Useful websites

England Handball	www.englandhandball.com
Scottish Handball	www.scottishhandball.com
British Handball Association	www.britishhandball.com

Context

5.6.22   Goalposts – fixed and portable – should not be improvised; they should comply with recognised safety standards and be made **secure** at all times in such a manner that they cannot fall forwards or backwards for any reason.

5.6.23   The court perimeter should be free from hazard with a safety zone surrounding the playing court of at least 1m along the sidelines and behind the goal lines. Protruding obstacles should be removed or made safe behind the lines of the court.

5.6.24   A safe, non-slip playing area should be maintained, particularly in attacking areas where perspiration from players making contact with the ground may constitute a hazard.

Organisation

5.6.25   Clear instruction should be given at all times, ensuring practices are well organised and that shooting drills in particular follow the correct progressions under supervision.

5.6.26   The normal **playing time** for teams:

- 16 years and above is two halves of 30 minutes with a half-time break of 10 minutes
- 12–16 years is two halves of 25 minutes with a 10-minute half-time break
- 8–12 years is two halves of 20 minutes with a 10-minute break.

5.6.27   In festivals and tournaments, the playing time equivalent of two full-length matches played in one day should not be exceeded.

5.6.28   Single-period playing times of up to 10 minutes are frequently played by teams in the 8–12 years age group. In the 12–16 age groups, teams frequently play single periods of 12–16 minutes.

Hockey

Useful websites

England Hockey	www.englandhockey.co.uk
Scottish Hockey	www.scottish-hockey.org.uk
Ulster Hockey	www.ulsterhockey.com
Hockey Wales	http://hockeywales.org.uk/

People

5.6.29   Goalkeepers should try to remain on their feet whenever possible.

Context

5.6.30   Shin pads and mouth guards are highly recommended for match play and competitive practices and mandatory at junior representative level.

5.6.31   Goalkeepers need to be suitably equipped and protected with:

- pads and kickers
- gauntlet gloves
- body protectors
- a full helmet
- a throat guard.

5.6.32   Playing surfaces – whether grass or synthetic – need to be true and flat.

Organisation

5.6.33   Players should seek to develop and exercise good stick and ball control at all times.

5.6.34   Controlled pushing should be well established before the introduction of hitting.

Lacrosse

Useful websites

English Lacrosse	www.englishlacrosse.co.uk
Lacrosse Scotland	www.lacrossescotland.com
Welsh Lacrosse Association (WLA)	www.lacrossewales.co.uk

People

5.6.35   Players should protect their hands and wrists with suitably padded gloves/gauntlets.

Context

5.6.36   Head protection is recommended for men's lacrosse, but is not acceptable for women's lacrosse. **Mouth guards** are recommended in both versions of the game.

5.6.37   Goalkeepers should be suitably protected with PPE for both the head and body.

Netball

Useful websites

England Netball	www.england-netball.co.uk
Netball Scotland	www.netballscotland.com
Welsh Netball	www.welshnetball.co.uk

People

5.6.38   Players should keep fingernails short and well trimmed.

Context

5.6.39   Posts need to be stable, with suitably weighted bases, where used, which should not project on to the court area.

5.6.40   During competitive matches, **gloves** may only be worn at the discretion of the umpire.

5.6.41   There should be at least 2m of space between adjacent courts.

Rugby football (league and union)

Useful websites

Rugby Football League (RFL)	www.rfl.uk.com
Rugby Football Union (RFU) (England)	www.rfu.com
Scottish Rugby	www.scottishrugby.org
Ulster Rugby	www.ulsterrugby.com
Welsh Rugby Union (WRU)	www.wru.co.uk

Context

5.6.42   Goalpost uprights should be protected by padding.

5.6.43   Corner flags should be flexible and sufficiently high so as not to constitute a hazard to falling players.

5.6.44   **Mouth guards** are strongly recommended for all players at all levels and mandatory at junior representative level. The wearing of other forms of PPE (eg shin pads, shoulder pads, padded helmets) should be encouraged following appropriate risk assessment.

5.6.45   A suitable playing surface is essential and should be soft enough to safely accommodate falls during tackles.

Organisation

5.6.46   **Contact** versions of the game should only be introduced and managed by suitably experienced staff and coaches following recognised teaching progressions, guidelines and governing body of sport (RFU and RFL) regulations.

5.6.47   Mixed-gender competition is generally suitable for children of primary age, but is not appropriate for secondary-age students.

Additional safety information for net/wall and racket games

5.6.48   Net/wall and racket games are comparatively safe compared to other types of game, but injuries do occur, predominantly involving eye damage. The most common causes of accidents include:

- being struck by a racket or fast-moving missile
- tripping or slipping
- collision with obstacles, equipment or another player
- crossing a court when in use.

Badminton

Useful websites

Badminton England	www.badmintonengland.co.uk
Badminton Ireland	www.badmintonireland.com
BADMINTONscotland	www.badmintonscotland.org.uk
Badminton Wales	www.badmintonwales.net

Context

5.6.49   Rackets with broken strings should not be used.

5.6.50   Nets should be in good condition and free from holes and tears.

5.6.51   Portable posts should be stored and positioned safely.

5.6.52   There should be sufficient space on court to accommodate group practice and to avoid students playing over post bases.

5.6.53   **Background lighting** should permit clear visibility of the shuttle in flight.

Squash and racketball

Useful websites

England Squash and Racketball	www.englandsquashandracketball.com
Irish Squash	www.irishsquash.com
Scottish Squash	www.scottishsquash.org.uk
Squash Wales	www.squashwales.co.uk

People

5.6.54   Protective **eye shields** are advisable to protect from eye injury.

5.6.55   Short-lever rackets are recommended for beginners.

Organisation

5.6.56   Squash is played in a confined area. A **maximum** of six students per court is recommended for coaching and practice sessions.

5.6.57   Safe procedures should be established for entering and leaving the court.

5.6.58   Players should only move on to doubles play when a high standard of singles play has been achieved.

Tennis

Useful websites

Lawn Tennis Association (LTA) (England)	www.lta.org.uk
Tennis Ireland	www.tennisireland.ie
Tennis Scotland	www.lta.org.uk/in-your-area/Scotland/

Context

5.6.59   Lighter, shorter rackets and sponge balls, or other types of soft ball, are recommended where space is limited.

5.6.60   Broken wire surround **fencing** is particularly hazardous, and students should maintain a safe distance until it is repaired.

5.6.61   When posts are removed, **caps** should be used to cover the holes, particularly on multi-use areas.

5.6.62   Courts should be arranged in the same **direction** of play in order to avoid the possibility of being hit by a ball from another game.

Organisation

5.6.63   When students are practising serving, smashing or lobbing, safe procedures should be adopted. During service practice, there should be a maximum of six students behind the baseline. For smashing practice, feeders should be safely positioned, never directly in front of the player practising the smash. Waiting players should remain alert, off the court.

5.6.64   A court may be used safely by two groups for rallying purposes, although care needs to be taken by players moving backwards.

5.6.65   Players should be encouraged not to look round at a serving player, jump over a net or attempt to play strokes outside their designated playing area.

Volleyball

Useful websites

Northern Ireland Volleyball (NIVB)	www.nivb.com
Scottish Volleyball Association (SVA)	www.scottishvolleyball.org
Volleyball England	www.volleyballengland.org

Context

5.6.66 Weighted posts should be made secure by **retaining wires** to adjacent walls above head height; bases should not protrude on to the court.

5.6.67 Free-standing or weighted posts are not acceptable for competitive matches.

5.6.68 All lights above the court should have a guard fitted.

Organisation

5.6.69 Players practising smashes or serves should be well spaced out and direct the ball to empty spaces on the court.

5.6.70 Balls should be rolled back during match play and carried back when both sides of the court are used for practice.

Additional safety information for striking and fielding games

5.6.71 Striking and fielding games involve throwing, running, bowling, catching and striking using an implement. Potential risk is increased when using a hard ball. The most common causes of accidents are:

- being unintentionally struck with a fast-moving hard ball
- being unintentionally struck with a bat or stick
- collision with another player or an item of equipment.

Cricket

Useful websites

Cricket Scotland	www.cricketscotland.com
Cricket Ireland	www.irishcricket.org
England and Wales Cricket Board (ECB)	www.ecb.co.uk
Welsh Cricket Association	www.welshcricket.org

Context

5.6.72 Batters, wicketkeepers and fielders close to the bat should wear appropriate **PPE**, including helmets.

5.6.73 The wicket – grass or synthetic – should be reasonably true and well maintained.

5.6.74 Practice netting should be free of gaps, holes and tears, positioned so players in adjacent areas are not at risk, and preferably include roof netting.

Organisation

5.6.75 Rules administered by the cricket governing bodies of sport relating to **close-in fielding** by junior players should be strictly enforced.

5.6.76 Bowlers should bowl in a controlled order and always ensure the batsman is fully ready.

5.6.77 Waiting batsmen should observe from a safe position.

5.6.78 Care needs to be taken when retrieving balls from the netting and should only happen when bowling has been halted.

5.6.79 A suitable space should be left between the nets and other activity areas to allow for billowing when a ball hits the net at speed.

Rounders, softball and baseball

Useful websites

| BaseballSoftball*UK* (BSUK) | www.baseballsoftballuk.com |
| Rounders England | www.roundersengland.co.uk |

Context

5.6.80 Rounders posts should be of **appropriate height** and have secure bases and rounded tops.

5.6.81 Catching mitts/gloves should be worn as appropriate for baseball and softball.

5.6.82 The ball should not be pitched until all players are fully ready.

5.6.83 Rounders bats should be **carried** when running between bases and never thrown down.

5.6.84 Backstops should consider the use of head and body protection and always position themselves so as to avoid backswing.

Additional safety information for target games

5.6.85 Target games involve striking or projecting a missile, often at great speed, towards a designated area. Consequently, most accidents are caused by:

- other players, spectators or passers-by inadvertently wandering into the line of shot

- waiting players standing too close to the hitter and being struck by an implement

- a lack of skill causing the ball or implement to go off line and possibly into an area where other players or spectators are standing.

Archery

Useful website

| Archery GB | www.archerygb.org |

5.6.86 Archery in schools should always be organised and supervised by suitably qualified and experienced personnel. Advice on training, accreditation and safe procedure can be obtained from the governing body of sport for archery, Archery GB.

Golf

Useful websites

English Golf Union	www.englishgolfunion.org
Golfing Union of Ireland (GUI)	www.gui.ie
Golf Union of Wales	www.golfunionwales.org
Scottish Golf Union (SGU)	www.scottishgolf.org

Context

5.6.87 Golf activities should take place on a golf course or driving range.

5.6.88 When a net is being used for practice:

- a well-maintained special net with fine mesh that is at least 2.5m high and hangs clear of any supports should be used

- only light (airflow) balls should be used when students are practising on both sides of the net

- suitable protective mats should be used when indoors.

Organisation

5.6.89 When practising in group situations, care needs to be taken to ensure all players have sufficient space and can hit the ball in a safe direction.

5.6.90 Individual players should always ensure they have sufficient personal space around them to swing safely.

5.6.91 Balls should only be retrieved on a given signal after all players have completed their shots.

5.6.92 Careful supervision is essential to ensure students' actions and behaviour do not create a hazard for other students.

Additional safety information for other game-type activities

5.6.93 These activities – usually competitive in nature – are normally found in primary school and are frequently used as warm-up activities to develop speed, agility and spatial awareness. Accidents are commonly caused by:

- students inadvertently colliding with each other or an obstacle of some kind

- slipping or falling.

Relay racing and tag games

Context

5.6.94   Clear boundary markings are necessary for tag-type activity.

Organisation

5.6.95   In relays, walls are unsuitable for turning points; lines and marker discs provide a safe alternative.

5.6.96   Highly challenging skills (eg running backwards at high speed) should only be practised with advanced performers.

5.7 Gymnastics and Trampolining Activities

Useful website

5.7.1 See the British Gymnastics (BG) website for detailed guidance on the safe organisation and risk assessment of age-related gymnastics and trampolining activities:

BG	www.british-gymnastics.org

5.7.2 Gymnastics activity involves subjecting the body to a wide experience of movement challenges, which might include at various times managing the body in flight, climbing, hanging, descending, swinging, inverting and balancing, often at some distance from the ground, and rolling on sloping and narrow surfaces. The aim of gymnastics activity is to develop and refine a broad range of movement skills using the floor and large gymnastics apparatus.

5.7.3 It is recognised that work on apparatus provides a potentially more hazardous environment, with the majority of recorded incidents typically involving falls or misjudged descents from gymnastics equipment. However, work at a low level – on the floor or when using benches and mats – requires equally rigorous risk management.

5.7.4 Most primary schools deliver a curricular gymnastics activity programme of study through a task-centred or problem-solving approach, building in some direct teaching where progress and safety issues require a specific focus. The ability of staff to set realistic and appropriate movement challenges based on the existing abilities of their students is key to safety in this approach.

5.7.5 In secondary schools, partly reflecting the specialist physical education training of the staff involved, there is often more recourse to direct instruction of recognised formal gymnastics skills, typically associated with vaulting and agility, that may lead to acrobatic, artistic, rhythmic, tumbling and cheerleading versions of the sport and gymnastics for people with a disability. A sound knowledge of technical progression relating to specified skills is essential to safe practice here.

5.7.6 In addition, trampolining can offer a challenging and developmental gymnastics experience to students of all abilities. Trampolines and trampettes, however, have proved to be unforgiving pieces of equipment in the absence of adequate control of body movement by performers at all levels. Well taught and soundly learned techniques that are well controlled will minimise the likelihood of injury occurring either when moving or assembling the trampoline or performing on it.

5.7.7 Because of the highly technical nature of the activity and the potential risks associated with rebound jumping, trampolines and trampettes are not considered suitable for use in primary schools.

General gymnastics issues

People

5.7.8 Staff should work at a level in gymnastics at which they feel comfortable about their own expertise.

5.7.9 An appropriate BG coaching award is strongly advised for staff wishing to offer formal gymnastics, in primary or secondary schools, through an out-of-hours club when seeking to involve students in, and prepare them for, competitive involvement.

5.7.10   Students should be involved in **moving and assembling apparatus** from the earliest ages in a manner appropriate to their age, ability, physical development and safety awareness. This requires simple manual handling skills to be taught and closely monitored by the teacher.

5.7.11   Clothing should allow free, unrestricted movement without being loose. Very loose clothing may snag on equipment and cause injury.

5.7.12   **Barefoot work** is preferable for gymnastics where the surface is appropriate. Soft-soled, flexible gymnastics slippers are also appropriate to enable the 'feel' of a movement. Thick-soled training shoes are not suitable. Socks should never be worn on a polished surface.

Context

5.7.13   Apparatus should conform to appropriate standards, and be purchased from reliable sources and stored in a manner that allows ready access.

5.7.14   Apparatus should be **inspected** at least annually by a specialist company. The condition of equipment should be monitored regularly by a member of staff responsible for, and experienced in, the teaching of gymnastics and checked visually by the teacher prior to students commencing work.

> **More information on apparatus inspection can be found on the CD-ROM in *Appendix 20: Quality Assurance and Quality Standards on the Inspection and Maintenance of Gymnastics, Fixed Play, Sports and Fitness Equipment.***

5.7.15   Defective equipment must not be used. It needs to be identified, labelled and taken out of use such that it cannot be reintroduced until repaired. Where repair is not feasible, all **condemned** apparatus must be disposed of such that it cannot be reintroduced at all. Keeping condemned apparatus for alternative uses, such as benches or mats for sitting on only, creates a hazard of possible reintroduction that places a serious liability on the school.

5.7.16   The work surface should be clean, free from obstruction or hazard and non-slip, with sufficient space to match the needs of the group and the use of apparatus.

> **General information on gymnastics apparatus can be found in *Section 3: Safe Management Principles*, paragraphs 3.6.33-3.6.36, pages 114-115.**
>
> **Information on the use of mats in gymnastics can be found in *Section 3: Safe Management Principles*, paragraphs 3.6.47-3.6.55, pages 118-119.**

Organisation

5.7.17   On no account should any gymnastics lesson ever be left **unsupervised**.

5.7.18   In the event of the teacher needing to resolve any emergency or organisational problem, activity should stop until the teacher deems it safe to continue.

5.7.19   Organisation of lessons needs to take account of accommodating large groups in a limited space, such as with compact apparatus arrangements or alternating periods of observation with practical involvement.

5.7.20   Lessons would typically progress from the development or consolidation of skills using the floor or mats followed by application and further consolidation of the skills on to apparatus.

5.7.21   Physical **support** may be necessary in the learning of more complex skills, usually to prevent under- or over-rotation. Guidance on physical contact should always be followed.

> General information on physical contact can be found in *Section 2: Safe Teaching Principles, paragraphs 2.3.186-2.3.191, pages 48-49, and Section 3: Safe Management Principles, paragraphs 3.4.92-3.4.100, pages 74-75.*

5.7.22   The frequency, intensity and duration of training sessions for students progressing towards competitive situations need to reflect the physical and mental maturity of those involved.

Trampolining issues

People

5.7.23   As a higher-risk activity, those teaching trampolining are strongly advised to be able to show up-to-date and appropriate **qualifications and expertise** that demonstrate knowledge of the basic skills, techniques and mechanics of the moves they teach.

5.7.24   Staff who wish to teach or coach trampolining to a more advanced level (eg forwards or backwards rotational movement in a horizontal plane) or enter students in competitions should attend courses organised or approved by BG and be **appropriately qualified** with at least a Level 2 coaching award or BG Teachers Trampoline Award. Where alternatives to governing body of sport qualifications are offered, the employer needs to clearly determine the standards and expertise offered by any alternative agency before agreeing to accept them.

5.7.25   With experience, staff can safely supervise a number of trampolines at once. In such instances, the importance of positioning to maximise observation and frequent scanning of the whole activity area, so intervention and advice may be provided, cannot be overemphasised.

5.7.26   Beginners with little or no confidence or previous experience and those learning new skills should always be directly supervised.

5.7.27   Students used as **spotters** may be positioned one or two at each side. It is essential that anyone fulfilling this role is suitably strong, mature, responsible and trained in spotting. Spotters should not distract the performer by giving vocal encouragement.

> More information on spotters can be found on the CD-ROM in *Appendix 24: Summary of British Gymnastics' Advice on the Use of Spotting.*

5.7.28   Suitable clothing is similar to that used in gymnastics, with a long-sleeved top advised to prevent friction burns when performing a front drop.

5.7.29   Non-slip trampoline **slippers** are necessary to prevent toes entering the gaps in the webbed bed. Cotton or wool socks are acceptable though nylon socks on a webbed nylon bed may not provide adequate traction.

Context

5.7.30　Trampolines should be **sited** well away from walls, fire exits and overhead obstructions (a minimum clearance height of 5m is recommended for curriculum and recreational standards, increasing to 8m for competition).

5.7.31　Positioning, assembling and **folding** a trampoline should always be undertaken by at least two trained staff. Where older students, sufficiently mature and strong enough, have been trained, they may carry out the folding and unfolding of trampolines under the close supervision of qualified staff ready to give immediate hands-on assistance if needed. There have been several accidents where younger students, lacking the necessary strength and physique, have been left to carry out this task without direct staff involvement. It is important that, in circumstances with such students, qualified staff are directly physically involved as part of the process. Training shoes should be worn when folding or unfolding a trampoline. Clear communication, awareness and a responsible attitude are essential, particularly in the phase where the end of the trampoline has been opened, to ensure it is held with sufficient force to counter the tension of the springs. Elbows and forearms should be kept away from the gap between the folding ends and frame while lowering under control.

5.7.32　During use, roller stands should be stored securely well away from the working area.

5.7.33　The frame and springs or cables should be covered by fixed **coverall pads**, which should be checked regularly for wear and tear.

5.7.34　**Non-slip mats** of a suitable thickness and consistency should be positioned on the floor to the sides of the trampoline to a distance of about 2m in width, with cushioned 'end decks' placed at the ends of the trampoline.

5.7.35　Two trampolines may be positioned end to end with a large weight-absorbing mattress covering the frames and frame pads at the adjoining ends.

5.7.36　An overhead support rig may be used to teach students movements involving rotations or twists on the trampoline. The supporter (usually an adult) needs to be competent in the use of the rig and capable of holding the weight to control the descent of the student. BG offers specific training for the use of an overhead rig within the Teachers Trampoline Award Level 2 course or as an add-on module.

5.7.37　The positioning of the trampoline and rig needs to be checked to ensure the centre of the rig is vertically aligned to the centre of the trampoline.

5.7.38　Damaged trampolines should never be used until repaired or replaced.

General information on trampolining equipment can be found in *Section 3: Safe Management Techniques, paragraphs 3.6.37–3.6.42*, pages 116–117.

Organisation

5.7.39　Teaching should emphasise the basic skills, correct techniques and quality of movement, with graduated progression according to the ability, confidence and responsible attitude of the individual student, avoiding unnecessary risks and over-rapid progress.

5.7.40　Basic skills should be learnt and consolidated in isolation before being combined into routines.

5.7.41	Basic straight jumps should be consolidated before any performer progresses to rotational movements.
5.7.42	Rebounding should take place as near to the **centre** of the bed as possible and at a height that enables the maintenance of full control.
5.7.43	Where loss of control occurs, the student should flex at the knee and hip joints on the very next contact of the feet with the bed to deaden the jumping.
5.7.44	Typically, beginners should work for about 30 seconds, gradually increasing to about a minute, but stop if tired or losing concentration.
5.7.45	On no account should students ever be left **unsupervised**.
5.7.46	Large groups using few trampolines does not provide for worthwhile levels or quality of experience unless those waiting for a turn on the trampoline are deployed to useful, related exercises and activities.
5.7.47	There should never be any alternative, unrelated activities taking place in the same area that could distract, or create other risks to, the participants on the trampolines.
5.7.48	Any competition or display routine should consist only of movements successfully **practised and consolidated** during training. It is not acceptable to place students at risk by changing their routines in a bid for higher marks during a competition.
5.7.49	Only one student at a time should normally be allowed on the trampoline. Work should only begin when everyone is appropriately positioned and ready.
5.7.50	**Tag-on-type games**, in which students in turn add a movement to the routine, are not recommended as they may encourage students to jump beyond their ability or endurance.

> **Information on trampolining for students with SEND can be found in *Section 3: Safe Management Principles, paragraphs 3.5.33-3.5.34*, page 87.**

Trampette issues

People

5.7.51	Appropriate **footwear** is needed when using trampettes with webbed beds.

Context

5.7.52	Trampettes should always be inclined and not flat when approached from the floor.

Organisation

5.7.53	Basic trampette skills are the same as those for trampolining, except forward travel occurs, and landing takes place on a thick weight-absorbing mattress.
5.7.54	Basic jumping from a double-footed take-off **on the floor** should be well developed before progressing to the trampette.
5.7.55	Beginners should approach the trampette in an unhurried and controlled manner from a short approach of only a few steps.

5.7.56   Each trampette skill should be thoroughly practised and consolidated before progressing to the next.

5.7.57   Support should be provided that is appropriate to the skill being practised. It should provide a physical check for the students as they land, preventing them from pitching forwards or falling backwards. Responsible students may be trained to provide support.

5.7.58   **Rotational skills** in the horizontal or vertical plane during flight from a trampette are potentially dangerous and should never be attempted by beginners. The same applies to forward rolls after landing.

5.7.59   **Direct supervision** is required where somersault actions are being learned. These are more safely learned on a trampoline using an overhead support rig, followed by competent support when transferred to the trampette, until the movements are thoroughly consolidated.

5.7.60   The use of single trampettes is recommended. Using double trampettes (where two or more precede the final action of flight and landing) is only suitable for advanced performers.

5.7.61   When a trampette is used as part of one activity within a gymnastics lesson, close attention should be paid to the performance of basic trampette skills. Frequent observation and maintaining control of the class as a whole is essential.

5.7.62   It is recommended that trampettes are not used during vaulting activities as students who are not specifically trained in their use find it difficult to cope with the added height and rotation provided by the trampette.

5.8 Health-related Physical Activities

Useful websites

5.8.1 See the following websites for detailed guidance and information about safe and effective practice, organisation and risk assessment of health-related physical activities:

British Heart Foundation National Centre for Physical Activity and Health (BHFNC)	www.bhfactive.org.uk
Learning About Healthy Active Lifestyles	www.learningabouthal.co.uk
YMCA Fitness Industry Training (YMCAfit)	www.ymcafit.org.uk
Department of Health	www.dh.gov.uk

5.8.2 Health-related physical activity (HRPA) is physical activity associated with health enhancement and disease prevention. HRPA in schools should involve the teaching of knowledge and understanding, motor and behavioural skills, the development of positive attitudes and the social and emotional skills and confidence required to make informed decisions about lifelong participation in physical activity.

5.8.3 The latest physical activity guidelines from the Department of Health Chief Medical Officer, published in July 2011, give the following recommendations for 5–18-year-olds:

- All children and young people should engage in moderate to vigorous intensity physical activity for at least 60 minutes and up to several hours every day.

- Vigorous intensity activities, including those that strengthen muscle and bone, should be incorporated at least three days a week.

- All children and young people should minimise the amount of time spent being sedentary (sitting) for extended periods.

5.8.4 An understanding of HRPA should permeate learning in and through all aspects of the physical education curriculum, as well as being delivered through specific activities such as aerobics, step, skipping, circuit training, weight training and fitness testing. Health and fitness activities are growing in popularity in schools and are important in terms of their links with the recreational habits of young adults, and their relevance as a vehicle for learning about the importance of maintaining a healthy lifestyle.

General issues

People

5.8.5 **Staff** should:

- be qualified or experienced in the specific activities (QTS is sufficient to be able to teach students in fitness suites, although additional professional learning is recommended)

- be familiar with the safe use of equipment

- be inducted in the use of new or unfamiliar equipment

- provide appropriate supervision to students working in **fitness facilities**

- provide progressive learning within HRPA appropriate to students' individual abilities, needs and interests

- teach safe, effective and efficient technique

- use student-centred interactive teaching methods, involving students in learning that is relevant and meaningful to their lifestyle contexts

- review student **medical records** to ensure they are not at risk from vigorous or strenuous physical activity

- know the appropriateness of specific exercises and avoid those considered to be controversial or **contraindicated**, such as straight leg sit-ups or deep knee bends, and offer safer alternatives

- be able to adapt tasks and exercises to be appropriate to the developmental stage of students, such as by offering different versions of an exercise at different intensities

- ensure they can be heard over any accompanying music.

5.8.6 **Students** should:

- be taught how to safely store equipment

- be taught how to use equipment safely and adjust loads to suit individuals

- be taught how to **adapt** exercises to make them safe and appropriate for their own needs at different ages, stages and, for different activities, be competent at performing exercises in their own time before being asked to perform at speed or in competitive contexts

- wear clothing that allows unrestricted movement without being so loose as to catch on equipment

- have supportive footwear when performing **high impact** and vigorous cardiovascular activities, such as skipping, star jumps or step ups, and when using weights

- be taught the mental, physical and social benefits to be gained through maintaining a healthy, active lifestyle appropriate to their age, stage and ability.

Context

5.8.7 **Equipment** should be:

- stored safely and securely when not in use

- maintained in good condition by specialist contractors

- checked regularly

- repaired or replaced as appropriate

- compatible with the age, size, strength, ability and experience of the students involved.

5.8.8 The **facility** should:

- be hazard-free and conducive to safe practice

- offer sufficient space for safe exercise

- provide mats or a matted floor area for strength and endurance exercises and stretches performed in sitting or lying positions

- be secured to prevent **unauthorised access** where specific equipment (such as weight machines or free weights) is available.

5.8.9 **Organisation** should:

- focus on **quality** of technique rather than the quantity of exercise

- take account of the space available and numbers involved to ensure safe movement

- accommodate individual needs for the frequency, intensity and duration of exercise, particularly for prepubescent students and those with any specific special needs

- develop activity over time, following carefully planned and graduated progression, such as from using one's own body weight to light equipment and on to fixed equipment

- take account of the Department of Health's national guidelines in relation to quantity, type and intensity of physical activity appropriate at each stage

- ensure issues such as diet, nutrition and maintaining a healthy body weight are delivered sensitively.

Specific activities

Preparation for, and recovery from, activity

Organisation

5.8.10 Lessons should include safe preparation for, and recovery from, activity that includes exercises:

- of gradually increasing intensity in a warm-up and gradually decreasing intensity in a cool-down

- designed to enhance mobility and flexibility

- specifically related to the demands of, and skills inherent in, the main activity

- covering mobility, cardiovascular and stretching exercises relating to the joints, energy systems and muscles associated with the activity

- for warm-up that commence with low-impact, low-intensity activities related to the main activity followed by gradually more energetic activities and static stretches of the major muscle groups associated with the activity, held for 6–10 seconds and showing good technique

- for cool-down that decrease in intensity to low-impact activities followed by static stretches of the main muscle groups worked in the activity, holding these with good technique for up to 30 seconds.

5.8.11 Students should be involved in designing, conducting and evaluating their own and other students' preparation for, and recovery from, activity, having been taught the required knowledge base over time. Teachers should monitor student-led warm-up sessions to ensure the warm-up is effective, accurately performed and safe.

Resistance exercise

Organisation

5.8.12   This form of exercise is recommended for students of all ages and includes, according to age, ability and development:

- weight-bearing activities
- body-weight exercises
- weight training
- weightlifting.

5.8.13   Primary students will benefit from upper-body exercises (climbing, throwing, pushing, pulling), with older primary students also doing low-level, lower-body exercises involving their own body weight (curl ups with bent legs and hands reaching towards the feet) but not using specific fitness equipment.

5.8.14   Younger secondary students (11–14 years) can safely use low to medium resistance external weights such as light dumb-bells, elastics and tubing.

5.8.15   Only older secondary students (14–18 years) should use medium to high resistance external weights, such as multi-gyms, dumb-bells and barbells, with a focus on endurance work.

5.8.16   Only students of 16 years old or more should be involved with lifting heavy loads or near-maximal weights, and they should:

- receive tuition in correct technique because the risk of joint and spinal injuries is high
- gradually progress from light, easily manageable weights to heavier weights
- use trained, alert spotters
- maintain a record of progressive resistance exercise programmes to show an appropriate rate of progression.

5.8.17   Students should never be allowed to weight train or weightlift alone. Weight training and weightlifting should always be supervised appropriately.

5.8.18   Competitive **weightlifting** for students should focus on style rather than weight lifted.

5.8.19   Weightlifting should only be taught by adults with a specific qualification in the activity.

Information on the use and storage of weights in fitness rooms can be found in *Section 3: Safe Management Principles*, paragraph 3.7.18, page 123.

Fitness testing

Organisation

5.8.20   A thorough and relevant warm-up is essential prior to performing fitness tests.

5.8.21   Maximal tests, such as the **Multistage Fitness Test** ('bleep test') and Abdominal Curl Conditioning Test, were designed for elite adult performers, requiring participants to exercise to exhaustion.

5.8.22   Maximal tests are problematic to use with groups of students because:

- they can impose inappropriate physiological demands

- self-imposed and peer pressure can encourage exercise beyond safe limits

- screening is required prior to such tests

- close and continuous monitoring is essential.

5.8.23   Tests more appropriate for the school context include:

- maximal tests such as **time/distance** runs and timed muscular or **endurance tests**, which allow students to pace themselves during the time or distance allowed

- **sub-maximal tests**, such as step-ups.

5.8.24   Sub-maximal tests make more appropriate demands on developing systems and provide more information for learning about fitness components.

5.8.25   **Age-related norms** are not suitable for comparing students' fitness test scores due to the wide range of physical development within the same chronological age. Criterion-referenced health and fitness standards and monitoring physical activity levels are more appropriate.

Staff personal use of fitness rooms

5.8.26   Where schools accept a policy that staff may use fitness rooms for personal activity, they should be given a suitable induction before working on the fitness equipment independently.

5.8.27   Where such use is unsupervised, it should be made known to the staff that they use the fitness room at their own risk, with only occupiers' liability on the part of the school that the facility is safe for the purpose it is being used for.

5.8.28   Where staff use is supervised, they need to recognise that only third party liability for negligence on the part of the supervisory staff or faulty facility/equipment would be provided.

5.8.29   Staff using the facility should be made aware that free weights (barbells, loose weights) require closer supervision and care in use.

5.8.30   The employer (local authority [LA] or school governors or sponsor) should be made aware of the use of the facility in this way but that is the responsibility of the head teacher.

5.8.31   It is recommended that staff complete a short participation agreement, indicating that they suffer from no ailments to which participation in the fitness room might prove harmful and that they know whom to seek advice from about appropriate progressions and guidance.

5.8.32   A procedure for managing emergencies needs to be in place as does a system that prevents a lone participant using the facility without anyone else being in a position to initiate emergency procedures instantly. This would usually assume a qualified member of staff being available (though not necessarily directly supervising).

Information on fitness rooms can be found in *Section 3: Safe Management Principles, paragraph 3.7.18*, page 123.

5.9 Physically Active Play in the School Environment

5.9.1 Opportunities for physical play abound in the school environment and may take a number of forms, depending on the age and developmental stage of students.

5.9.2 Structured physical play within the taught curriculum typically involves the youngest children using a range of mobile and static equipment, has predetermined learning outcomes and assumes direct supervision and intervention, where necessary, by suitably qualified staff.

5.9.3 Playground activity occurring at break and lunchtime, preschool or at the end of the school day is much more varied and involves students of all ages. Activity may be student-regulated, with minimum levels of adult supervision, or directly controlled and supervised by a member of staff. It may consist of highly creative activity or be based on traditional sports and games.

5.9.4 Schools should have in place a clearly communicated policy relating to all aspects and dimensions of play for which they have responsibility. The information below will assist in compiling such a policy with a view to ensuring consistency and safe practice across the full extent of provision.

People

5.9.5 Those responsible for supervising physically active play should be suitably qualified, trained and competent to do so. The level and type of supervision to be undertaken should be clearly understood and not exceeded.

5.9.6 All supervisory adults should be fully aware of emergency procedures and how to rapidly access first aid in the event of an accident.

5.9.7 Staff should be competent in setting out any equipment where required to do so.

5.9.8 Students need to comply with behavioural expectations and any **code of conduct**.

5.9.9 Any student given **leadership responsibility** for play activity must work under the direct supervision of a member of staff.

5.9.10 Suitable footwear that provides grip and traction should be worn, with laces securely tied.

Context

5.9.11 All equipment should meet any appropriate and relevant British Standards/European Norm requirements, such as EN 1176.

5.9.12 Where no formal standard exists, the piece of equipment should be installed and safety tested by a specialist contractor before use, with written confirmation of correct installation and testing obtained.

5.9.13 Periodic regular inspection should occur throughout use. All repairs should be by a qualified and competent person.

5.9.14 Particular attention needs to be paid to any possibilities of entrapment.

5.9.15 Signs displaying instructions and guidance can assist safe supervision.

5.9.16 All climbing equipment should be appropriate for the age and developmental needs of the students who will use it.

5.9.17   Outdoor climbing frames should not be used in inclement weather.

5.9.18   Soft play shapes should offer firm and predictable support, with replacement as wear and tear takes place.

5.9.19   The surfaces of soft play equipment should be cleaned periodically.

5.9.20   Playing surfaces need to be acceptably safe and free from hazard.

5.9.21   An appropriate **safety surface** should be provided beneath and around all climbing equipment with a fall height greater than 600mm, whether indoors or outdoors. All-purpose gymnastics mats may be used to provide a temporary safety surface where the climbing equipment is located indoors.

5.9.22   Appropriate impact-absorbing surfaces have been shown to reduce injuries. Recommended sizes of impact-absorbing surfaces increase in line with the critical fall height, typically:

Critical Fall Height	Free Fall Space Needed
1.5m	1.5m diameter
2.0m	1.85m diameter
2.5m	2.15m diameter
3.0m	2.5m diameter

5.9.23   The types of **hazard** that may be encountered include those outlined below in Table 10.

Table 10: Potential hazards relating to play areas

Play-area Surface	Surrounding Plants/Shrubs etc
• Uneven or cracked • Loose grit • Slippery in wet weather • Vegetation growing on or through • Litter • Patches of silt from poor drainage	• Possibility of students overrunning into plants/shrubs etc • Type of plants/shrubs etc (eg shrubs with large thorns) • Possibility of poisonous berries adjacent to play area
Play-area Drainage	**Access to Play Area**
• Standing water after rain • Drain grids below or above surface level • Drain grids with oversized spaces • Drain grids broken or missing	• Possibility of unauthorised student access • Possibility of vehicular access • Vehicular deposits on play area if used as a car park outside school hours • Use as public right of way • Secure to prevent access by unauthorised adults

Play Area Built on Sloping Ground	Fixed Climbing Equipment
• Steep steps	• Lack of inspection and repair schedule
• Lack of secure handrail	• Peeling paint and rust
• Condition of steps	• Inappropriate or lack of safety surfaces
• Presence of rubbish or vegetation on steps	• Proximity to other hazards (eg windows, projections)
• Possibility of students overrunning play area	• Excessive fall height
• Possibility of stones etc rolling on to play area	

Buildings Around Play Area
• Exposed external corners adjacent to play areas
• Projections below head height (adult)
• Outward-opening windows
• Outward-opening doors
• Non-toughened glass

Organisation

5.9.24 **Zoned play areas** should be known and respected, and activities restricted to their particular designation. Quiet areas should not be intruded upon.

5.9.25 Sufficient space should be allocated for specific activities, particularly those involving rapid movement and sudden changes of direction.

5.9.26 Wherever practical, students should be **grouped** for play activities according to age and developmental stage.

5.9.27 No adult should be placed in sole charge of a lunchtime play area and climbing equipment at the same time.

5.9.28 The maximum number of students who can use a climbing area at any one time should be determined by a risk assessment and communicated to staff and students.

5.9.29 It is advisable to provide separate use of climbing frames for younger, more timid students from older, more adventurous ones.

5.9.30 **Wheeled equipment**, such as trikes, should be confined to designated areas.

5.9.31 The use of **bats and balls** can prove hazardous in confined areas. Careful planning and supervision are necessary to ensure students are not exposed to unnecessary risk.

Index

Note:

- Acts of Parliament, regulations and titles of publications are shown in *italics*.
- Tab indicates table.
- Numerals in parentheses denote page numbers. Page numbers are given where they provide a more precise location than paragraph numbers.
- The terms *people*, *context* and *organisation* are explained on page 16.

1st4sport Qualifications 3.4.36

abseiling and climbing 5.1.173
accepted practice *see* regular and approved practice: accepted practice
access routes *see* evacuation, exits and access; transportation and walking routes
accidents *see* emergencies and accidents
Acquired Immune Deficiency Syndrome (AIDS) 3.5.41–3.5.43
activity areas *see* playing and working areas
adults supporting learning (ASLs) *see* support staff and adults supporting learning (ASLs)
advanced planning *see* planning
adventure activities 5.1.1–5.1.5, 5.1.163–5.1.184 *see also* off-site activities; outdoor activities
 Adventure Activities Licensing Regulations 2004 5.1.156
 buoyancy aids 5.1.92, 5.1.131
 cold water immersion 5.1.131
 expeditions 5.1.22, 5.1.38, 5.1.177
 long-term planning 5.1.27
 medium-term planning 5.1.28
 Mountain Leadership Training (MLT) 5.1.38–5.1.39, 5.1.87–5.1.88, 5.1.147, 5.1.173, 5.1.177
 mountaineering 5.1.173
 pre-visit 5.1.17, 5.1.140, 5.1.144
 safety boats 5.1.128, 5.1.134, 5.2.82
 short-term planning 5.1.29
 stoves 5.1.46
 tour operators 5.1.25
 wind chill 5.1.53, 5.1.90, 5.2.74
Affutu-Nartay versus Clark (1994) 2.3.191
age disparities in sports 3.9.14–3.9.17
agency staff and coaches *see* support staff and adults supporting learning (ASLs)
AIDS (Acquired Immune Deficiency Syndrome) 3.5.41–3.5.43
aikido 5.4.64–5.4.69
analytical skills 2.2.1 (21), 2.3.40–2.3.43
Anderson versus Portejolie (2008) 2.3.169
angling 5.1.30–5.1.37
 context 5.1.33–5.1.34
 organisation 5.1.35–5.1.37

 people 5.1.31–5.1.32
 websites 5.1.30
approved practice *see* regular and approved practice
aquatic activities 5.2.1–5.2.91 *see also* swimming
 context 5.2.21–5.2.30
 diving 5.2.46–5.2.65
 hydrotherapy pools 5.2.84–5.2.91
 lifesaving 5.2.66–5.2.67
 organisation 5.2.31–5.2.45
 people 5.2.6–5.2.20
 personal survival skills 5.2.68–5.2.69
 swimming in open water 5.2.70–5.2.83
archery 5.6.86
Association for Physical Education (afPE) qualifications 3.4.36
AstroTurf/synthetic grass 3.7.51, 5.6.10, 5.6.32, 5.6.73
athletics 5.3.1–5.3.78
 context 5.3.2–5.3.9
 cross-country 5.3.61
 discus 2.3.94, 2.3.98, 5.3.25, 5.3.31
 equipment transportation 2.3.94
 high jump 3.6.56, 5.3.19, 5.3.40, 5.3.42–5.3.43
 hurdles 5.3.11, 5.3.56
 indoor events 5.3.62–5.3.65
 javelin 2.3.94, 5.3.25, 5.3.28
 jumping events 5.3.38–5.3.55
 landing modules 3.6.56–3.6.57
 long jump 3.7.56
 organisation 5.3.10–5.3.20
 pole vault 5.3.19, 5.3.44–5.3.45
 running events 5.3.56–5.3.61
 sand landing areas 2.3.94, 2.3.125, 3.7.56, 5.3.43, 5.3.46–5.3.55
 shot 2.3.94
 sports days 5.3.69–5.3.78
 throwing events 5.3.21–5.3.37
 websites 5.3.1
aural difficulties 3.5.21
 hearing aids 2.3.53
away fixtures Tab 7 (102), 3.10.35–3.10.41

badminton 5.6.49–5.6.53

barefoot activities 2.3.21
baseball 5.6.80–5.6.84
basketball 5.6.16–5.6.19
Bassie versus Merseyside Fire and Civil Defence Authority (2005) 3.7.53
Beaumont versus Surrey County Council (1968) 3.6.43
Begum versus the Head Teacher and Governors of Denbigh High School (2006) 3.10.31
behaviour *see* discipline and class control skills
behavioural difficulties 3.5.25–3.5.27
best practice *see* regular and approved practice: best and good practice
body piercing *see* personal effects (including jewellery, cultural and religious adornments)
body protection and armour 3.5.81
Bolam versus Friern Hospital Management Committee (1957) 3.4.29
Bolton versus Stone (1951) 3.4.34
boxing 5.4.30–5.4.36
    websites 5.4.30
bullying 3.5.115
Burton versus Canto Playgroup (1989) 3.4.66

camping 5.1.38–5.1.50
    context 5.1.41–5.1.43
    organisation 5.1.44–5.1.50
    people 5.1.39–5.1.40
    websites 5.1.38
canoeing, kayaking and paddle sports 5.1.170–5.1.171
    websites 5.1.171
cars 3.8.31–3.8.40 *see also* transportation and walking routes
case law
    adherence to procedures 2.3.112
    coach hire 3.8.53
    competence and qualifications 3.4.46–3.4.49
    discipline and class control skills 3.4.78–3.4.80
    duty of care 3.4.24–3.4.34
    equipment 3.6.43–3.6.46
    footwear 2.3.29–2.3.30
    group work 2.3.150, 3.4.78–3.4.80
        sizes 3.9.9
    insurance, indemnity and liability 3.4.113–3.4.114
    organisational care 2.3.98
    parental consent 3.5.7
    personal effects 2.3.55
    planning 2.3.36
    playing and working area surfaces 3.7.51–3.7.56
    programme management
        religious and cultural issues 3.10.31–3.10.32
    progression (staged development) 2.3.169
    protective clothing and equipment 3.5.7
    regular and approved practice 2.3.175–2.3.176
    risk assessment 3.11.19–3.11.22

of working areas 2.3.127
    risk management 1.2.1–1.2.2
    risk reporting, recording and communication 3.11.29–3.11.31
    safe management policies 3.1.10
    staff participation and physical contact 2.3.191
    supervision
        and observation of students 2.3.117, 2.3.195–2.3.198, 3.4.78–3.4.80
        of support staff 3.4.65–3.4.66
    training in safe practice 3.4.86
    violent play 3.5.152–3.5.156
caving and mine exploration 5.1.172
changing facilities 2.3.74–2.3.81, 3.7.2
    inspection of 2.2.1 (22), 2.3.80
    supervision of 2.3.76–2.3.79, 3.4.74–3.4.75
    for swimming pools 3.7.25
child abuse 3.5.126–3.5.127 *see also* safeguarding
child protection *see* safeguarding
class control skills *see* discipline and class control skills
climbing and abseiling 5.1.173
clothing 2.2.1 (21) *see also* footwear; personal effects (including jewellery, cultural and religious adornments); protective clothing and equipment
    for activity 2.3.2–2.3.6, 3.5.44–3.5.48
    additional provision of 2.2.1 (24)
    for staff 3.4.89–3.4.91
    and weather considerations 2.3.4, 3.5.126
coaches from agencies *see* support staff and adults supporting learning (ASLs)
coasteering 5.1.174
Code of Practice for Sports Coaches (sports coach UK) 2.3.173
codes of conduct 3.5.8–3.5.12
cognitive difficulties 3.5.28
combat activities 5.4.1–5.4.99
    aikido 5.4.64–5.4.69
    boxing 5.4.30–5.4.36
    context 5.4.13–5.4.16
    fencing 5.4.37–5.4.48
    GO/FENCE 5.4.49–5.4.51
    ju-jitsu 5.4.76
    judo 5.4.52–5.4.62
    karate 5.4.70–5.4.75
    kendo 5.4.76
    kung fu 5.4.76
    martial arts 5.4.63–5.4.81
        mats for 3.6.58–3.6.59
    organisation 5.4.17–5.4.29
    people 5.4.7–5.4.12
    self-defence 5.4.82–5.4.83
    taekwondo 5.4.77–5.4.81
    wrestling 5.4.84–5.4.99
compensation 2.3.48, 3.4.5
competence and qualifications 2.2.1 (21), 2.3.7–2.3.11, 3.4.35–3.4.49 *see also* training
    1st4sport Qualifications 3.4.36
    definition of 3.4.44

initial teacher education (ITE) 3.4.42–3.4.43
revalidation 3.4.85
of support staff 3.4.59, Tab 2 (70)
training in safe practice 3.4.81–3.4.85
case law 3.4.86
computer use and Internet Tab 7 (103)
cyber-bullying 3.5.115
email, appropriate use of 3.5.114
mobile telephones 3.5.111–3.5.112
power points and wiring for 3.7.13
social networking 3.5.118–3.5.120
contingency planning 2.2.1 (24), 2.3.33,
2.3.128–2.3.130, 3.10.21, 3.10.37,
3.11.12, 3.11.29
Continental Sports 3.7.36
contributory negligence *see* negligence:
contributory negligence
control *see* discipline and class control skills
cool-down from activities *see* warm-up for and
cool-down from activities
coping strategies for individual and special
needs 3.5.20, 3.5.23
cover supervisors 3.4.1, 3.4.61
cricket 5.6.72–5.6.79
helmet standards 3.5.75
Criminal Records Bureau (CRB) checks
3.5.122–3.5.123 *see also* safeguarding
crisis management plans *see* emergencies and
accidents: injuries and critical incidents
critical incidents *see* emergencies and accidents:
injuries and critical incidents
cultural adornments *see* personal effects
(including jewellery, cultural and
religious adornments)
cyber-bullying 3.5.115 *see also* computer use
and Internet
cycling and mountain biking 5.1.51–5.1.64
context 5.1.53–5.1.56
organisation 5.1.57–5.1.64
websites 5.1.52

dance activities 5.5.1–5.5.10
context 5.5.7–5.5.8
floor area recommendations 3.7.8
and footwear 2.3.21
organisation 5.5.9–5.5.10
people 5.5.5–5.5.6
websites 5.5.1
dangerous occurrences (near misses) 2.3.156 *see
also* emergencies and accidents: injuries
and critical incidents
dangerous play 3.5.146–3.5.156
case law 3.5.152–3.5.156
Data Protection Act 1998
and photography and imagery
3.5.93–3.5.95
demonstrations of sports movements
2.3.131–2.3.133
*Denbighshire County Council versus McDermott
(2005)* 2.3.36
*Dickinson versus Cornwall County Council
(1999)* 3.5.152

dietary supplements 3.5.157–3.5.159 *see also*
drug abuse
digital images *see* photographs and images:
digital images
dinghy sailing 5.1.176
disability considerations *see also* individual and
special student needs
cognitive difficulties 3.5.28
eyesight difficulties 3.5.21
hearing difficulties 3.5.21
language difficulties 3.5.19
physical difficulties 3.5.23–3.5.24
wheelchair users 3.5.35
disaster management plans *see* emergencies
and accidents: injuries and
critical incidents
discipline and class control skills 2.2.1 (21),
2.3.12–2.3.18, 3.4.67–3.4.80
see also supervision
case law 3.4.78–3.4.80
codes of conduct 3.5.8–3.5.12
and officiating at sports events 3.4.77
student required knowledge 4.3.10
disclaimers 3.5.2, 3.5.65
Disclosure and Barring Service (DBS) checks
3.5.122–3.5.123
diving 5.2.46–5.2.65
context 5.2.48–5.2.57
organisation 5.2.58–5.2.65
people 5.2.46–5.2.47
dog fouling dangers 3.7.45
doors of playing and working areas 3.7.16
*Douch versus Reading Borough Council
(2000)* 3.7.54
drinking and eating, dangers of during
activity 2.3.68
driving *see* transportation and walking
routes: driving
drug abuse Tab 7 (104) *see also*
dietary supplements
duty of care 3.4.2–3.4.34
case law 3.4.24–3.4.34
higher duty of care 3.4.14
legal age limitation 3.4.12
responsibilities of teaching and support staff
when working together 3.4.50
dyspraxia 3.5.24

email, appropriate use of 3.5.114 *see also*
computer use and Internet
eating and drinking, dangers of during
activity 2.3.68
education of teachers 3.4.42–3.4.43
see also training
Edwards versus NCB (1949) 3.11.31
electrical equipment
care and maintenance of 2.2.1 (23)
power points for 3.7.13
testing and certification of 2.3.82–2.3.86
portable appliance test (PAT) 3.6.18
emergencies and accidents 3.9.18–3.9.37
see also reporting, registers and

record keeping
causal analysis of 3.1.1
evacuation, exits and access 2.2.1 (22),
    2.3.100–2.3.101, 3.7.16, 3.7.37
fire 2.3.99–2.3.101, 3.7.16
injuries and critical incidents
    2.3.103–2.3.107
'no-fault' injuries and accidents 3.1.1, 3.4.15
policies and procedures 2.3.103, 2.3.107,
    3.8.4, 3.9.33–3.9.37
procedural awareness 2.2.1 (22)
*Reporting of Injuries, Diseases and
Dangerous Occurrences Regulations 1995
(RIDDOR)* 3.9.31
emergency equipment, care and maintenance
    of 2.2.1 (23)
emergent, new or hybrid activities 3.10.8–3.10.17
employees
    and duty of care
        legal obligations 3.4.23
    and *Health and Safety at Work Act
    1974* 3.4.19
    responsibilities of 1.1.5
employers, local authorities and governors *see
    also* head teachers
    and duty of care 3.4.9, 3.4.21–3.4.22
        legal obligations 3.4.22
    and *Health and Safety at Work Act
    1974* 3.4.19
    and responsibilities for support staff 3.4.55
    responsibilities of 1.1.3–1.1.4, 1.1.7,
        3.1.5–3.1.9, 3.4.71
        for negligence of employees 3.4.41, 3.4.65
    and vicarious liability 3.4.17
English as an additional language (EAL) 3.10.30
equipment 3.6.1–3.6.59 *see also* electrical
        equipment; emergency equipment;
        protective clothing and equipment;
        rescue equipment
    acquisition and quality of 3.6.7–3.6.13
    assembly of 3.5.33, 3.6.34
    beanbags 3.6.30
    care and maintenance of 2.2.1 (23),
        3.6.14–3.6.18
    case law 3.6.43–3.6.46
    cones 3.6.30, 3.6.32
    correct and appropriate use of 2.3.95,
        2.3.174, 3.6.32
    fixed 2.3.88, 3.6.1, 3.6.12, 3.6.28, 3.6.33,
        3.7.12, 5.6.10, 5.6.15, 5.6.22, 5.8.9,
        Tab 10 (255)
    gymnastics apparatus 3.6.33–3.6.58,
        Tab 8 (115)
    inspection of 2.3.87–2.3.88, 2.3.100, 3.6.12,
        3.6.14, 3.6.16–3.6.17
    lifting and carrying of 3.6.6, 3.6.23, 3.6.27,
        3.6.31, 3.6.34
    mats 3.6.47–3.6.59
    movement of 3.6.7–3.6.42
    netting 2.3.98, 3.6.24, 3.7.35, 5.6.74, 5.6.78
    in primary schools 3.6.9, 3.6.33

purchase of 3.6.7–3.6.42
safeguards for when condemned 2.3.91
specialist equipment 3.6.19–3.6.59, Tab 8 (115)
storage of 2.3.92, 2.3.100, 3.6.2–3.6.6
student required knowledge 4.3.9
trampolines and trampettes 3.6.37–3.6.42
transportation of 2.3.93–2.3.94
unauthorised access to 2.3.125, Tab 7 (104),
    3.6.6, 3.7.7, 5.4.16, 5.8.8
evacuation, exits and access 2.2.1 (22),
    2.3.100–2.3.101, 3.7.16, 3.7.37 *see also*
    fire safety; transportation and
    walking routes
EVOLVE 5.1.29
exercise safety 3.11.35, 4.3.2, 4.3.6
exhaustion *see* fatigue
exits *see* evacuation, exits and access
eye safety when swimming 3.5.82–3.5.90
eyesight difficulties 3.5.21

facility management *see also* changing facilities;
        playing and working areas
    policies and procedures 3.7.1
*Farmer versus Hampshire County Council
    (2006)* 2.3.29
fatigue 2.2.1 (24), 2.3.42, 2.3.134–2.3.137,
    2.3.168
    through heat exhaustion 2.3.179
fencing 5.4.37–5.4.48
    GO/FENCE 5.4.49–5.4.51
    websites 5.4.37
fire safety 2.2.1 (22), 2.3.99–2.3.101, 3.7.16,
    3.7.37 *see also* evacuation, exits
    and access
first aid 2.3.105–2.3.106, 3.9.23–3.9.25,
    Tab 7 (102)
    required student knowledge 4.3.5
1st4sport Qualifications 3.4.36
fitness rooms 3.7.18 *see also* health-related
        physical activities
    staff use of 5.8.26–5.8.32
fitness testing 5.8.20–5.8.25 *see also*
        health-related physical activities
fixtures 3.10.33–3.10.41
floors and floor areas *see* playing and
        working areas
fluid intake 2.2.1 (24), 2.3.177–2.3.179, 3.5.126
football 5.6.13–5.6.15
footwear 2.2.1 (21), 2.3.19–2.3.28,
        3.5.49–3.5.57
    case law 2.3.29–2.3.30
Forest School activities 5.1.65–5.1.80
    context 5.1.68–5.1.73
    organisation 5.1.74–5.1.80
    people 5.1.67
    website 5.1.66
forethought *see* planning
forward planning *see* planning
freestyle gymnastics 3.10.13
further assistance for staff 1.1.24
Futcher versus Hertfordshire LA (1997) 3.7.56

G (a child) versus Lancashire County Council (2000) 3.5.7
Gaelic games 5.6.20–5.6.21
games activities 5.6.1–5.6.96
   archery 5.6.86
   badminton 5.6.49–5.6.53
   baseball 5.6.80–5.6.84
   basketball 5.6.16–5.6.19
   context 5.6.7–5.6.10
   cricket 5.6.72–5.6.79
   fielding games 5.6.71–5.6.84
   football 5.6.13–5.6.15
   Gaelic games 5.6.20–5.6.21
   golf 5.6.87–5.6.92
   handball 5.6.22–5.6.28
   hockey 5.6.29–5.6.34
   invasion games 5.6.12–5.6.47
   lacrosse 5.6.35–5.6.37
   net, wall and racket games 5.6.48–5.6.70
   netball 5.6.38–5.6.41
   organisation 5.6.11
   people 5.6.5–5.6.6
   racketball 5.6.54–5.6.58
   relay racing 5.6.94–5.6.96
   rounders 5.6.80–5.6.84
   rugby 5.6.42–5.6.47
   softball 5.6.80–5.6.84
   squash 5.6.54–5.6.58
   striking games 5.6.71–5.6.84
   tag games 5.6.94–5.6.96
   target games 5.6.85–5.6.92
   tennis 5.6.59–5.6.65
   volleyball 5.6.66–5.6.70
gender, issues when mixed in sports 3.9.10–3.9.13
glasses (spectacles), wearing of 2.3.53
GO/FENCE 5.4.49–5.4.51
goalposts 3.6.19–3.6.28
   case law 3.6.44, 3.6.46
goggles and eye safety when swimming 3.5.82–3.5.90
golf 5.6.87–5.6.92
good practice *see* regular and approved practice: best and good practice
governing bodies of sports
   and protective clothing and equipment 3.5.69–3.5.71, Tab 6 (92)
   and recommended designs for sports facilities 3.7.36
governors *see* employers, local authorities and governors
Gower versus LB of Bromley (1999) 3.4.30
Gravil versus Carroll (1) and Redruth RFU Club (2) (2008) 3.5.155
Greenwood versus Dorset County Council (2008) 3.6.45
groups, group work and management 2.3.138–2.3.150, 3.9.1–3.9.37 *see also* discipline and class control skills
   case law 2.3.150, 3.4.78–3.4.80
   and learning outcomes 2.3.142–2.3.143

   lesson structure for 2.3.144–2.3.145
   matching of students within 2.2.1 (24), 2.3.146–2.3.149
   mixed-age sport 3.9.14–3.9.17
   mixed-gender activities 3.9.10–3.9.13
   policies and procedures 3.9.1
   risk assessment 3.9.6
   sizes of 3.9.2–3.9.8
      amendment 3.4.76, 3.9.7
      case law 3.9.9
   staff to student ratios 3.9.2–3.9.3
   supervision 3.4.67–3.4.80, 3.9.4
gymnastics 5.7.1–5.7.22
   apparatus for 3.6.33–3.6.58, Tab 8 (115)
   and clothing 2.3.3
   context 5.7.13–5.7.16
   floor area recommendations 3.7.8
   and footwear 2.3.21
   freestyle 3.10.13
   organisation 5.7.17–5.7.22
   people 5.7.8–5.7.12
   physical support 5.7.21
   website 5.7.1
gyms (fitness training) *see* fitness rooms

hair care 2.2.1 (21), 2.3.54, 3.5.58
Hall versus Holker Estate Co Ltd (2008) 3.6.46
handball 5.6.22–5.6.28
   context 5.6.22–5.6.24
   organisation 5.6.25–5.6.28
   websites 5.6.22
Handsam 5.1.6, 5.1.29
Harris versus Perry (2008) 2.3.195
Harrison versus Wirral MBC (2009) 3.4.34
Hattingh versus Roux (2011, South Africa) 3.5.154
head teachers *see also* employers, local authorities and governors
   and duty of care 3.4.9, 3.4.11, 3.4.20
   and fire safety 3.7.38
   and management and recruitment of support staff 3.4.54, Tab 1 (66–69)
   and negligence resulting from a lack of staff competence 3.4.41
   responsibility for correct deployment of staff 3.4.71
headwear *see* protective clothing and equipment: helmets and headwear
Health and Safety at Work Act 1974 1.2.2, 3.10.23, 3.11.10, 3.11.22
   and duties imposed 3.4.19
Health and Safety Executive (HSE)
   and competence 3.4.39
health-related physical activities 5.8.1–5.8.32
   aerobics 5.8.4
   context 5.8.7–5.8.8
   fitness rooms 3.7.18
      staff use of 5.8.26–5.8.32
   fitness testing 5.8.20–5.8.25
   high impact activities 5.8.6
   Multistage Fitness Test (bleep test) 5.8.21–5.8.22

organisation 5.8.9
people 5.8.5–5.8.6
physical activity guidelines 5.8.3
preparation and recovery 5.8.10–5.8.11
resistance exercise 5.8.12–5.8.19
sub-maximal tests 5.8.23–5.8.24
websites 5.8.1
weightlifting 5.8.12, 5.8.17–5.8.19
hearing aids
wearing of 2.3.53
hearing difficulties 3.5.21
heating of playing and working areas 3.7.17
Heffer versus Wiltshire County Council (1996)
3.4.48
helmets and headware 3.5.75, 3.5.80
higher duty of care 3.4.14
higher-risk activities 2.3.18, 3.4.68,
3.10.18–3.10.21, 5.1.167
Hippolyte versus Bexley London Borough (1994)
2.3.112
HIV (human immunodeficiency virus)
3.5.41–3.5.43
hockey 5.6.29–5.6.34
context 5.6.30–5.6.32
organisation 5.6.33–5.6.34
people 5.6.29
websites 5.6.29
horse riding and pony trekking 5.1.81–5.1.86
context 5.1.82–5.1.84
organisation 5.1.85–5.1.86
websites 5.1.81
human immunodeficiency virus (HIV)
3.5.41–3.5.43
hybrid, emergent or new activities
3.10.8–3.10.17
hydration 2.2.1 (24), 2.3.177–2.3.179, 3.5.126
hydrotherapy pools 5.2.84–5.2.91
context 5.2.89
organisation 5.2.90–5.2.91
people 5.2.85–5.2.88
hypothermia
risk of during evacuation incidents 2.3.101

images *see* photographs and images
impairment considerations *see*
disability considerations
improvisation 2.2.1 (23), 2.3.95, 2.3.174,
3.10.21
in loco parentis 3.4.6
in service training *see* training
indemnity *see* insurance, indemnity and liability
individual and special student needs
3.5.13–3.5.35 *see also*
disability considerations
planning 2.2.1 (24), 2.3.102, 2.3.182,
2.3.184–2.3.185, 3.4.73, Tab 3 (84), Tab
4 (85), Tab 5 (86)
therapeutic exercise for 3.5.33–3.5.35
indoor activities
athletics 5.3.62–5.3.68
and footwear 2.3.24
inexperience 2.3.36, 3.4.9, 5.1.109

initial teacher education (ITE) 3.4.42–3.4.43
injuries 2.3.103–2.3.107
'no-fault' injuries and accidents
3.1.1, 3.4.15
policies and procedures 2.3.103, 2.3.107,
3.8.4, 3.9.33–3.9.37
*Reporting of Injuries, Diseases and
Dangerous Occurrences Regulations 1995
(RIDDOR)* 3.9.31
instructions, clarity of 2.3.34, 2.3.36
insurance, indemnity and liability
3.4.102–3.4.114
case law 3.4.113–3.4.114
and parental consent 2.3.48, 3.5.2
and parental requests to wear swimming
goggles 3.5.89
and student retrospective claims after
reaching adulthood 3.5.2
of visiting staff 3.9.8
Internet *see* computer use and Internet
invasion games 5.6.12–5.6.47

jewellery *see* personal effects (including
jewellery, cultural and
religious adornments)
*Jones versus Cheshire County Council
(1997)* 3.9.9
*Jones versus Manchester Corporation
(1958)* 3.4.46
*Jones versus Monmouthshire County Council
(2011)* 3.7.51
*Jones versus Northampton Borough Council
(1990)* 3.4.114
ju-jitsu 5.4.76
judo 5.4.52–5.4.62
mats for 3.6.58–3.6.59
jumping events 5.3.38–5.3.55
context 5.3.39–5.3.55
people 5.3.38

karate 5.4.70–5.4.75
kayaking *see* canoeing, kayaking and
paddle sports
kendo 5.4.76
*Kenyon versus Lancashire County Council
(2001)* 3.4.49
kung fu 5.4.76

lacrosse 5.6.35–5.6.37
landing modules, athletics 3.6.56–3.6.57
language difficulties 3.5.19
laws of sports and games 2.3.180
legal responsibilities
employees 1.1.5
employers 1.1.3
schools 1.1.4
liability *see* insurance, indemnity and liability
lifesaving 5.2.66–5.2.67
equipment and swimming pools 3.7.34
lighting of playing and working areas 3.7.14
litter, dangers of 3.7.44–3.7.46
*Liverpool City Council versus The Adelphi Hotel
(2010)* 3.11.22

local authorities *see* employers, local authorities and governors
Lyes versus Middlesex County Council (1962) 3.4.28

McDougall versus Strathclyde Regional Council (1995) 2.3.196
managers
    application of safe practice and standards by 1.1.8–1.1.10, 1.1.13–1.1.14
martial arts 5.4.63–5.4.81
    aikido 5.4.64–5.4.69
    ju-jitsu 5.4.76
    karate 5.4.70–5.4.75
    kendo 5.4.76
    kung fu 5.4.76
    mats for 3.6.58–3.6.59
    taekwondo 5.4.77–5.4.81
matching of students within group work 2.2.1 (24), 2.3.146–2.3.149
mats 3.6.47–3.6.59
medical concerns Tab 7 (101)
    information and needs 3.5.36–3.5.43
    wristband identification 3.5.62
medication 3.5.31, Tab 7 (101–102), 3.10.38, 3.10.51, 5.1.29, 5.2.20
mine exploration and caving 5.1.172
minibuses 3.8.7–3.8.30
mixed-age sport 3.9.14–3.9.17
mixed-gender activities 3.9.10–3.9.13
mobile telephones 3.5.111–3.5.112 *see also* computer use and Internet
Moore versus Hampshire County Council (1981) 2.3.117
Morrell versus Owen (1993) 2.3.98
mountain biking *see* cycling and mountain biking
Mountford versus Newlands School (2007) 2.3.150
mouth guards 3.5.77–3.5.78

National College for Professional Learning (NCPL) 1.1.24
near misses (dangerous occurrences) 2.3.156 *see also* emergencies and accidents: injuries and critical incidents
negligence 3.4.2–3.4.5, 3.4.15 *see also* insurance, indemnity and liability
    contributory negligence 3.4.17
    defences against charge of 3.4.17–3.4.18
    employers' responsibility for as a result of staff competence 3.4.41, 3.4.65
    resulting from lack of competence 3.4.41
    standard of proof for compensation 3.4.16
    vicarious liability 3.4.17, 3.5.147
    voluntary assumption of risk 3.4.17
net, wall and racket games 5.6.48–5.6.70
netball 5.6.38–5.6.41
netball posts 3.6.31
non-accidental injuries 3.5.126–3.5.127
Norfolk County Council versus Kingswood Activity Centre (2007) 3.4.86

observation *see also* discipline and class control skills; supervision
    following student absence 2.3.115
    and intervention 2.3.40–2.3.43
    positioning and scanning for 2.2.1 (24), 2.3.13–2.3.14, 2.3.199
occupational therapists (OT) 3.5.24, 3.5.29
Occupiers' Liability Acts 1957 and 1984 3.7.19
off-site activities 2.2.1 (23), 3.9.26 *see also* adventure activities; evacuation, exits and access; outdoor activities; residential visits; transportation and walking routes
    sports festivals 3.10.42–3.10.48
    sports fixtures 3.10.33–3.10.41
    sports tours 3.10.49–3.10.51
optional activities
    and parental consent 2.3.44–2.3.48
Orchard versus Lee (2009) 2.3.198
orienteering 5.1.98–5.1.113
    context 5.1.100–5.1.106
    organisation 5.1.107–5.1.113
    people 5.1.99
    website 5.1.98
outdoor activities 5.1.6–5.1.184 *see also* adventure activities; off-site activities
    angling 5.1.30–5.1.37
    camping 5.1.38–5.1.50
    canoeing, kayaking and paddle sports 5.1.170–5.1.171
    caving and mine exploration 5.1.172
    climbing and abseiling 5.1.173
    coasteering 5.1.174
    context 5.1.11
    cycling and mountain biking 5.1.51–5.1.64
    dinghy sailing 5.1.176
    and footwear 2.3.25
    Forest School activities 5.1.65–5.1.80
    horse riding and pony trekking 5.1.81–5.1.86
    organisation 5.1.12–5.1.29
    orienteering 5.1.98–5.1.113
    overseas expeditions 5.1.177
    people 5.1.7–5.1.10
    problem-solving activities 5.1.114–5.1.125
    rafting 5.1.126–5.1.134, 5.1.178
    at residential centres 5.1.155–5.1.162
    rowing 5.1.179
    skating 5.1.135–5.1.146
    skiing and snowboarding 5.1.180–5.1.181
    sub-aqua 5.1.182
    surfing 5.1.183
    traversing (bouldering) 5.1.147–5.1.154
    walking 5.1.87–5.1.97
    water and rock activities 5.1.175
    websites 5.1.6
    windsurfing 5.1.184
over-exercising 3.5.126, Tab 7 (101–102)
overseas expeditions 5.1.177

paddle sports *see* canoeing, kayaking and paddle sports
Palmer versus Cornwall County Council (2009) 2.3.197

parents *see also* support staff
    consent of 2.2.1 (22), 2.3.44–2.3.48,
      3.5.2–3.5.7, 3.8.5
      case law 3.5.7
    contacting of 3.5.113
    and medical information 3.5.36
    and off-site activities 2.3.122
    and requests to wear swimming
      goggles 3.5.89
    responsibilities of for protective
      equipment 2.3.58
    and staff acting in loco parentis 3.4.6
    and voluntary assumption of risk 3.4.17
personal effects (including jewellery, cultural
    and religious adornments) 2.2.1 (21),
      2.3.49–2.3.54, 3.5.58–3.5.65,
      3.10.24–3.10.25 *see also* clothing
personal protective equipment (PPE) *see*
    protective clothing and equipment
personal survival skills 5.2.68–5.2.69
photographs and images
    CD-ROM, DVD and CCTV storage
      precautions 3.5.103, 3.5.109–3.5.110
    and *Data Protection Act 1998* 3.5.93–3.5.95
    digital images Tab 7 (103)
      care and storage 3.5.97, 3.5.99–3.5.103,
        3.5.107–3.5.108
      distribution and publishing 3.5.103,
        3.5.105–3.5.106
     guidelines for creation of 3.5.104
     parents and school photographs
      3.5.93–3.5.96
physical difficulties 3.5.23–3.5.24
physical education and sport (PES)
    safety aspects of 1.1.2
physically active play 5.9.1–5.9.31
    critical fall heights 5.9.22
    safety surfaces 5.9.21
    wheeled equipment 5.9.30
physiotherapists 3.5.24
pitch (level of demand) 1.1.20–1.1.21, 2.2.1
    (23), 2.3.115–2.3.116, 2.3.158–2.3.169
planning 2.2.1 (21) *see also* policies and
    procedures; programme management;
    risk assessment
    case law 2.3.36
    for contingencies 2.2.1 (24), 2.3.33,
      2.3.128–2.3.130
    of lesson structure for group work
      2.3.144–2.3.145
    off-site, outdoor activities 5.1.27–5.1.29
    and progression (staged development)
      2.3.159–2.3.161
    of safe lessons 2.2.1 (23–25), 2.3.31–2.3.35
      for special and individual student needs
        see individual and special student
        needs: planning
    transportation and walking routes 2.3.122,
      3.8.2–3.8.5
planning, preparation and assessment (PPA) time
    3.4.25, 3.4.60
playground and informal play activities
    5.9.1–5.9.31

    context 5.9.11–5.9.23
    hazards in play areas Tab 10 (254–255)
    organisation 5.9.24–5.9.31
    people 5.9.5–5.9.10
playing and working areas *see also*
    swimming pools
    care of playing fields 3.7.43–3.7.50
    case law 3.7.51–3.7.56
    ceilings of 3.7.11
    design recommendations by sports governing
      bodies 3.7.36
    doors of 3.7.16
    fitness rooms 3.7.18
    fixtures and fittings in 3.7.12–3.7.13
    heating of 3.7.17
    inspection of 2.2.1 (22), 2.3.125
    lighting of 3.7.14
    markers for 3.6.29–3.6.30
    security of 3.7.7
    sports halls 3.7.35
    surfaces of 3.7.3–3.7.56
      case law 3.7.51–3.7.56
      risk assessment 3.7.3–3.7.5
      size and recommended areas of
        2.3.126, 3.7.8
    and vehicular access 3.7.40–3.7.41
    walls of 3.7.15
policies and procedures 2.3.108–2.3.112 *see*
    also planning
    application of 2.2.1 (22), 2.3.61–2.3.64
    and case law 3.1.10
    critical incidents 2.3.107
    emergencies, accidents and critical incidents
      2.3.103, 2.3.107, 3.8.4, 3.9.18–3.9.21,
      3.9.33–3.9.37
    equipment management 3.6.1
    facilities management 3.7.1
    generic policy statement 3.2.1–3.2.3
    group work and management 3.9.1
    procedural guidance 3.3
    programme management 3.10.1
    protective clothing and equipment 3.5.92
    risk management 3.11.1
    safe management 3.1.5–3.1.14
    and safeguarding 3.5.125
    safety education 4.1.1
    and students 3.5.1
    for teachers as drivers 2.3.123
    transport management 3.8.1
Poppleton versus Portsmouth Youth Activities
    Committee (2008) 3.11.30
Porter versus City of Bradford MBC
    (1985) 3.4.78
potholing, caving and mine exploration 5.1.172
problem-solving activities 5.1.114–5.1.125
    context 5.1.117–5.1.121
    organisation 5.1.122–5.1.125
    people 5.1.115–5.1.116
    website 5.1.114
professional learning 3.4.81–3.4.86
programme management 3.10.1–3.10.60 *see*
    also planning; policies and procedures;
    programme management; risk assessment

club links 3.10.52–3.10.58
emergent activities 3.10.8–3.10.17
higher-risk activities 3.10.18–3.10.21
off-site activities 3.10.33–3.10.51
policies and procedures 3.10.1
religious and cultural issues 3.10.22–3.10.32
    case law 3.10.31–3.10.32
schemes of work 2.3.181–2.3.185,
    3.10.2–3.10.7
progression (staged development)
    2.3.158–2.3.169
case law 2.3.169
Protection of Freedoms Act 2012 3.5.123
protective clothing and equipment 2.2.1 (21),
    2.3.56–2.3.60, 3.5.66–3.5.92 *see also*
    clothing; equipment
body protection and armour 3.5.81
case law 3.5.7
and governing bodies of sports 3.5.69–3.5.71
    Tab 6 (92)
helmets and headwear 3.5.75, 3.5.80
mouth guards 3.5.77–3.5.78
policy documentation 3.5.92
shin pads 3.5.79, 5.6.14
standards of manufacture and
    maintenance 3.5.75
swimming goggles and eye safety
    3.5.82–3.8.90
*Provision and Use of Work Equipment
    Regulations 1998 (PUWER)* 3.6.12
pupils *see* students

qualifications *see* competence and qualifications

*R (ex parte Roberts) versus the Chair and
    Governors of Cwnfelinfach Primary
    School (2001)* 2.3.55
R versus Brooks (2007) 3.5.143
R versus Calton (1998) 3.5.153
*R versus Chargot and Ruttle Contracting
    (2008)* 1.2.2
R versus Church (2008) 3.5.138
R versus Drake (2011) 3.5.140
R versus Ellis (2003) 3.11.29
R versus HTM (2008) 3.11.21
R versus Kite (1996) 3.4.47
R versus Lister (2005) 3.5.144
R versus Porter (2008) 1.2.1
R versus Stafford (2009) 3.5.156
R versus Thompson (2008) 3.5.141
R versus Unsworth (2000) 3.5.145
R versus Unwin (2011) 3.8.53
R versus Walsh (2007) 3.5.142
racket, net and wall games 5.6.48–5.6.70
racketball and squash 5.6.54–5.6.58
rafting 5.1.126–5.1.134, 5.1.178
    context 5.1.129–5.1.131
    organisation 5.1.132–5.1.134
    people 5.1.127–5.1.128
    websites 5.1.126, 5.1.178
record keeping *see* reporting, registers and
    record keeping

registers *see* reporting, registers and
    record keeping
regular and approved practice 2.3.170–2.3.176
    accepted practice 3.4.7–3.4.8
    best and good practice 1.1.22–1.1.23
    case law 2.3.175–2.3.176
rehydration 2.2.1 (24), 2.3.177–2.3.179, 3.5.126
relay racing 5.6.94–5.6.96
religious adornments *see* personal effects
    (including jewellery, cultural and
    religious adornments)
religious and cultural issues
    fasting 3.10.24, 3.10.26–3.10.28
    festivals 3.10.24, 3.10.26, 3.10.28
reporting, registers and record keeping
    2.3.113–2.3.117, 3.9.27–3.9.32
    for group work 3.4.72
    maintenance of 2.2.1 (22)
    procedures
        compromised changing facilities 2.3.81
        equipment 2.3.89
        first aid 2.3.106
        risk 3.11.23–3.11.31
    of support staff 3.4.58
*Reporting of Injuries, Diseases and Dangerous
    Occurrences Regulations 1995
    (RIDDOR)* 3.9.31
rescue equipment
    care and maintenance of 2.2.1 (23)
    lifesaving equipment for swimming
        pools 3.7.34
    pre-activity awareness checks 2.3.96
residential visits *see also* off-site activities;
    transportation and walking routes
    to centres 5.1.155–5.1.162
        organisation 5.1.160–5.1.162
        people 5.1.159
        websites 5.1.155
    with host families 3.5.130–3.5.137
resistance exercise 5.8.12–5.8.19
responsibilities for health and safety 1.1.3
risk
    definition of 1.1.1
    education 3.11.35
    reporting, recording and communication of
        3.11.23–3.11.31
    required student knowledge 4.3.4
    residual, real or fanciful and hypothetical
        1.1.18, 1.2.1
    voluntary assumption of 3.4.17
risk assessment 1.1.21, 2.2.1 (25),
    2.3.151–2.3.157, 3.11.7–3.11.22,
    Tab 9 (157–160)
    case law 3.11.19–3.11.22
    of combined classes 3.4.64
    fire 2.3.99
    and groups 3.9.6
    and playing surfaces 3.7.3–3.7.5
    of support staff supervision 3.4.59
    and transport and walking routes 3.8.3
risk-benefit analysis 1.1.20, 2.3.151, 3.11.2–3.11.6

risk control 1.1.21, 3.11.32–3.11.34
risk management 1.1.17–1.1.24, 3.11.1–3.11.35
    case law 1.2.1–1.2.2
    and continuum of increasing risk
        1.1.19, 1.1.21
        higher-risk activities 2.3.18, 3.4.68,
            3.10.18–3.10.21
        misunderstandings of by staff 1.1.22
        model 1.1.15–1.1.16
        policies and procedures 3.11.1
rock and water activities 5.1.175
rock climbing 5.1.173
rounders 5.6.80–5.6.84
rowing 5.1.179
Royal Society for the Prevention of Accidents
        (RosPA) 1.1.22, 3.8.17
rugby 5.6.42–5.6.47
rules of sports and games 2.3.180
running 5.3.56–5.3.61
run-off areas 2.3.125, 3.4.77, 3.4.79, 3.7.6,
        3.7.35, 3.7.47, 5.4.40, 5.6.10

safe management
    and duty of care 3.4.2–3.4.34
    policies 3.1.5–3.1.14
        generic statement 3.2.1–3.2.3
    principles of 3.1.1–3.11.35
        organisation (134)
    procedural guidance 3.3
    staff management 3.4.1
safe practice and standards
    application of by teachers, managers and
        students 1.1.8–1.1.10, 1.1.13–1.1.14,
        4.3.1–4.3.10, 4.4.1–4.4.8
    communication of 3.4.87–3.4.88, 3.9.22,
        3.11.23–3.11.31
    competence see competence
        and qualifications
    generic principles of 1.1.11–1.1.12
    principles
        safe teaching 2.1–2.3
    qualifications see competence
        and qualifications
    rationale of 1.1.6
safe teaching
    overview 2.1
    principles of 2.1–2.3
        context 2.2.1 (22–23), 2.3.74–2.3.127
        organisation 2.2.1 (23–25)
        people 2.2.1 (21–22), 2.3.2–2.3.73
    teaching safely 1.1.8, 1.1.23, 4.4.1
safeguarding 2.3.61–2.3.64, 3.5.121–3.5.129,
        4.3.3, Tab 7 (101–104) see also policies
        and procedures
    intentional harm 2.3.63–2.3.64,
        3.5.125–3.5.128
    intimate care 2.3.64, 3.5.128, Tab 7 (102)
    neglect 2.3.63, 3.5.126, Tab 7 (101)
    physical abuse 3.5.126
    unintentional harm 2.3.64, 3.5.125, 3.5.128
    welfare plans 3.5.132
safety, definition of 1.1.1

safety and rescue equipment see
        rescue equipment
safety education 4.1.1–4.4.8
    policies and procedures 4.1.1
    teaching safety 1.1.8, 1.1.23, 3.11.35, 4.4.1
sailing, dinghy 5.1.176
schemes of work 2.3.181–2.3.185,
        3.10.2–3.10.7 see also planning
security 3.7.7
self-defence 5.4.82–5.4.83
sensory difficulties 3.5.21
    hearing aids 2.3.53
Shaw versus Redbridge LBC (2005) 2.3.176
shin pads 3.5.79, 5.6.14
sight difficulties 3.5.21
skating 5.1.135–5.1.146
    context 5.1.138–5.1.141
    organisation 5.1.142–5.1.146
    people 5.1.136–5.1.137
    websites 5.1.135
skiing and snowboarding 5.1.180–5.1.181
    helmets 3.5.80
Smolden versus Whitworth (1996) 3.4.80
snowboarding see skiing and snowboarding
social networking 3.5.118–3.5.120 see also
        computer use and Internet
socks, safety recommendations 2.3.22
softball 5.6.80–5.6.84
special educational needs coordinators
        (SENCOs) 3.5.29
special needs students see individual and special
        student needs
specialist skills 3.4.7
spectacles, wearing of 2.3.53
speech and language therapists (SALTs) 3.5.29
speech difficulties 3.5.19
sporting governing bodies
    and protective clothing and equipment
        3.5.69–3.5.71, Tab 6 (92)
sports days 5.3.69–5.3.78
    context 5.3.70–5.3.71
    organisation 5.3.72–5.3.78
    people 5.3.69
sports facilities, areas and halls see playing and
        working areas
sports festivals 3.10.42–3.10.48
sports fixtures 3.10.33–3.10.41
sports governing bodies see governing bodies
        of sports
sports halls 3.7.35
sports tours 3.10.49–3.10.51
squash and racketball 5.6.54–5.6.58
staff see support staff and adults supporting
        learning (ASLs); teaching staff
staff to student ratios
    group work 3.9.2–3.9.3
    walking routes 3.8.6
staff without qualified teacher status (QTS) see
        support staff and adults supporting
        learning (ASLs)
staged development see progression
        (staged development)

standard of care 3.4.6, 3.4.9–3.4.10
Steed versus Cheltenham Borough Council (2000) 3.6.44
Stokes versus Guest, Keen and Nettleford (Bolts and Nuts) Ltd (1968) 3.4.31
street surfing 3.10.15
striking and fielding games 5.6.71–5.6.84
student to staff ratios
    group work 3.9.2–3.9.3
    walking routes 3.8.6
students *see also* individual and special student needs
    application of and responsibilities for safe practice 1.1.8–1.1.10, 1.1.13–1.1.14, 2.3.65–2.3.68, 3.11.35, 4.3.1–4.3.10, 4.4.1–4.4.8
    behaviour of *see* discipline and class control skills
    and codes of conduct 3.5.8–3.5.12
    with disabilities and impairments 3.4.73
    knowledge about held by teaching staff 2.3.37–2.3.39
    management of 2.2.1 (21–22), 3.5.1–3.5.159
        context-related principles (109)
    matching of within group work 2.2.1(24), 2.3.146–2.3.149
    as minors 3.4.63
        legal age limitation 3.4.12
        and retrospective claims after reaching adulthood 3.5.2
    over-exercising of 3.5.126
    procedures for 3.5.1
    and reporting of equipment faults 2.3.90
    residentials with host families 3.5.130–3.5.137
    special and individual needs of 2.2.1 (24), 2.3.102
    and transportation of equipment 2.3.93
sub-aqua 5.1.182
sun protection 2.2.1 (24), 2.3.177–2.3.179, 3.5.91
supervision 2.3.192–2.3.198, 3.4.67–3.4.80
    see also discipline and class control skills; observation
    case law 2.3.195–2.3.198, 3.4.78–3.4.80
    of changing facilities 2.3.76–2.3.79
    of groups 3.4.67–3.4.80, 3.9.4
    of support staff 3.4.56–3.4.66, Tab 2 (70)
supplements to diet 3.5.157–3.5.159
support staff and adults supporting learning (ASLs) 2.3.69–2.3.73, 3.4.50–3.4.66
    awareness of policies and procedures by 2.3.111
    competence of 2.3.11, 3.4.59, Tab 2 (70)
    and duty of care *see* duty of care
    and employers' responsibilities for 3.4.55
    management of 2.2.1 (21), 3.4.1
    recruitment criteria and guidance 3.4.53–3.4.55, Tab 1 (66–69)
    risk assessment of 3.4.59
    role of 3.4.51
    and safeguarding 3.5.122

supervision of 3.4.56–3.4.66, Tab 2 (70)
surfing 5.1.183
swimming *see also* aquatic activities
    and clothing 2.3.5
    glare 2.3.125, 3.7.14, 3.7.21, 5.2.30
    goggles and eye safety 3.5.82–3.5.90
    in open water 5.2.70–5.2.83
        context 5.2.72–5.2.75
        organisation 5.2.76–5.2.83
        people 5.2.70–5.2.71
    programmed 5.2.4, 5.2.10–5.2.11, 5.2.32
    unprogrammed 5.2.4, 5.2.11, 5.2.32
    and religious and cultural issues 3.10.29
swimming pools 3.7.19–3.7.34
    changing facilities for 3.7.25
    emergency action plan (EAP) 5.2.14, 5.2.38, 5.2.40, 5.2.43
    and lifesaving equipment 3.7.34
    normal operating procedures (NOPs) 5.2.14, 5.2.38–5.2.39
    pool safety operating procedures (PSOPs) 5.2.38
    temperatures of 3.7.27

tag games 5.6.94–5.6.96
target games 5.6.85–5.6.92
taxis 3.8.41–3.8.47
Taylor versus Corby Borough Council (2000) 2.3.127, 3.7.55
teacher education, initial (ITE) 3.4.42–3.4.43
teachers *see* teaching staff
teaching assistants *see* support staff and adults supporting learning (ASLs)
teaching safely *see* safe teaching: teaching safely
teaching safety *see* safety education
teaching staff *see also* employees
    application of safe practice and standards by 1.1.8–1.1.10, 1.1.13–1.1.14
    and codes of conduct 3.5.8–3.5.12
    and combined classes 3.4.64
    and communication of safe practice 3.4.87–3.4.88, 3.9.22, 3.11.23–3.11.31
    competence *see* competence and qualifications
    and driving procedures 2.3.123
    and duty of care *see* duty of care
    further assistance for 1.1.24
    and importance of having knowledge about students 2.3.37–2.3.39
    initial teacher education (ITE) 3.4.42–3.4.43
    intervention to safeguard Tab 7 (101)
    management of 3.4.1
    participation and physical contact 2.3.186–2.3.191, 3.4.92–3.4.101
        case law 2.3.191
    qualifications in safe practice *see* competence and qualifications
    specialist skills of 3.4.7
    and support staff supervision 3.4.56–3.4.66, Tab 2 (70)
    trainees 2.3.70, 3.4.45, 3.4.62
telephones, mobile 3.5.111–3.5.112

266   **Safe Practice** in Physical Education and Sport 2012 Edition

tennis 5.6.59–5.6.65
therapeutic exercise for special needs students 3.5.33–3.5.35
thinking ahead *see* planning
throwing events 5.3.21–5.3.37
    context 5.3.21–5.3.29
    organisation 5.3.30–5.3.37
tiredness *see* fatigue
trainee teaching staff 2.3.70, 3.4.45, 3.4.62
training *see also* competence and qualifications
    in safe practice 3.4.81–3.4.85
        case law 3.4.86
    for special needs 3.5.30
trampolining 5.7.23–5.7.62
    apparatus 3.6.37–3.6.42
        case law 3.6.43, 3.6.45
    context 5.7.30–5.7.38
    and footwear 2.3.23, 5.7.51
    organisation 5.7.39–5.7.50
    people 5.7.23–5.7.29
    trampette issues 5.7.51–5.7.62
        context 5.7.52
        organisation 5.7.53–5.7.62
        people 5.7.51
transportation and walking routes
    2.3.118–2.3.124, 3.8.6, Tab 7 (104)
    see also evacuation, exits and access
    awareness of 2.2.1 (23)
    buses 3.8.48–3.8.50
    car seats/child restraints Tab 7 (104), 3.8.39–3.8.40
    case law 3.8.53
    coaches 3.8.48–3.8.50
    driving
        cars 3.8.31–3.8.40
        minibuses 3.8.7–3.8.30
        taxis 3.8.41–3.8.47
        by teaching staff 2.3.123
    management 3.8.1–3.8.53
    public transport 3.8.51–3.8.52
traversing (bouldering) 5.1.147–5.1.154
    context 5.1.148–5.1.150
    organisation 5.1.151–5.1.154
    website 5.1.147

unqualified staff (without qualified teacher status [QTS]) *see* support staff and adults supporting learning (ASLs)

van Oppen versus the Clerk to the Bedford Charity Trustees (1988) 3.4.113
vetting 3.4.53, 3.5.114, 3.5.122–3.5.123, 3.5.137, 5.1.27, 5.2.42
Viasystems (Tyneside) Ltd versus Thermal Transfer (Northern) Ltd (2005) 3.4.65
vicarious liability 3.4.17, 3.5.147
    see also negligence
Villella versus North Bedfordshire Borough Council (1983) 2.3.30
violent play 3.5.146–3.5.156
    case law 3.5.152–3.5.156
visiting staff 3.4.50–3.4.66 *see also* support staff and adults supporting learning (ASLs)

and duty of care 3.4.9, 3.4.11
and group sizes 3.9.8
and insurance 3.9.8
and safeguarding 3.5.122
visual difficulties 3.5.21
voluntary assumption of risk *see* negligence: voluntary assumption of risk
volunteer staff 3.4.50–3.4.66 *see also* support staff and adults supporting learning (ASLs)
and safeguarding 3.5.122

walking 5.1.87–5.1.97
    context 5.1.88–5.1.92
    organisation 5.1.93–5.1.97
    websites 5.1.87
walking routes *see* transportation and walking routes
wall, racket and net games 5.6.48–5.6.70
walls of playing and working areas 3.7.15
warm-up for and cool-down from activities 2.3.200–2.3.201
    health-related physical activities 5.8.10–5.8.11
water and rock activities 5.1.175
Watkins-Singh versus the Governing Body of Aberdare High School and Rhondda Cynon Taff Unitary Authority (2008) 3.10.32
weather considerations 2.2.1 (24), 2.3.178, 3.10.7, 3.10.59–3.10.60, Tab 7 (102–103)
    and clothing 2.3.4, 3.5.126
wheelchair users 3.5.35
Williams versus Eady (1893) 3.4.27
windsurfing 5.1.184
Woodbridge School versus Chittock (2002) 3.4.32
Woodland versus Swimming Teachers' Association (STA) and others (2011) 3.4.25–3.4.26
Woodroffe-Headley versus Cuthbertson (1997) 2.3.175
Wooldridge versus Sumner (1962) 3.4.79
working areas *see* playing and working areas
wrestling 5.4.84–5.4.99

Young versus Plymouth City Council (2010) 3.7.52

Notes

Notes

afPE Safety Poster Downloads: An Example of Involving Students in Safe Practice

afPE, funded by the Child Safety Education Coalition (CSEC), has developed and produced materials to support student safety education within the context of physical activity.

After discussing key safety messages, the students made it clear which messages held meaning for them. From this, they selected the most popular. These tended to be the ones where they could take some responsibility. Once the messages had been decided on, the students agreed on the style of posters, graphics and words they felt would have the most impact with this age group.

From this work, three posters were created, viewed, and approved by the students. Aimed at 11–14-year-olds, schools can use these posters around the physical education and sport facilities as a reminder of the students' responsibility to consider health and safety issues.

Staff can also make use of the posters to cover key elements of teaching about safe practice in physical education and sport.

The three key messages illustrated in the posters are:

1 Preparation is key in physical education. Have you checked your equipment?

2 Physical education – have fun but keep focused.

3 Physical education – prepare with care. Have you checked your kit?

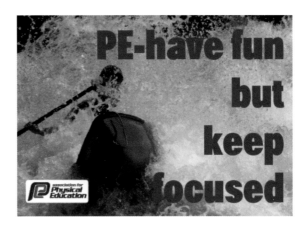

Price: £2.99

This includes a set of three PDF posters and MS Word accompanying guidance notes.

On receipt of payment, the posters and guidance notes will be emailed out to the relevant contact.

How to place your order:

Order now at www.afpe.org.uk or call **01905-855 584.**

Alternatively, email enquiries@afpe.org.uk for more information.